W9-BEN-709

ALSO BY HAL VAUGHAN

Doctor to the Resistance
FDR's 12 Apostles

SLEEPING WITH THE ENEMY

SLEEPING WITH THE ENEMY

COCO CHANEL'S SECRET WAR

HAL VAUGHAN

ALFRED A. KNOPF   NEW YORK 2011

THIS IS A BORZOI BOOK
PUBLISHED BY ALFRED A. KNOPF

Copyright © 2011 by Hal Vaughan

All rights reserved. Published in the United States by Alfred A. Knopf,
a division of Random House, Inc., New York, and in Canada by
Random House of Canada Limited, Toronto.

www.aaknopf.com

Knopf, Borzoi Books, and the colophon are registered trademarks
of Random House, Inc.

Library of Congress Cataloging-in-Publication Data
Vaughan, Hal.
Sleeping with the enemy : Coco Chanel's secret war / by Hal Vaughan.
p. cm.
Includes bibliographical references and index.
ISBN 978-0-307-59263-7
1. Chanel, Coco, 1883–1971. 2. Fashion designers—France—Biography. 3. World War,
1939–1945—Secret service—Germany. 4. Espionage, German—History—20th century.
I. Title.
TT505.C45V38 2011
746.9'2092—dc23
{B}   2011020430

Back-of-jacket photograph of Coco Chanel, age fifty-six, by George Hoyningen-Huene, 1939.
© Horst / Courtesy Staley-Wise Gallery

Jacket design by Carol Devine Carson

Manufactured in the United States of America

FIRST EDITION

This book is dedicated to those French men and women

who, though bent by the Nazi yoke, refused to collaborate.

And as always, for Phuong.

I long to hear the story of your life,
which must captivate the ear strangely.

—SHAKESPEARE, *THE TEMPEST*

CONTENTS

ILLUSTRATIONS

PROLOGUE

D ESPITE HER AGE she sparkles; she is the only volcano in the Auvergne that is not extinct . . . the most brilliant, the most impetuous, the most brilliantly insufferable woman that ever was.

Gabrielle Chanel had barely been laid to rest in her designer sepulcher at Lausanne, Switzerland, when the city of Paris announced that France's first lady and Chanel's admirer and client, the wife of French president Georges Pompidou, would open an official exhibit celebrating Chanel's life and work in Paris in October 1972. Shortly before, Hebe Dorsey, the legendary fashion editor of the *International Herald Tribune,* reported the "homage to Chanel" probably would be canceled or, at the very least, postponed. Dorsey revealed that Pierre Galante, an editor at *Paris Match,* would soon expose shocking documents from French counterintelligence archives. Dorsey alleged that Chanel had had an affair during the German occupation of Paris with Baron Hans Günther von Dincklage: "a dangerous agent of the German information service—likely an agent of the Gestapo."

Chanel, the epitome of French good taste, in bed with a Nazi spy—worse yet, involved with an agent of the hated Gestapo? To the French, and especially to French Jews, veterans of the Resistance, and survivors of SS-run concentration camps, German collaborators were pariahs or, worse, fit to be spat upon. Granted, for years fashionable Paris had gossiped that Chanel had shacked up during the occupation with a German lover called Spatz— German for sparrow—at the chic Hôtel Ritz where Nazi bigwigs like Hermann Göring and Joseph Goebbels were pampered by the Swiss management. But the Gestapo? Hadn't Chanel dressed Mme Pompidou? Hadn't she been honored at the Élysée Palace? How could such an icon of French society have bedded a "German spy"? It was hard to believe. Even though tens of thousands of French men and women *collabos* had escaped punishment, being a willing bedmate and helpmate of a German officer still reeked of treason in 1972. Their liaison would last over ten years, leading one observer to wonder if Chanel "cared about political ideology but wanted instead to be loved and to hell with politics."

The timing for the proposed national celebration of Chanel's life and work could hardly have been worse. On top of everything else, the U.S. publisher Alfred A. Knopf had just released *Vichy France: Old Guard and New Order, 1940–1944* by American historian Robert O. Paxton. This study of the Vichy regime under Marshal Philippe Pétain left many French scholars chagrined and upstaged on their own academic home turf. Based on material from German archives—because the French government had forbidden access to the Vichy archives—Paxton's book proved that Pétain's collaboration with this particular cohort of full-blooded Nazis had been voluntary rather than forced on Vichy.

For the Pompidou political machine facing an election in just twenty-four months and for the Chanel organization confronting allegations that its founder had been linked to the Gestapo, postponement of the "homage to Chanel" was the only option. There was also solid and damning evidence of her collaboration in an upcoming biography by Pierre Galante—scheduled for publication in Paris and New York. A former resistance fighter and husband of English actress Olivia de Havilland, Galante claimed his information was based on access to French counterintelligence sources.

Le Tout-Paris was talking about the book before it was even published. Edmonde Charles-Roux, a Goncourt Prize–winning novelist, was outraged by Galante's revelations. She labeled his claims nonsense: [Dincklage] "was not in the Gestapo." Spatz and Chanel, she maintained, just enjoyed an amorous friendship. (Madame Charles-Roux was also writing a Chanel biography and presumably did not have access to Galante's sources.)

Marcel Haedrich, an earlier Chanel biographer, claimed that Spatz was merely a bon vivant who "loved eating, wines, cigars, and beautiful clothes . . . thanks to Chanel he had an easy life . . . he waited for her in her salon . . . he would kiss Chanel's hand and murmur: " 'how are you this morning?' "—and because the two spoke English together she would say, "He is not German, his mother was English."

Asked by *Women's Wear Daily,* the New York garment industry paper, in September 1972: "[W]as Chanel, Paris's greatest couturière, really an agent for the Gestapo?" Charles-Roux replied, "[Dincklage] was not in the Gestapo. He was attached to a commission here [in Paris] and he did give information. He had a dirty job. But we must remember, it was war and he had the misfortune to be a German." Years later, Charles-Roux learned that she had been duped—manipulated by Chanel and her lawyer, René de Chambrun.

THE LIBERATION OF PARIS in August 1944 began with bloody street fighting, pitting German troopers against a scruffy, ragtag band of General Charles de Gaulle's irregular street fighters called Forces Françaises de l'Intérieur (the FFI), which Chanel would dub "les Fifis." They were joined by Communist fighters, Francs-Tireurs et Partisans (FTP), and civilian police officers. Facing German forces, some resistants were armed only with light police weapons; others had World War I–vintage revolvers and rifles; a few had Molotov cocktails and weapons seized from dead Boches. The street fighters were often young students, their sleeves rolled up on bony arms and wearing sandals. Their FFI, FTP, and police armbands served as uniforms.

In the last week of August the U.S.-equipped Free French Army, led by General Leclerc, nom de guerre for Philippe de Hauteclocque, relieved the Paris insurgency, and the German garrison surrendered. After four years of often-brutal occupation, Paris was liberated—free from the threat of arrest, torture, and deportation to concentration camps. Church bells rang, whistles blew; people danced in the streets. Except for some provinces, such as Alsace and Lorraine, France was under General Charles de Gaulle's Free French.

A thirst for revenge gripped the nation in the last days of August. Four years of shame, pent-up fear, hate, and frustration erupted. Revengeful citizens roamed the streets of French cities and towns. The guilty—and many innocents—were punished as private scores were settled. Many alleged collaborators were beaten; some murdered. "Horizontal collaborators"—women and girls who were known to have slept with Germans—were dragged through the streets. A few would have the swastika branded into their flesh; many would have their heads shaved. Civilian *collabos*—even some physicians who had treated the Boche—were shot on sight. The lucky were jailed, to be tried later for treason. Finally, General de Gaulle's soldiers and his provisional magistrates put a stop to this internecine war.

The twentieth-century *monstre sacré* of fashion, Chanel was among those marked for vengeance. The French called it *épuration*—a purge, a cleansing of France's wounds after so many had died and suffered under Nazi rule.

Within days after the last German troopers left Paris, Chanel hurried to give out bottles of Chanel No. 5 to American GIs. Then the Fifis arrested her. Truculent young men brought her to an FFI headquarters for questioning.

Chanel was released within a few hours, saved by the intervention of Winston Churchill operating through Duff Cooper, the British ambassador to de Gaulle's French provisional government. A few days later, she fled to Lausanne, Switzerland, where she would later be joined by Dincklage—still a handsome man at forty-eight. Chanel was sixty-one years old.

DE GAULLE'S government soon ordered Ministry of Justice magistrates to use special courts to try those suspected of aiding the Nazi regime—a crime under the French criminal code. Among the first to be tried were Vichy chief Philippe Pétain and his prime minister, Pierre Laval. Both were found guilty of treason and sentenced to death. De Gaulle spared Pétain because of his old age, but Laval was shot.

During the postwar process of cleansing, French military and civilian courts tried or examined 160,287 cases in all. While 7,037 people were condemned to death, only about 1,500 were actually executed. The rest of the death sentences were commuted to prison sentences.

It took nearly two years after the Liberation before a French Court of Justice issued an "urgent" warrant to bring Chanel before French authorities. On April 16, 1946, Judge Roger Serre ordered police and French border patrols to bring her to Paris for questioning. A month later he ordered a full investigation of her wartime activities. It wasn't Chanel's relations with Dincklage that attracted Serre's attention. Rather, the judge had discovered that

Chanel had cooperated with German military intelligence and had been teamed with a French traitor, Baron Louis de Vaufreland. French police had identified the baron as a thief and wartime German agent who was tagged as a "V-Mann" on German Abwehr documents—meaning, in the parlance of the Gestapo and German intelligence agencies, that he was a trusted agent.

Serre, forty-eight years old and with more than twenty years of experience as a magistrate, grilled Vaufreland for months. Serre also learned from French intelligence officers how Vaufreland and Chanel had collaborated with the German military. Slowly, Serre, a painstaking investigator, turned up details of Chanel's Abwehr recruitment, her collaboration with Vaufreland, and how she and the German spy had embarked on an Abwehr mission to Madrid in 1941.

During her interrogation and testimony, Chanel would claim Vaufreland's stories were "fantasies." But French police and court documents tell another story: while French Resistance fighters were shooting Germans in the summer of 1941, Chanel was recruited as an agent by the Abwehr. Fifty pages of minute detail describe how Chanel and the trusted Abwehr agent F-7117— Baron Louis de Vaufreland Piscatory—were recruited and linked together by German agent Lieutenant Hermann Niebuhr, alias Dr. Henri Neubauer, to travel together in the summer of 1941 on an espionage mission for German military intelligence. Vaufreland's job was to identify men and women who could be recruited, or coerced, into spying for Nazi Germany. Chanel, who knew Sir Samuel Hoare, the British ambassador to Spain, via her relations with the Duke of Westminster, Hugh Grosvenor, was there to provide cover for Vaufreland's work.

It is doubtful that Judge Serre ever learned the extent and depth of Chanel's collaboration with Nazi officials. It is unlikely he saw the British secret intelligence report documenting what Count Joseph von Ledebur-Wicheln, an Abwehr agent and defector, told MI6 agents in 1944. In the file, Ledebur discussed how Chanel and Baron von Dincklage traveled to bombed-out Berlin in 1943 to offer Chanel's services as an agent to SS Reichsführer Heinrich Himmler. Ledebur also revealed that Chanel, after visiting Berlin, undertook a second mission to Madrid for SS general Walter Schellenberg, Himmler's chief of SS intelligence. Serre would never learn that Dincklage had been a German military intelligence officer since after WWI: Abwehr agent F-8680.

It is also unlikely that Judge Serre ever discovered the depth of Chanel's collaboration with the Nazis in occupied Paris or that she was a paid agent of Walter Schellenberg. Nor did he know that Dincklage worked for the Abwehr and the Gestapo in France and for the Abwehr in Switzerland and, later, during the occupation of Paris.

SLEEPING WITH THE ENEMY

ONE

METAMORPHOSIS —
GABRIELLE BECOMES COCO

If you're born without wings, do nothing to preclude them
from growing . . .
Get up early, work hard. It won't hurt: your mind will be
busy, your body active . . .

—COCO CHANEL

GABRIELLE CHANEL, who would grow up to be the
essence of French chic, was born in a hospice for the poor at
Saumur, in France's Pays de la Loire, on a blistering hot August
afternoon in 1883. She was descended from a tribe of peasants
who lived on the edge of a chestnut forest in the Cévennes and
were driven by the blight to become itinerant peddlers. Her name
was registered at birth as "Chasnel." Quite possibly, this was a
slip of an official pen; or, more likely, it was the ancient spelling
of the family name, softened later to please the ear. (The added "s"
would cause some confusion in later police documents.)

Her mother, Jeanne Devolle, unwed at Chanel's birth, and her
street-hawker father, Albert Chanel, were finally married a few
years later. For the twelve years before Jeanne died, the family, a
brood of three sisters—Julia-Berthe, Gabrielle, and Antoinette—
and two brothers, Alphonse and Lucien, lived here and there in
shabby lodgings as Albert drove a horse-drawn goods-wagon
from one market town to another. Upon Jeanne's death at age
thirty-three in 1895, Albert put his two sons out to hire on a farm

and sent Gabrielle, age twelve, and her two sisters to the stark Corrèze region of central France. There, at the Aubazine convent-orphanage founded in the twelfth century by Étienne d'Aubazine, the Chanel sisters became wards of Catholic nuns.

Years later, when reflecting upon her humble beginnings at the convent, Chanel recalled: "From my earliest childhood I've been certain that they have taken everything away from me, that I'm dead. I knew that when I was twelve. You can die more than once in your life."

None of her biographers have speculated about how twelve-year-old Chanel found life at the convent. She never talked about her years as a ward of the nuns or about the long years of Catholic discipline—the hard work, the frugal life. At the time, Catholic doctrine and theology stressed sin, penitence, and redemption. We also know that at the turn of the twentieth century, Catholic institutions such as Aubazine indoctrinated Catholic youth to loathe Jews. Chanel was no exception. She was often given to anti-Semitic outbursts. Well-known French author and editor in chief of the French fashion magazine *Marie Claire,* Marcel Haedrich, tells of a conversation he had with Chanel over his book *And Moses Created God.* Chanel asked Haedrich, "Why Moses? You can't believe that ancient stories are still of interest? Or you hope Jews will like your story? They won't buy your book!" When the conversation turned to how new fashion boutiques were springing up like mushrooms in Paris, Chanel declared, "I only fear Jews and Chinese; and the Jews more than the Chinese." Haedrich observed, "Chanel's anti-Semitism was not only verbal; but passionate, demoded, and often embarrassing. Like all the children of her age she had studied the catechism: hadn't the Jews crucified Jesus?"

Christian religious beliefs for centuries held that Jews were the Christ killers. From the Middle Ages, Europeans preached that "Jews are bad luck" and excluded them from professions and corporations. Jews were banned in England in Shakespeare's time and considered socially inferior and fit only for collecting taxes—not work that would endear them to peasant families such as the Chanels. Later, the Nazis and even many less fanatical Europeans fervently believed in a Judeo-Bolshevik conspiracy, blaming the Jews for inventing Communism.

At eighteen, Chanel moved to a Catholic pension for girls at Moulins. It was at a time when the French were still debating the Dreyfus affair, a scandal that divided France for nearly a decade. The saga evolved from the 1894 arrest, trial, and conviction for high treason based on false evidence of Captain Alfred Dreyfus, a young French artillery officer of Alsatian-Jewish descent. The condemned Dreyfus was banished to a penal colony at Devil's Island in French Guiana; later he was retried and finally in 1906 exonerated. Restored to the French Army with the rank of major, Dreyfus served honorably in World War I, retiring as a lieutenant colonel in 1919.

The Dreyfus affair laid bare the anti-Semitic passions of the day and the decisive influence of the Catholic Church and their allies the monarchists and nationalists. During Chanel's teens at the convent and later in the Catholic community at Moulins, "anti-Semitism was in full froth." The widely read Catholic Assumptionist daily *La Croix* (The Cross) "raged against Jews." A typical spokesman for the Church's position was the Jesuit priest Father Du Lac, the spiritual guide to the anti-Semitic publicist Édouard Drumont, author of *La France juive* (Jewish France). Drumont coined the slogan "France for the French"—words that still echo today in French politics, particularly in the campaigns of Jean-Marie Le Pen and his daughter Marine, now head of the powerful and extreme-right Front National party.

Chanel could not have escaped the Catholic Church's propaganda campaign against the Jewish officer Dreyfus. Later, her fear and hatred for Jews was noxious and notorious—even to those who themselves practiced a more genteel form of anti-Semitism.

AT TWENTY, Chanel was put to work as a seamstress and, in her spare time, sang at a cafe patronized mostly by cavalry officers. There she became "Coco," a name taken from a ditty she sang, or perhaps drawn from the shorthand version of the French word for a kept woman: *cocotte.*

It was her burning black eyes, striking silhouette, and slim good looks bordering on the juvenile that eventually captured the heart of a rich ex–cavalry officer, Étienne Balsan. Chanel put needle, thread, cafe coquetry, and a life destined for drudgery aside. At twenty-three, she became Balsan's paramour, liv-

A faked scene of jealousy: left to right, Boy Capel in a satin kimono threatens
Léon de Laborde, who shields a sleepy Chanel in bathrobe, ca. 1908.

ing for the next three years at his château and racing stable near
Compiègne—seventy-five kilometers from Paris. In the dense forest of Compiègne, among heath and moor, pond and bog, Chanel,
her lover, and his friends rode Balsan's stable horses on hunting
paths used by the kings of France.

Balsan, the son of a wealthy industrialist family of fabric mak-
ers who had supplied uniforms to the French army, saw to it that
Chanel developed solid equestrian skills—riding astride and
sidesaddle—and taught her how to manage the stables. Pictures
of Chanel on horseback show her proud carriage; one in particular shows her mounted on a fine great bay hunter, a bowler hat
settled on braided hair—her torso proud and confident. Her love
of horses and skills at riding would serve her well when, years
later, she hunted with Hugh Grosvenor, the Duke of Westminster, known as Bendor, and his friends, among them Winston
Churchill and his son, Randolph.

Chanel's life had changed in the space of a few months. One
has only to scan pictures taken of her at the time: Chanel on
horseback; in the arms of the elegant Léon de Laborde as Étienne
Balsan looks on; with Arthur Capel (her future lover) dressed in a
satin kimono and wielding a large stick as a pajama-clad Laborde

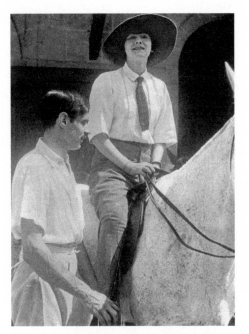

Arthur "Boy" Capel with Chanel on
horseback at Balsan's Château Royallieu,
set in the forest of Compiègne. In 1908,
they would begin an eleven-year romance.

playfully shields Chanel from a mock attack by Capel. In one
picture, Chanel wears the look of a little girl who just got out
of bed—with coal-black hair tumbling down her shoulders and
flowing over her white bathrobe. One, taken later that summer
of 1912, shows the Balsan set clad in flimsy pajamas and robes
at breakfast: Capel, Laborde, Gabrielle Dorziat, Balsan, Chanel,
Lucien Henraux, and Jeanne Léry.

In 1908, Chanel fell in love with Arthur Capel, Balsan's riding partner and friend. Nicknamed "Boy," Capel was from the
English upper class—handsome, rich, and mercurial. In 1908,
Boy installed Chanel in a Paris apartment and helped her to
launch a business making ladies' hats. Balsan may have lost a
mistress—he had many—but he would remain friends with Chanel for a lifetime.

Boy Capel and Chanel were now soul mates. A generous Capel
arranged for his mistress's nephew, André Palasse, to attend a fine
English boarding school after his mother, Chanel's older sister,

SEM's illustration of Chanel at Boy Capel's
mercy, ca. 1910.

Julia-Berthe, committed suicide. Later, when Chanel moved into
ladies' fashion wear, Capel would finance boutiques for her in
Paris, Deauville, and Biarritz.

Between 1914 and 1918, the years of the Great War, Chanel
took an apartment overlooking the Seine and the Trocadéro; she
was on her way to acquiring enormous wealth. Soon she would
employ up to three hundred workers making a line of dress wear
in jersey fabric. Later, she opened her landmark Paris boutique-
residence behind the elegant Place Vendôme at 31, rue Cambon.
There she began building the House of Chanel into a hallmark
of French style, refinement, and craftsmanship. As business prospered Chanel would later create "les Tissus Chanel" to reproduce
high-quality fabrics.

For eleven years Chanel enjoyed being Boy Capel's lover and
pal—but given her lowly origins she could hardly become the
wife of a socially connected upper-class Englishman. In 1918,
Boy married the daughter of an English lord. Still, he and Chanel
remained lovers. Then, at Christmas, returning home to be with
his wife and newborn child, Boy died in a road accident. Chanel

was devastated at Boy's death—and all the more so when she discovered she was not his only mistress. The *Times* of London revealed in February 1920 how Capel had left Chanel and another—an Italian countess—handsome bequests. Overwhelmed by feelings of betrayal and grief Chanel sank into an agonizing period of mourning. Twenty-five years later, exiled in Switzerland, she confided to her friend and biographer Paul Morand, "His death was a terrible blow to me. In losing Capel, I lost everything. What followed was not a life of happiness I have to say."

THE SCENT OF A WOMAN

A woman who doesn't wear perfume has no future.

—PAUL VALÉRY

MARIE SOPHIE OLGA ZÉNAÏDE GODEBSKA— "Misia" to the Paris Bohemian elite—was, like Chanel, banished at age ten to a Catholic convent. As a child, her skill at the piano delighted composers Franz Liszt and Gabriel Fauré. Tutored by stern nuns, Misia over time became an accomplished pianist. "Neglect taught Misia independence and loneliness taught her courage."

Unhappy and oppressed by convent life, Misia escaped to Victorian London at eighteen and engaged in a series of trysts with older men. Eventually, she rejoined her family in Belgium where, barely twenty, she inherited a large sum of money from a rich uncle. A year later, Misia married twenty-five-year-old Thadée Natanson. The couple moved to Paris, where her beauty combined with a tart's "above-it-all iconoclast attitude" brought her full sail into the free and easy Bohemian lifestyle at the turn of the century. For the next few years, Misia lived a rough-and-ready life with "speech peppered with four-letter words," seducing some of the most creative talent in Paris. Marcel Proust portrayed her as Princess Yourbeletieff, whom he found as dazzling and seductive as the Ballets Russes itself. Misia and husband Thadée quickly joined a band of what were then considered unconventional artists. She became a favorite model for Vuillard, Bonnard, Toulouse-Lautrec, and Renoir. Each artist painted her many times over.

The face that would fascinate world-
renowned French painters:
Misia Godebska, 1905.

Today, portraits of Misia at the piano, at a table, and at the theater
hang in some of the world's most important museums. Attracted
to the performing arts, Misia entered the world of theater and ballet, becoming the close friend of ballet impresario Serge Diaghilev.
Misia's biographers describe her as "enthroned at his [Diaghilev's]
side, the eminence rose of the Ballets Russes."

To know Misia was to be admitted to Diaghilev's exclusive
circle and the post–World War I elite of Paris. But Misia was not
the princess drawn by Proust. In her three marriages, she was
Madame Thadée Natanson; Madame Alfred Edwards (a very rich
businessman and notorious coprophiliac who forced Natanson to
relinquish Misia in payment for a debt); and, finally, wife of Spanish painter José-Maria Sert.

Chanel met Misia when they were guests at a dinner offered
by renowned Comédie-Française actress Cécile Sorel. Years later
Misia remembered their first meeting and described the event in
an unpublished memoir:

[I] was drawn to a very dark-haired young woman . . . she did
not say a word [but] radiated a charm I found irresistible . . . she
was called Mademoiselle Chanel. She seemed to me gifted with

Igor Stravinsky and Vaslav Nijinsky, at the Théâtre
du Châtelet, Paris, attending the premiere of the
1911 ballet *Petrushka,* produced by Diaghilev.

infinite grace . . . when I admired her ravishing fur—she put it
on my shoulders, saying with charming spontaneity she would be
only too happy to give it to me . . . her gesture had been so pretty
that I found her completely bewitching and thought of nothing
but her.

When I visited her boutique on the rue Cambon, two women
were there talking about her, calling her "Coco" . . . this name
upset me . . . my heart sank . . . I had the impression my idol was
being smashed. Why trick out someone so exceptional with so
vulgar a name? [Suddenly] the woman I had been thinking about
since the night before appeared . . . magically the hours sped
by . . . it was I who did most of the talking, for she hardly spoke.
The thought of parting from her seemed unbearable . . . that

same evening Sert and I dined at her apartment . . . in the midst of countless Coromandel screens, we found Boy Capel.

Sert was really scandalized by the astonishing infatuation I felt for my new friend. I was not in the habit of being carried away like this . . . Then [on the death of Boy Capel] Coco felt [the loss] so deeply that she sank into a neurasthenic state; and I tried desperately to think of ways to distract her . . . Sert and I took her to Venice the following summer . . .

Something had clicked between these two beautiful women. Gabrielle Chanel and Misia Sert's atoms had hooked, as the French say. Of Misia, Chanel would remember: "I remained forever a mystery to Misia—and therefore interesting. She was a rare being who knew how to be pleasing to women and artists. She was and is to Paris what the goddess Kali is to the Hindu pantheon—at once the goddess of destruction and creation."

Misia's biographers, Arthur Gold and Robert Fizdale, summed up how they believe she valued Chanel in those early years of their intimate friendship:

Chanel's designs imposed an expensive simplicity—an almost poor look on rich women—and she made millions in the process. Her genius, her generosity, her madness combined with her lethal wit, her sarcasm, and her maniacal destructiveness intrigued and appalled everyone.

Over the years Misia and Chanel's friendship would ebb and rise with time; nevertheless, they maintained a twosome sharing innumerable secrets, including the morphine they used to keep going, not to live but to hold on.

AS THE OLD WORLD of privileged aristocracy drew to a close, Chanel became a symbol of a new age. At thirty-five Chanel began inventing Coco—a woman of the Roaring Twenties. She launched her casual or "poor look" line of expensive women's wear: traveling suits of wool jersey with a tailored blouse, sports dresses, and low-heeled shoes.

The magazines of the day reproduced her creations. It was all about jersey as America discovered Chanel. In 1918, she could afford to pay 300,000 gold francs to purchase a sumptuous villa at Biarritz—the headquarters of her business in the south of France.

Misia, ca. 1910.

As early as 1915, *Harper's Bazaar* declared, "The woman who hasn't at least one Chanel is hopelessly out of fashion . . . This season the name of Chanel is on the lips of every buyer."

If Chanel was on the lips of fashion editors, victory against the Boche was on the minds of the Allies: English, French, Italians, and a host of others. U.S. president Woodrow Wilson entered his second term in office in March 1917 and persuaded the Congress to declare war on Germany in April. The Teddies, as the French called the Yanks, led by General John J. "Black Jack" Pershing, sailed to France as rich Parisians fled to Deauville and Biarritz, flocking to Chanel's boutiques to try on her women's wear.

Momentous events rocked Europe. The October 1917 revolution brought Lenin and Trotsky's Bolsheviks to power; Turkey surrendered to the Allies; and at home, Germans were starving. By 1918 the Allies, reinforced by American troops, stopped the Kaiser's spring offensive on the Western Front. On November 11,

1918, the Allies signed an armistice with Austria-Hungary and Germany. World War I had come to an end.

As demobilized German troops began the long slog back to their homes, Champagne corks popped in Paris. Chanel was wearing "big loose jerseys that were as simple as a boarding school girl's frock, and extraordinarily chic." She was also being driven about in a Rolls-Royce limo while her customers were paying 7,000 francs for a gown—the equivalent of $3,600 in today's money.

But in Europe inflation was beginning to haunt the Continent's financial institutions. In simple terms the cost of a loaf of bread in Germany, expressed in U.S. dollars, had doubled from 13 cents a loaf in 1914 to 26 cents in 1919. Thereafter the cost doubled, tripled, and reached an inconceivable level. The German economy was headed for a devastating crash.

TWO GERMAN CAVALRY OFFICERS, thousands of miles from Paris, were struggling to return home. Lieutenants Baron Hans Günther von Dincklage and Theodor Momm, fellow officers and friends serving in Hannover's elite Königs-Ulanen Regiment, were among the millions of defeated German and Austrian soldiers trying to make a new life after four years of war. Each had fought on the Eastern Front as mounted cavalry officers and later in the mud and gore of the trenches as dismounted "cavalry rifles." They returned from the east to a defeated homeland and chaotic politics. The Bolshevik Revolution in Russia and a revolt at the German naval base at Wilhelmshaven had spread across the country and forced the abdication of Kaiser Wilhelm II. A long-standing British blockade brought widespread starvation to the country.

In June 1919, a newly formed German Republic agreed to the terms set out by Britain, France, Italy, and the United States in the Treaty of Versailles. Germans would come to believe that the reparations demanded by the terms of the treaty were the cause of the coming devastating economic and financial hardships. Adolf Hitler would tear up the treaty when he came to power over a Germany scorched by defeat; a nation that hungered for the restoration of German greatness. "A people continually torn

Lieutenant Hans Günther von Dincklage (center) and fellow officers on the Russian front, ca. 1917.

by inner contradictions which make them uncertain, unsatisfied, frustrated and anxious to be released from the strain of individual decision and choice. Their greatest luxury is to have someone else make the decisions and take the risks."

Theodor Momm's wealthy family had owned a successful textile business in Germany and Belgium before the war. Returning to civilian life in early 1919 he took over the firm in Bavaria. Over the years Momm prospered with business ventures in Germany, Holland, and Italy. With the coming to power of Hitler, Momm joined the National Socialist Party of Germany (NSPD)—the Nazi party—and became a supporting member of the paramilitary Schutzstaffel (SS), in 1938.

Dincklage, the aristocrat and descendant of two generations of German army officers, joined the German military intelligence service. His grandfather Lieutenant-General Georg Karl had fought in the Franco-Prussian war (1870–1871) when German armies battered the forces of Napoleon III and annexed the territories of Alsace-Lorraine. Dincklage's father, Hermann, held the rank of major of cavalry, and both father and son fought against the Allies in World War I—Spatz on the Russian front with his Königs-Ulanen cavalry regiment. Dincklage's English-born mother, Lorry Valeria Emily, was the sister of a senior German naval officer, Admiral William Kutter. The Dincklages shared with many Germans, and certainly the German officer corps, a sense of Völkisch—a nationalistic and racist culture of war, dramatized by the trauma of 1914–1918.

With the execution of Czar Nicholas II and his family in Soviet Russia, the German Revolutionary Communist Workers' Party was founded in Berlin. Dincklage joined a body of German officers to fight Communists with the far-right Free Corps. In 1919, members of the Free Corps murdered the intellectual leader of the German Communists, Rosa Luxemburg. Later, Hermann Göring would label the Free Corps "the first soldiers of the Third Reich." Years later when Heinrich Himmler became Hitler's chief of the SS, he honored the Free Corps, claiming that its officers were spiritually united with his SS.

ACCORDING TO FRENCH COUNTERINTELLIGENCE, sometime after 1919 Dincklage was recruited by German military intelligence as agent No. 8680F, working for the Weimar Republic. This parliamentary regime would last until March 1933, when the newly elected Nazi-run government put an end to the Republic.

Dincklage was the perfect candidate for a career in military intelligence and work as a clandestine agent. He was fluent in English and French, had the impeccable good manners of the old school, used men and seduced women without mercy, and turned his recruits into informers and agents. Blond, blue-eyed, of medium height (five foot eight), graceful in manner, and urbane, Spatz Dincklage had brooding good looks and a warm, outgoing personality that appealed to both sexes. But Spatz was certainly no Aryan playboy, as some biographers have cast him. He was trained by his masters in Berlin to be what every spy must be: resourceful, observant, cool, sensitive, empathetic, and able to blend in with his surroundings. He hid his end game, attracting useful targets to betray their countries by collecting strategic and tactical information and documents useful to German military and naval intelligence.

Although a spy, Dincklage was never really in danger in pre–World War II France or later, in Poland or Switzerland. Operating as a German diplomat, he was shielded by the cloak of diplomatic immunity. The worst thing that could have happened to him in peacetime was expulsion. But neither the French nor the Swiss saw much benefit to be gained from creating a fuss with the prickly Nazi regime by expelling one of its diplomats.

IN THE WINTER–SPRING of 1919–1920, the splendor of Venice cast a spell over Chanel. With its serpentine canals and alleyways opening onto grandiose, often sunny *piazze* and *campi,* Venice was a magical place in every season. Misia and José-Maria Sert would recall how Chanel prayed and wept, torn by the sorrow and humiliation of knowing that she had not been alone in Boy Capel's affections—just as surely as the Italian countess must have wept at the news. Isabelle Fiemeyer described how Chanel prayed under the dome of the seventeenth-century church, the Santa Maria della Salute, while a thousand candles burned and flickered in the gloom under the watchful eyes of Titian's five saints.

As winter gave way to spring, Chanel's spirit returned. Under the spell of the Serts' good humor and the city's charm Chanel came out of the dark and brooding mood that had possessed her.

IN THE TURBULENT TRANSITION from war to peace, the automobile became an affordable toy of the rich and a danger for pedestrians. As President Woodrow Wilson was awarded the Nobel Peace Prize, prohibition was enacted in the United States; hordes of wealthy Americans bore down on Paris; Benito Mussolini entered Italian politics; and Communism and the Soviet revolution infected Europe, terrifying the middle and upper classes. Meanwhile, at a German military hospital in Pomerania, a little man with a toothbrush mustache was recuperating from wounds to his eyes suffered in an English gas attack at Ypres on the Western Front. His name was Adolf Hitler.

Paris was at the epicenter of the postwar cultural earthquake— a period that the French would call Les Années folles. F. Scott Fitzgerald called it the Jazz Age; Gertrude Stein and Ernest Hemingway, the Lost Generation. Chanel biographer Pierre Galante called this moment in time "The Crazy Years: when artists hungered for glory; and the man on the street sought pleasure; and the joy of being alive after the terrors of the war to end all wars."

By 1920, Paris was a Mecca for all those who wrote, painted, composed, and sculpted. Artists, musicians, composers, and writers were drawn to this now-jubilant city. They sought to be part of a new era—to drink and taste a life brimming with joy, amusements, and creative inventions. Parisian society met in street cafes, ateliers, and at soirees animated by brilliant conversation, music, and a passion for the arts. The city had "forgotten the black years." Natives and expats such as Hemingway begged for something new. In painting, sculpture, discourse, and literature, there was a hunger for original work. Painters such as Picasso, Modigliani, Braque, and Marie Laurencin were the rising stars. Le Corbusier offered something brand new in dwellings; Ravel and Stravinsky in music; Diaghilev and Nijinsky in dance; Gide, Cocteau, Mauriac in literature. Jazz symbolized the heedless gaiety of the Années folles; and with the birth of mass industries, automobiles, flapper dancers, radio, and popular sports, utopia was in the air. Rich Europeans developed a credo of progress, unchained individualism, and extravagance. Money jingled and jangled in bourgeois pockets, begging to be spent. In Paris's Montmartre and Montparnasse neighborhoods, Hemingway drank and dined with fellow expat writer Henry Miller, soaking up the ambience and plugging snapshots of the moment into their work. The F. Scott Fitzgeralds got to France in 1921 and were bored by it all. They never learned to speak but a few words of French, and Zelda and Scott returned home so their baby could be born in America in October 1921. The couple returned to France in April 1924. A year later Fitzgerald's *The Great Gatsby* was published, and the couple settled in Paris, where they would meet Ernest Hemingway in May 1925.

The decade brought joy to some and terror to others. For Chanel, the twenties began with a family tragedy. In a letter from Canada, her younger sister, Antoinette, poured out her distress over a souring marriage to a handsome Canadian officer. The man had brought Antoinette from France to a miserable existence in the hinterland of Ontario. Adored by Chanel, the lovely and fragile Antoinette had helped launch the Chanel boutiques. But now she was begging Chanel for money to return to Paris. Despite

Chanel, 1920, the year her younger sister, Antoinette, died of the Spanish flu.

Antoinette's obvious unhappiness, Chanel urged her younger sister to stick with the marriage.

Instead, Antoinette escaped with a young, good-looking Argentinean—of all people, a man Chanel knew in Paris and recommended to Antoinette's Canadian family. They had taken the man in, and Antoinette fled with him to Buenos Aires in 1920. That same year, Antoinette died in Buenos Aires of the Spanish flu that would eventually kill more than 50 million people worldwide.

Back from Venice with Misia in the autumn of 1920, Chanel soon became a locomotive for Jazz Age fashion, determined to revolutionize women's wear. She was bent on turning ladies from powdered objects of glamour to lithe silhouettes wearing her little black dresses and a wardrobe of flexible tubular wear like the boa. She would make a fortune as the beacon of women's ambitions and emancipation: free to earn, to love, to live as they wished; not under the thumb of any man—"liberated from prejudices; and not disdaining homosexual adventures." Her designer clothes inspired flappers to wear sheer short-sleeved and sometimes sleeveless dresses and to roll down their stockings to just below their knees. French and American fashion magazines such as *Mademoiselle, Femina,* and *Minerva* celebrated her creations:

"Chanel launches the ravishing dark green sports suit. . . . Lady Fellowes sports a Chanel raw silk dress at the Ritz . . . Chanel launches the black tulle dress. . . . Chanel's creation for evening: a white satin sheath covered over with an embroidered and beaded cloak." Still, critics could be ferocious: "Women were no longer to exist . . . all that's left are the boys created by Chanel."

Harper's Bazaar featured Chanel in a mass of pearls (a gift from Grand Duke Dmitri Pavlovich) and clad in a short, dark tunic and pleated skirt. In another photograph, she sports black silk pajamas and is biting a pearl on her necklace; and in another, she is running the pearls through her sensuous lips while reclining in the exotic setting she loved: the Coromandel screens, the leather, the silks and satins, all the while watched by a Chinese fawn and bronze lion.

Ever on the prowl for male conquests, Chanel set her sights on Igor Stravinsky, Pablo Picasso, the Russian Grand Duke Dmitri Pavlovich, and the man she would love and be loved by for a lifetime, Pierre Reverdy. It's a shame that Chanel and Ernest Hemingway never got together. Her fingernails might have popped Papa's inflated macho ego. For however independent, Chanel, the creative dynamo, needed admiration and to be loved. She had to have a man at her side, always seeking love yet never finding satisfaction. In one of her maxims she wrote: "not to feel loved is to feel rejected regardless of age."

Misia Sert viewed her friend as an enigma: "For the wealthy woman she imposed an expensive simplicity . . . and made millions doing it. Chanel's genius, her generosity, the façade of the self-made woman, her devastating sarcasm, and her ferocious capacity for destruction terrified and intrigued everyone."

Terrified or not, Paris celebrated her genius for creating women's high fashion, costumes for ballet and amusements, decorations, and jewelry. Ever the innovator, Chanel created a feminine personage not seen before on the stage of Paris society.

She mastered the art of social climbing—and Parisians delighted in it. "An orphan denied a home, without love, without either father or mother . . . my solitude gave me a superiority complex; the meanness of life gave me strength, pride; the drive to win and a passion to greatness . . . and when life brought me lavish elegance and the friendship of a Stravinsky or a Picasso I never felt stupid or inferior. Why? Because I knew it was with such people that one succeeds." Such was the self-made image Coco had of herself and the legend she wanted the outside world to believe—that of a heroic Marianne audaciously battling daunting odds to achieve fame, wealth, power, and acceptance by the elite.

By the early 1920s Chanel was no longer a well-known tradesperson—she was now a celebrated patron of the arts. She underwrote *Le Sacre du Printemps,* a ballet choreographed and produced by Serge de Diaghilev, and took into her new house, Bel Respiro in the Paris suburb of Garches, the family of Igor Stravinsky, the Russian composer and pianist. When Chanel wasn't dallying with Misia at her new apartment, a stone's throw from the Champs-Élysées, she enjoyed flirting with Stravinsky. The swank flat at 29, rue du Faubourg-Saint-Honoré was decorated by Chanel and Misia in tones of "beige, white and chocolate brown." In her designer residence with gardens stretching to the avenue Gabriel, Chanel created a center for Parisian cultural life—quite a step up from her days as just a clever playgirl in the Royallieu follies staged by Étienne Balsan. The crème de la crème of Paris— artists, aristocrats, the very rich and often notorious characters from the demimonde—mixed at her lunches, dinners, and soirees. Chanel's set often began the evening imbibing at the Boeuf sur le Toit (Ox on the Roof), a Right Bank night spot located on the rue Boissy-d'Anglas, just a few hundred meters from Chanel's residence. From the moment the Boeuf opened in 1922, it was "the place," boasting the smallest stage, "but the greatest concentration of personalities per square meter." The Boeuf became a Mecca for the Parisian creative elite, "a place where people threw their arms about each other to say hello while glancing over each other's shoulders to see who else was there . . . and where wit was as compulsory as Champagne: 'One cocktail and two Cocteau's.'" Later, Chanel and her entourage headed for supper chez Chanel or to dance at the Count de Beaumont's. "Love affairs between writers and artists (real or fake) and millionaires started and ended during those evenings. They drank, they danced, and loved." And Chanel held her own among them, including the Serts, the Beaumonts, Stravinsky, Picasso, Cocteau, Diaghilev, and Pierre Reverdy, a down-and-out modern poet of the day admired by art-

Sergei Diaghilev with Igor Stravinsky (1882–1971) in Seville during their
Ballets Russes collaboration, ca. 1923.

ists and writers Jean Cocteau, Max Jacob, Juan Gris, Braque, and
Modigliani. Chanel's newfound friends appreciated her "talent,
wit and intelligence . . . her minimalist approach to fashion was
not far from their abstract ideas of art."

Between 1921 and 1926 Chanel began an on-again off-again
love affair with Pierre Reverdy. In time their relations matured
into deep friendship that would endure more than forty years.
She often served as the poet's inspiration: "You do not know dear
Chanel how shadows reflect light; and it is from the shadows that
I nourish such tenderness for you. P."

But Reverdy the aesthetic, the poets' poet who enchanted Chanel with phrases like "What would become of dreams if people
were happy," couldn't swallow the everyday terrestrial world of
Chanel. On May 30, 1926, after burning a number of manuscripts
in front of a few friends, he retired to a little house just outside
the Benedictine abbey at Solesmes, where he lived for thirty years
with his wife, Henriette.

Chanel loved him and he loved her. Biographer Edmonde
Charles-Roux believed that Reverdy, who had converted to
Catholicism the same year, went into exile seeking inspiration
and God. His separation from Chanel was inevitable.

French poet, playwright, and film director Jean Cocteau (center) with (from left) Lydia Sokolova (born Hilda Munnings), English dancer and choreographer Anton Dolin, Leon Woizikowsky, and Bronislava Nijinska after the first performance of *Le Train bleu* in Britain, at the Coliseum Theatre, London. Costumes designed by Chanel.

Though she was hurt at first, Chanel eventually accepted fate. Nevertheless she never really lost Reverdy. He would visit Paris from time to time and somehow be available.

Over their long years of friendship Chanel gave Reverdy strength, confidence in his creative ability, and material assistance. She was generous and tactful, secretly buying up his manuscripts, financing him through his publisher, and underwriting his work. Despite her own success, Reverdy's darkest fears and somber view of life struck a melancholy chord in Chanel—a remembrance of her childhood. For Reverdy, son of a winegrower, was someone of her breed. Even though he had adopted a quasi-monastic lifestyle, their affair never seemed to end.

WHEN REVERDY WAS NOT available the handsome Russian Grand Duke Dmitri Pavlovich was. He had fallen out of favor in 1916 at the court of his first cousin, Nicholas II, emperor of all Russia. Nicholas was not amused when the twenty-one-year-old guardsman had a drawn-out homosexual love affair with his handsome, cross-dressing, and bisexual cousin, Prince Felix Yusupov. (Prince Felix chose Dmitri to help carry out the murder of Grigori Rasputin, the Russian monk whose influence on the Czarina was feared in court circles and the Russian parliament.) Dmitri was banished to the Persian front in the early days of World War I—an act of grace as it turned out, because it spared him the ravages of the Bolshevik Revolution of 1917 and probably saved his life. Dmitri eventually fled to France with few belongings but his stock of precious jewels, including strings of fabulous pearls. Some would end up draped around Chanel's neck, launching another Chanel fashion creation: costume jewelry.

Once in France, and a pretender to the Russian throne, the tall, elegant, and alcoholic Dmitri Pavlovich grieved with other Russian exiles over the annihilation of the Romanov family. But Dmitri could be lively and fun loving. His good looks, green eyes, long Romanov legs, and charm seduced Chanel. It was just what she needed after the intensity of Reverdy and a brief tryst with Stravinsky.

In late 1920, when the Grand Duke entered Chanel's intimate life, Paris wags dubbed her new adventure "Chanel's Slavic period." In homage to her new paramour, Coco wanted to create an authentic Russian line. She hired Dmitri's sister, the Grand Duchess Marie, and her exiled Russian royal friends. The Czarina's former ladies-in-waiting delivered embroidery and beadwork at far less cost than demanded by French artisans. They fashioned stunning combinations of needlework and fur, such as Chanel's own white coat embroidered and trimmed in Russian sable featured in a 1920 issue of *Vogue* magazine.

Augmenting her Slavic collection, Chanel included a component never before seen on the continent: Russian-inspired peasant dresses worn with a draping of pearls, some with square-neck tunic tops and elbow-length sleeves, Oriental embroideries, chenille knitted cloches, and stunning waterfall gowns of

Grand Duke Dimitri, Chanel's lover—who helped Chanel launch
her successful Chanel No. 5 perfume, 1910.

crystals and lignite jet. And for those wanting something more
classic, she brought out a line of modern garb: wool knits, dresses
cut from fine French muslin cotton, tulle for day wear and lamé
or metallic lace for an evening out. It was all very grand. Like her
jersey line before it, Chanel's "Russian look" was a great success.
It sold so well that she was soon employing fifty Russian seamstresses in addition to designers and technicians, all working at an
expanded atelier on the rue Cambon under her critical eye.

The Grand Duke brought Chanel something rare and more precious than a few strings of pearls. Just as Boy Capel's English knit
sweaters had inspired her to copy that mode for women, Pavlovich
helped to inspire her to create the Russian-Slavic collection—and
to venture into perfume.

During WWI, women were wedded to their grandmothers' lye
soap for personal hygiene. Later, they used scents extracted from a
combination of flowers—violets, roses, orange blossoms, jasmine—
or scents from animal sources. For a night out, more sophisticated women applied powder and sprayed their bodies with floral
mists. Men favored Bay Rum or Roger & Gallet cologne, liber-
ally splashed about to mask unpleasant odors. Rumors now spread
that Chanel was about to launch a "secret, marvelous eau Chanel."

The hallmark Chanel No. 5 flacon, illustrated by French artist SEM
(Georges Goursat), ca. 1921. The bottle entered the New York
Museum of Modern Art in 1959.

The secret, according to Paris gossip, was known to the fifteenth-
century Medici family of Florence. Women thought the perfumed
liquid preserved their skin while men used it to cure razor burns.

By this time, the younger set in France was already beginning
to wear Chanel's little black dresses, sweaters, and short, pleated
skirts. So why not marry a new fragrance to what was already
fashionable? When it came to daubing a pearl of scent behind a
feminine ear, on a wrist, or at the hollow of a shoulder curve, it
was all about the sweet smell of success; it embodied poet Paul

Valéry's statement: "A woman who doesn't wear perfume has no future." It was about knowing how to dress and having the thousand-dollar allure of a Parisian hostess.

Chanel set out with the help of Dmitri and a Russian chemist friend to devise a scent that would become part of the folklore of the interwar years: a fragrant emblem for *les garçonnes,* the boyish emancipated females sporting a unisex allure who danced the tango and Charleston, sometimes smoked opium, and embraced the art of Cocteau and Picasso. These women boasted short, manly haircuts, men's suit jackets and ties, culottes, and shift dresses shockingly cut to the knee, without sleeves but with Charleston fringes. Indeed, the right perfume would go along perfectly with makeup, fast cars, sports, travel, and the Charleston.

When Dmitri introduced Chanel to his Russian émigré friend, Ernest Beaux, the ex-czar's official perfumer, a new fashion venture was launched. The Moscow-born Beaux had fled St. Petersburg after the 1917 Bolshevik Revolution to fight the "Reds." He joined the anti-Bolsheviks' White Russian armies and landed in the far north, near the Arctic Circle where the sun shone at midnight and where lakes and rivers give off a refreshing perfume. In France, where he quickly became a respected chemist and specialist in concocting exotic perfumes, Beaux was just then experimenting with using synthetic compounds to enhance various natural mixtures. At his laboratory in the south of France at Grasse, known as the perfume center of the world, Beaux, under Chanel's watchful eye and delicate sense of smell, worked his magic. He insisted that he could capture the freshness of a sunny Arctic day in his test tubes.

Chanel found the perfumes of the day, extracted from violets, roses, and orange blossoms and put up in extravagant bottles banal. She told Beaux she wanted everything in the perfume— a scent that would evoke the femininity of a woman. Beaux's genius was then to add synthetic chemical components to enhance the natural scents and stabilize the perfume so that the scent lingered on the skin—unlike the natural scents.

In 1921, Beaux presented Chanel with a series of concoctions, numbered from 1 to 5 and 20 to 24. At first, she chose the twenty-second one and offered it for sale. But it was No. 5 that delighted Chanel, and she decided it must be introduced in 1921 along with her collection. She would call the new fragrance Chanel No. 5.

Except to a handful of the initiated, the formula for making Chanel No. 5 remains secret. It is known to be exceptionally complicated. The perfume was, and still is, constructed of approximately eighty ingredients. The most important one is high-quality jasmine found only in Grasse.

Chanel banished the idea of a baroque bottle design her competitors used—no sculpted cupids or flowers. Rather, Chanel chose a geometric cube minimalist bottle—her modern concept of packaging.

The name she chose, her fetish number 5, was a revolution. It was serpentine, recalling the divine five heads of Hinduism or the five visions of Buddha. (Chanel would celebrate the number 5 time and again. Her collections were invariably offered to the public on February 5 and August 5 of every year.)

To promote her new invention, Chanel—like the shrewd peasant she was—believed in "word of mouth." She tested Chanel No. 5 by inviting friends to dine with her at a posh restaurant near Grasse; there she furtively sprayed guests passing by her table—they reacted with surprise and pleasure. Pleased with the results, Chanel returned to Paris and quietly launched her new venture. She didn't announce its arrival in the press. She wore it herself and sprayed the shop's dressing rooms with it, giving bottles to a few of her high-society friends. Her perfume soon became the talk of Paris.

Chanel instructed Beaux to put No. 5 into production. "The success was beyond anything we could have imagined," recalled Misia Sert. "It was like a winning lottery ticket." And so Beaux's juice, a woman's perfume with a scent meant for a woman, was put into an Art Deco bottle and labeled "No. 5" with interlocking Cs back to back—and launched from Chanel's rue Cambon boutique on May 5, 1921. The Chanel-Beaux creation would withstand the vicissitudes of the Great Depression and World War II. It was a fragrance that grandmothers and mothers would pay a small fortune to wear, and one that young women could hope to acquire one day.

For the next three years, with the help of Grand Duke Dmitri, Chanel successfully promoted No. 5 as a luxury perfume. Soon, she realized that to fully exploit the growing demand for No. 5, her modest enterprise would have to expand production.

On a Sunday in the early spring of 1923, Chanel dressed for a day at the Longchamp racetrack. The site was and still is today an elegant meeting place, located in the Bois de Boulogne where the Seine curves around the western extreme of Paris. It's the place to go on a Sunday to see and be seen by Le Tout-Paris, to watch the "ponies" gallop around the oval, and to dine well after betting one's money on some "gentleman-owner's" horse.

But it was Pierre Wertheimer and his money that brought Chanel to Longchamp that afternoon. Théophile Bader, who kept in touch with the "world of frippery," arranged the meeting. As a prince of the French retail trade and one of the owners of Paris's major emporium, Les Galeries Lafayette, Bader wanted to be sure he could obtain a steady supply of the perfume from the Beaux laboratory—and in quantities to satisfy his customers. "You have a perfume that deserves a much bigger market. I want you to meet Pierre Wertheimer, who owns Bourjois perfumes and has a large factory in France and an important distribution network," he advised Chanel. (It is unknown if Bader revealed to Chanel that the Wertheimers were his business partners.)

Chanel's Longchamp meeting with Pierre Wertheimer was by all accounts short and to the point: "You want to produce and distribute perfumes for me?"

"Why not?" he replied. "But if you want the perfume to be made under the name of Chanel, we've got to incorporate."

Within the time it took to complete the legal work, Chanel turned over to a newly formed French company Les Parfums Chanel, S.A. the ownership and rights to manufacture Chanel perfumes along with the formulas and methods to produce the fragrances developed by Beaux. In return, she became president of the new entity and held a stake of two hundred fully paid-up shares—worth 500 French francs each. Her ownership represented 10 percent of the paid-up capital. She was also granted 10 percent of the capital of all companies that manufactured her perfumes outside of France. The majority of the remaining capital, 70 percent of the outstanding shares, went to the Wertheimer clan, who would finance production and assure worldwide distribution of the perfume from their corporate headquarters in New York. Bader's proxies (Adolphe Dreyfus and Max Grumbach) received 20 percent of the shares. One wonders if Chanel knew

Pierre Wertheimer, the younger Wertheimer brother, 1928. The
Wertheimers bought a majority of Chanel's perfume company in 1924.

that Bader was in effect getting a kind of finder's fee through
these intermediaries.

Chanel's nonchalance in reaching a deal with Pierre Wertheimer—and agreeing to use the same lawyer as the Wertheimers
to draw up contracts—borders on commercial recklessness. It may
be that after her hopeless affair with Pierre Reverdy, and having recently parted with Grand Duke Dmitri, she was just too
emotionally worked up to give the matter any serious attention.
Indeed, between 1923 and 1937, Chanel was "Mademoiselle Ballet," trapped in a whirlwind of hyperactivity. She poured her

The poet Pierre Reverdy, 1940—a man Chanel deeply
loved. Their friendship lasted more than fifty years.

creative energy into designing costumes for Sergei Diaghilev's
ballets—*Le Train bleu, Orphée, Œdipe roi*—and a host of other the-
atrical productions, many choreographed by Diaghilev with Vaslav
Nijinsky. Her costumes for *Le Train bleu* meshed beautifully with
the subtle sexual transgressions in the dance, the characters playing with gender stereotypes, androgyny, and homosexuality—
though in this case, the females were endowed with masculine
characteristics. The ballet was an open exploration of avant-garde
perversity—and Chanel must have been delighted to be part of
the production.

BY THE LATE 1920S, thanks to the production capabilities, marketing expertise, and distribution muscle of the Wertheimers, Chanel No. 5 had become a worldwide success—and nowhere more so than across the Atlantic. The perfume would become the most profitable and long-lasting result of her volcanic career, pumping out an ever-rising river of profits that would make both Chanel and the Wertheimers fabulously wealthy. But it would take a worldwide depression and later World War II for Chanel to realize the economic significance of her new perfume and the complications of her partnership with the Wertheimers. When she first signed the deal with the family, she did not and could not have imagined how Chanel No. 5 would become a fountain of riches.

And who were these Wertheimers?

France's defeat by German armies in the Franco-Prussian War of 1870–1871 split the Alsatian-Jewish Wertheimer family. Émile stayed in Alsace, now part of a united Second German Reich, while Julien and Ernest Wertheimer opted, as did some 15 percent of Alsatians, for French nationality. But it was brother Ernest who had the "nose." In 1898 he established E. Wertheimer & Cie. and, with Julien at his side, acquired a majority interest in A. Bourjois & Cie., manufacturers of *poudre de riz* Bourjois (ladies' powder), soap, and other beauty products distributed worldwide. They also acquired a production facility at Pantin, close to the Paris slaughterhouses of La Villette, known as "the city of blood." Ironically, during the Nazi occupation of Paris, it was from the Pantin rail yards that French and German police deported uncounted thousands of men, women, and children to Germany and to certain death.

Soon the brothers joined with other French Jews to invest in Galeries Lafayette, a large department store that would be run with great success by Théophile Bader, first on Paris's boulevard Haussmann and later in other locations throughout France. On the shelves of the Galeries, Bourjois products for ladies and men found a warm welcome.

Chanel was not an astute businesswoman. The whole idea of commerce, contracts, and paperwork "bored her to death." For her entire life, she would have a love-hate, chaotic relationship with the shrewd businessman Pierre Wertheimer. She would come to believe that she had been exploited, lamenting, "He screwed

me"—yet in a typical Chanel whisper, she would add, "that darling Pierre." Indeed, four years after inking the agreement with
the temperamental couturier, the Wertheimers engaged a lawyer
to deal with her while they kept an arm's-length relationship.

Still, the impoverished pupil of the sisters of the Congregation
of the Sacred Heart mined a seam of gold in forty-one-year-old
Paul and thirty-six-year-old Pierre Wertheimer. Between 1905
and 1920 the brothers had established some one hundred distribution arrangements for their products worldwide.

WHILE ENJOYING her new fame and wealth, Chanel had
yet to be accepted by the very top tier of French society; she
had yet to be "anointed" by English "royals." She was still an individual whose sexual promiscuity placed her outside of respectable
society—despite her having "revolutionized French fashion" since
1910. Her amorous pursuits didn't bother Pierre Wertheimer. He
knew all about the gossip that swirled around her. In fact, Pierre
had a crush on Gabrielle Chanel—still irresistible at forty-four
and looking ten years younger. Despite their future quarrels, legal
battles, and problems, Pierre would remain enamored of Chanel
for the rest of his life. In the end, he would be her savior.

FOR THE HOLIDAY SEASON of 1924–1925, Chanel drove
down to Monte Carlo with Sarah Gertrude Arkwright Bate. Sarah,
whom everyone called Vera, had been abandoned by her mother
and became the surrogate child of Margaret Cambridge, Marchio-
ness of Cambridge, daughter of the Duke of Westminster, and
related to King Edward VII and Sir Winston Churchill. Vera thus
acquired from childhood solid ties with the British royal family.
Her good looks, luminous skin, statuesque figure, and English
connections attracted Chanel. No one was more keenly appreciated by London high society . . . As a young woman Vera enjoyed
a host of suitors: a stream of Archies, Harolds, Winstons, and
Duffs at her side. Chanel hired this thirty-five-year-old darling
of English royals to handle public relations in London and Paris
society for the House of Chanel.

THE CÔTE D'AZUR was an animated, bubbling place to
celebrate the holiday season and the New Year. Wealthy Con-

tinentals rubbed elbows with the English elite—the Churchills and the Grosvenors, who in the 1920s boom enjoyed unheard of luxury at the watering holes of Monte Carlo, Deauville, and Biarritz in France. The Wertheimers, Pierre and Paul, preferred the racecourses of Tremblay, Ascot, and Longchamp. It had been a bonanza year for the brothers: their investment in Félix Amiot paid off when the French government nationalized Amiot's firm, earning the Wertheimers an unexpected windfall profit of 14 million francs. (Prophetically, Amiot, a future business partner, would protect the Wertheimer fortune in the bad days ahead.)

A year before, in 1923, Adolf Hitler organized the Munich Beer Hall Putsch. When it failed, Hitler was arrested, tried, convicted of high treason, and sentenced to serve five years' imprisonment with eligibility for parole in nine months.

In cell 7 of the Landsberg Prison fortress, Hitler dictated a part-biographical, part-political treatise to his acolytes. *Mein Kampf* (although often translated as "My Struggle" or "My Campaign," its meaning could also be conveyed as "My Fight") told of Hitler's "Four and a Half Years [of Fighting] Against Lies, Stupidity and Cowardice." Released in early 1925, the first volume, a bible for the NSPD, laid out the Nazi creed of nationalism, anti-Semitism, and anti-Communism. That same year Hitler reorganized the Nazi party; his often-brilliant oratory began exciting millions of Germans and Austrians—including many disaffected World War I veterans.

A few months later, Joseph Goebbels was appointed Nazi district leader of Berlin. As France and Britain celebrated joyfully the Christmas season of 1924, chaos and hyperinflation was devouring the social fabric of the Reich. Riots swept the country as people's savings were wiped out. In 1919 a U.S. dollar bought 5.20 German marks. By December 1924 the U.S. dollar fetched 4.2 trillion German marks. A loaf of bread in 1924 was now priced, unbelievably, at 429 billion marks. A kilo of fresh butter cost 6 trillion marks. Pensions became meaningless. People began demanding to be paid daily so they wouldn't see their wages devalued by a passing day. Thousands became homeless and German culture collapsed, destroying the German middle class.

THREE

COCO'S GOLDEN DUKE

Mademoiselle is more than a Grande Dame, she is a Monsieur.

—FRENCH *VOGUE*, MARCH 2009

T HE AFFAIR BEGAN when Vera Bate played cupid during that 1923 Christmas season. She begged Chanel to accompany her to dinner with her childhood chum, the Duke of Westminster, aboard his yacht anchored in the harbor of Monte Carlo. (One biographer claimed that the duke paid Vera handsomely for the introduction.) Chanel snubbed the invitation until her friend Grand Duke Dmitri arrived for a visit. He chided Chanel, "It would have amused me to visit the yacht." A few nights later, Vera and Dmitri, with Chanel in tow—perhaps feigning reluctance—were ferried out to the schooner *Flying Cloud.* Although the yacht had been built to resemble a seventeenth-century pirate vessel, it was now decked out with glittering Christmas decorations.

Gypsy violins, hired for the occasion, played on as the duke showed Chanel his four-mast sailing schooner with its decks of scrubbed white oak and pristine white sails. Belowdecks, cabins resembling a small English country home, paneled in pine and oak, were furnished with Queen Anne furniture, upholstery and curtains of hand-blocked fabrics. The ship's bulkheads sported a collection of fine paintings and prints. The setting befitted Bendor, born Hugh Richard Arthur Grosvenor. Six feet tall and broad-chested, Bendor had been a war hero, a hunter–horseman–slayer of stag and boar, and an ever-charming host with impeccable manners and vast wealth. Slowly, deliberately, the duke set out to capture Chanel's heart.

It is easy to imagine why Bendor was attracted to Chanel; she was petite, olive-complexioned, sexy, witty, and brainy, with an acid tongue. At forty-two, she often played a sexy tomboy imposing her own luxurious simplicity. Chanel could more than hold her own with a man who plied his charm with solemn English ladies or easy tarts.

Over a splendid dinner and late dancing at a Monte Carlo cabaret, Bendor discovered a woman who commanded masculine attention—her nostrils flaring in sudden anger, her gravelly voice rising and then returning to a benevolent lassitude. Sometimes the kitten, sometimes the vamp, and often the vixen, Chanel's moods shifted. She must have melted Bendor's knees. She later described him as "a man of great generosity and courtesy like many well-mannered Englishmen—at least until they land in France. The essence of refinement when ladies were present—and when they were not: a guttersnipe and a cunning hunter . . . he had to be to hold me for ten years."

Chanel was in the midst of designing the costumes for *Le Train bleu*—a Diaghilev-Cocteau dance-opera about to debut at the Ballets Russes in Paris. On board the *Flying Cloud* with its Christmas decorations in the background, Bendor and guests must have chatted about Cocteau's imaginary blue train. The opera's plot had everything to please the duke, who loved both Paris and the Riviera, and who a few months later would see the ballet and admire Chanel's costumes.

The real train was run by the French rail system and offered regular service for the British and French elite trying to escape a grim, wet, and cold London or Paris for the sun-drenched Côte d'Azur. Cocteau's play featured seaside romances, gigolos and their women dressed by Chanel in beach and tennis wear, boating outfits, golf knickers, and striped sweaters. The cast performed to the music of Darius Milhaud with background beach scenery by Henri Laurens. The main curtain was the work of Pablo Picasso. The whole production was intended to be a dip into new art and great fun.

The holiday soon ended. Chanel and Vera returned to Paris to prepare Chanel's spring collections and to finish *Le Train bleu* costumes. Coco insisted she had no time for Bendor, or pretended so to Vera, who was still acting as the duke's procurer. From Eaton Hall, Bendor's vast country estate in the village of Eccleston near Chester in England, the duke wooed Chanel with billets-doux carried to Paris by his footmen, along with baskets of strawberries, spring crocuses, gardenias, and orchids, all picked by his hand from the Hall's hothouses and gardens. He even plied her with fresh Scottish salmon caught on his property and flown to Paris.

Shortly after their outing with Bendor at Monte Carlo, and despite Bendor's ardent long-distance wooing of Chanel, Vera arranged for her to meet a handsome, blue-eyed, almost effeminate thirty-year-old friend of Bendor's, who also happened to be Vera's cousin and childhood friend—Edward, Prince of Wales. On the eve of Good Friday, Chanel and the prince met at a memorable dinner party hosted by the Marquis Melchior de Polignac and his wife, Nina Crosby, at Chez Henri, a chic Paris restaurant off the Cercle Gaillon behind the Paris Opéra. Chanel struck again. Edward, known to family and close friends as "David" or "Bunny," was smitten, begging Coco to call him "David."

The next evening, hours before another dinner both were to attend, David dropped by Chanel's apartment for a pre-dinner cocktail. Years later, Diana Vreeland, former editor in chief of *Vogue,* would insist that the "passionate, focused, and fiercely independent Chanel, a virtual tour de force" and the Prince of Wales "had a great romantic moment together."

But Bendor never gave up. The duke, who could defeat even the most hardened adversary, showed up in Paris a few weeks later. It was an early spring evening. Joseph, Chanel's butler, answered the doorbell and found an enormous bouquet of flowers hiding the face of the deliveryman. Legend holds that the butler, digging for a coin, told the messenger, "Put them down there." When he turned to tip the man, he recognized the Duke of Westminster. Soon after, no doubt persuaded by Bendor, the Prince of Wales called at Chanel's apartment on the rue du Faubourg-Saint-Honoré and pleaded Bendor's cause.

Chanel still had reservations about Bendor. She told Lady Iya Abdy: "The Duke frightened me." Chanel knew all about his sexual escapades; she wished to be loved as an equal. "I am not one of those women who belong to several men."

Vera Bate introduced Chanel into the glittering social set that revolved around the English royals: Westminster; Edward, Prince of Wales; Winston Churchill; and the crème of English society who had access to Buckingham Palace. Chanel and Bendor, two very different people, worlds apart, often antagonistic, were about to embark on a five-year love affair and adventure. Chanel was "a little like Cinderella . . . a flirt . . . pretending to be captivated, when suddenly, pfft!—she seemed to disappear!" Bendor was "the buccaneer searching for adventures . . . a man who loved his women—but [who], above all, loved to love."

Chanel was acutely aware of how conventional French society viewed and maligned her. To them, she was "the former demimondaine" who kept the Grand Duke Dmitri, while also publicly carrying on with French politicians, the Prince of Wales, and, according to a French police report, Lord Rothermere, Harold Harmsworth, owner with his brother Alfred of the London *Daily Mail.* In one of her more sarcastic moods, Chanel told friends, "I wanted to be a woman of a harem, and between my three 'guys,' the Prince of Wales, Grand Duke Dmitri, and the Duke of Westminster, I chose the man [Bendor] who would protect me—the simplest of men."

Bendor and Chanel secretly slipped aboard the *Flying Cloud,* anchored at Bayonne harbor on the Bay of Biscay in the late spring of 1924. She would say of their first days together: "He had a yacht, and that's the best thing for running away to start a love affair. The first time you're clumsy, the second you quarrel a bit, and if it doesn't go well, the third time you can stop at a port." Those first days must have been magical in the enchanted world Bendor created. When they reached the Mediterranean, an orchestra from Monte Carlo was brought aboard the ship so they could dance every night—something Bendor loved. He showered Chanel with precious jewels and other gifts; and Chanel told a confidante: "I loved him or I thought I loved him, which amounts to the same thing."

Bendor's extraordinary wealth surely enhanced his attractiveness for Chanel. This cousin to King George V owned outright Eaton Hall, an estate of some 11,000 acres where legions of gardeners cultivated roses, carnations, orchids, and exotic fruits and

Lady Dunn with Chanel and Gigot, ca. 1926.

vegetables all year round. A railroad spur on the estate connected it to the main line. Bendor even owned a private train to go from Eaton Hall up to London, where he owned Grosvenor House (later leased to the U.S. government for its embassy) and Bourdon House, plus income-producing properties around London's Kensington Gardens and vast holdings in Australia and Canada.

For Bendor's sea voyages, he could choose between the *Cutty Sark*, a converted naval vessel, and the spacious schooner *Flying Cloud*. There were stables of horses; hunting lodges in Scotland and France; Rolls-Royce and Bentley automobiles. The family jewels included the Westminster tiara and the Arcot diamonds.

Bendor, like his lifelong friend Winston Churchill, was born into a world where British noblemen were considered (and considered themselves) little less than godlike. He and the other scions of the great landed aristocracy entered manhood knowing their destiny was to rule the greatest empire the world had ever seen.

One of Bendor's chums, a fellow lord, described the duke as "a good-humored fellow, like a Newfoundland puppy, much given to riotous amusements and sports, with horses, motors, and ladies. The fast life clearly suits him, for he looks the model of health and strength." Churchill thought Bendor "excelled at hunting and knew everything about the habits of wild game . . . in war and in sport an intrepid companion . . . little given to self expression and public pronouncements; he was a man who thought deeply with a rare quality of wisdom and sound judgment. I always held his opinion in high esteem."

A French lady described Bendor as "a pure Victorian who had eyes for his shotgun, his hunters, jumpers and race horses, his dogs—while English women, of his day, had only to give birth to children and please their masters . . . a man who played at dropping a bit of sugar in its paper wrapper into hot coffee and with a chronometer in hand, timing how long it took to melt . . . a man who enjoyed hiding diamonds under the pillow of his mistresses . . . a man who could brutalize women . . ."

Whatever Chanel's views on Bolshevism before 1925, Bendor tutored her on the evils of Communism and confirmed her antipathy toward Jews. He shuddered at the word "Marxism." He was also notoriously homophobic. When his homosexual brother-in-law advocated free trade unions as a leader of the Liberal Party, Bendor revealed him to be gay to the king, George V, ruining his sister's marriage and the man's political career.

Chanel could match Bendor's homophobia. She is quoted as telling Paul Morand while in exile in Switzerland in the winter of 1946 at St. Moritz, "Homosexuals? Are they not always hanging around women: 'my beauty, my little one, my angel'—continually strangling them with flattery? I have seen young women ruined by these awful queers: drugs, divorce, and scandal. They will use any means to destroy a competitor and to wreak vengeance on a woman. The queers want to be women—but they are lousy women. They are charming!"

IN THE SUMMER OF 1924, when Violet Rowley formally separated from Bendor, he brought Chanel to Eaton Hall for a

Bendor, Duke of Westminster, and Chanel at the Grand
National racetrack, May 1924. Chanel's love affair with
Bendor lasted five years, their friendship a lifetime.
Both feared Communism and were anti-Semitic
and pro-German.

season of soirees, tennis parties, riding in the English countryside, and lounging about the splendid gardens. The autumn was
given to hunts in France and salmon fishing in Scotland. Pictures
taken during this period show a range of Chanel cameos: smiling broadly, she was forty-one years old to his forty-seven. Wearing her version of a Fair Isle sweater, she appears confident of her
ability to charm the greatest English lords and ladies. In another
picture, taken by Baron Adolf Gayne de Meyer, creator of American fashion photography, Chanel poses for a portrait wearing an
"exquisite" necklace of pearls—a gift from Bendor. In a *Vogue*
photo, Chanel smiles wearing a classic jersey suit with a cardigan
jacket, her beautiful neck draped in ropes of pearls. In one rare

A smiling Chanel (left) and Vera Bate (later Vera
Lombardi), ca. 1925, after fishing on Bendor's
Scottish estate. Vera told Winston Churchill
how she betrayed Chanel as a Nazi agent
to the British at Madrid, 1944.

photo, she is smoking a cigarette—a habit she never broke. (She
smoked Camels "incessantly" when she could get them.) Another
snapshot shows Chanel and Vera Bate dressed in baggy pants and
heavy tweeds for fishing. The two are caressing a hunting dog
as Chanel clutches a fishing gaff, its point protected by a cork.
There is also a delightful November 1929 snapshot of Winston
Churchill and Chanel, arm in arm at a hunting party at Eaton
Hall.

Bendor and Chanel frequently returned to Paris for gala evenings and the opera. When the duke showed up at a rehearsal
of *Le Train bleu,* a gossip columnist for *The Star* wrote in October 1924: "Rumor is busy with the future of the Duke . . . when
trouble between the duke and his duchess first began, it was said
that the next duchess would be a very good-looking girl whose

With Sir Winston Churchill at the Duke of Westminster's Eaton Hall
estate, early winter 1929. Their friendship would last a lifetime.

parents have become prominent . . . Now gossip has it that she
will be a clever and charming Frenchwoman who presides over a
very exclusive dressmaking establishment in Paris."

What the duke willed he got, and nothing Chanel wanted
was denied her. "My real life began with Westminster," she said
in a moment of weakness. "I'd finally found a shoulder to lean
on . . . he didn't know the meaning of the word 'snobby.' He was
simplicity itself." Some thirteen years earlier, Chanel and Étienne
Balsan had enjoyed riding the forest paths at Compiègne, where
she lived for three years as a courtesan at the Château de Royallieu. Now, Coco was received as the unofficial mistress of Eaton
Hall. Vera Bate was often there, helping her friend with English
ways and manners. But in typical Chanel fashion she made everyone speak French—even Bendor, who spoke it with an atrocious
accent—while she secretly studied English.

Life with Bendor, for a time at least, amounted to an ever-
lasting holiday celebration. They were gracious hosts to royal
cotillions with fifty or sixty guests often in attendance. At these
musical dinners, an orchestra in red coats and patent leather slippers played far into the night. A battalion of valets and femmes de

Chanel in hunting dress with Winston Churchill and
his son, Randolph, in France, 1928. Churchill's friendship
and admiration for Chanel lasted some thirty years;
historians claim Churchill saved Chanel from trial as a
German collaborator when Paris was liberated in 1944.

chambre, butlers, cooks, kitchen staff, gardeners, and attendants
for every sport worked around the clock for the pleasure of the
duke's guests—no guest needed to lift a finger at Eaton Hall.
Its fifty-four bedrooms, stables, and seventeen Rolls-Royces were
ruled over by Bendor's stern and commanding steward, Percy
Smith. He held responsibility for the staff, the hall, and the mas-
terpieces by Rubens, Raphael, Rembrandt, Hals, Velázquez, and
Goya that decorated the walls.

Chanel shared Bendor's love for riding, hunting, fishing, sailing, and gay parties. In their headlong pursuit of pleasure, Chanel
and Westminster ignored the mass labor unrest of the mid- and
late 1920s and the Great Depression of the 1930s—it was all too
tedious. She was, after all, now a member of the privileged class.
For the duke, Chanel, and their set, the band played on, including taking parties to the ultra chic and exclusive Embassy club to
dance to Ambrose's orchestra and where the maître d'hôtel, Luigi,

always reserved a table for Bendor and Chanel with its view of the balcony and curved wooden staircase.

In 1928, the fairy tale continued as Chanel hunted wild boar with Churchill at Westminster's lodge, Mimizan, south of Bordeaux. Churchill, then the chancellor of the Exchequer, and his son, Randolph, are portrayed in a *Daily Mail* news clipping showing Coco in greatcoat, bowler hat, and booted with riding crop in hand. She stands like a queen between the two Churchills, surrounded by a pack of beagle hunting dogs. A copy of the article is annotated in Chanel's hand: "A very charming picture . . . the feather in your cap is missing. *Daily Mail,* 11 Jan. 1928." Churchill marked the occasion in a letter to his wife, Clementine:

> The famous Chanel turned up and I took great fancy to her—a most capable and agreeable woman—much the stronger personality Benny [Bendor] has been up against. She hunted vigorously all day, motored to Paris after dinner, and today is engaged in passing and improving dresses on endless streams of mannequins. All together 200 models have to be settled in almost three weeks. She does it all with her own fingers, pinning, cutting, looping. Some have to be altered ten times. With her is Vera Bate, nee Arkwright, Yr chief of staff? Non—One of your lieutenants? Non, Elle est là. Voilà tout.

Later, Winston wrote Clementine again from Stack Lodge in Scotland: "Chanel is here in place of Violet [Bendor's second wife] . . . she fishes from morn to night and has killed fifty salmon (sometimes weighing 24 pounds). She is very agreeable—really a great and strong being, fit to rule a man and an empire. Benny is very well and I think extremely happy to be mated with an equal. Her ability is balancing his power."

Churchill, clearly captivated by Chanel, was on the mark. Her creative energy seemed limitless. She would play, ride, fish, slake Bendor's lust, and then return to her mannequins to create ravishing outfits, such as her sexy and famously simple "little black dress," which was hailed by fashion cognoscenti. Among them, Janet Wallach, Chanel biographer and fashion director, wrote: "[Chanel] created elegant clothes and elegant settings at once comfortable, luxurious and chic; and she entertained an extraordinary number of friends. Her interests ranged from athletics to the intellectual—she [even claimed] to have read all the books in her library." Summing up, Wallach said, "She had a quick mind, a quicker tongue and a wit to amuse the most jaded of men."

Chanel had a genius for exploiting everything and everyone she came in contact with and went about inventing a lifestyle based on Westminster's manner and his dash. But her career and ambitions kept the couple apart. Bendor missed Chanel and resented the time she devoted to her work. Her friend Lady Iya Abdy said, "She really had two real loves . . . herself . . . and her fashion house . . . everything else was merely passion, weakness, adventures without a future, calculated liaisons."

Mademoiselle knew full well that Bendor's desire to "look after her" was shorthand for "you will have no obligation but me." Frustrated by her absences, Bendor begged Vera to help keep Chanel in London. His scheme was to convince Chanel to open a London boutique where she would be kept busy—and conveniently close to him.

The London House of Chanel was an immediate success. The Duchess of York, future Queen of England, and a host of prominent English noble ladies and socialites became her clients. Chanel was the name on everyone's lips. And from her ateliers in Paris, Chanel produced the toque, a pillbox hat. It was a perfect addition to her dress in black crêpe de chine with long sleeves— Chanel's proverbial little black dress.

It was during this London period that Chanel introduced her early version of the classic jersey suit with a cardigan jacket, low-belted pullover top, and pleated skirt. Every motif and article of clothing that came to her eye was food for inspiration, from Bendor's tweeds to his sailor's caps to his valet's vests. Bold and inventive, she personally wore bell-bottom trousers and crewneck sweaters, projecting a sexy, at-ease look. A picture taken at her La Pausa retreat shows Chanel, her waist pinched by a decorative belt, smiling and happy while her Great Dane, called Gigot (a gift from Bendor; the name means "leg of lamb" in French), looks at the camera.

DESPITE OCCASIONAL SPATS, Bendor never stopped showering Chanel with gifts: works of art, precious jewels, a house in Mayfair, and a five-acre plot near Roquebrune at Cap-Martin between Menton and Monte Carlo. Bendor purchased it in 1928 for 1.8 million francs (over $3 million today) and then deeded it to Chanel on February 9, 1929. There, they built La Pausa, at the top of Roquebrune near Monte Carlo, their ideal villa. (When completed by Chanel sometime in 1929, the total investment in La Pausa would amount to 6 million francs—the equivalent of almost 12 million dollars in 2010.)

Chanel's metamorphosis was now complete. In her forties, this onetime waif, impoverished orphan, and concubine had been transformed into a middle-aged fairy princess.

The duke's only son had died at the age of four in 1909, and Bendor desperately wanted a male heir. As early as 1926 he began insisting Chanel give up her career and become a full-time companion. But it's very difficult to believe that he ever truly intended to make Chanel his wife, a duchess, and the mother of an heir to his dukedom. The chance of Chanel giving birth to a child after forty was slim, indeed. She would later tell a German journalist why she had never married: "Because of my work, I suppose. The two men I loved never understood that. They were rich and didn't understand that a woman, even a rich woman, might want to work. I could never have given up the House of Chanel. It was my child. I created it starting from nothing. I once said to the Duke of Westminster, 'Why should we marry? We're together . . . people accept it.' I never wanted to weigh more heavily on a man than a bird."

Chanel's friends thought she was timid with children, didn't understand them, and didn't know how to talk to them. Still, Chanel and Boy Capel unofficially adopted Chanel's nephew, André Palasse—and sent him to an English boarding school to have the best education. Later, she became a loving aunt and surrogate mother to André's eldest daughter, Gabrielle "Tiny" Palasse—"Gabrielle" to honor Chanel.

Neither Chanel nor Bendor ever really insisted on a marriage. To prove her independence, Chanel eventually returned his unused checkbook to his secretary. "I have used my own money." She steadfastly refused to be seen as any man's kept woman.

When Bendor invited Princess Stephanie von Hohenlohe, an

accomplished sportswoman and a startling Viennese beauty, to fish with him in Scotland, Chanel reacted by meeting her former poet lover, Pierre Reverdy in Paris—throwing Bendor into a jealous rage. He declared, "Chanel is crazy" as he bombarded her apartment with letter after letter. Chanel would reply, "All I want from you are wildflowers picked by your own hands." The Duke then showered her with flowers—under the leaves of which were hidden yet more precious jewels.

It is doubtful that the beautiful and wealthy Stephanie was ever a competitor of Chanel's. The Viennese princess was of partial Jewish descent—and Bendor was fervently anti-Semitic. In a notorious breach of etiquette, he went so far as to refer to the British royal family as "those Jews," falsely believing that Queen Victoria's Prince Consort, Albert of Saxe-Coburg-Gotha, had Jewish origins. After a number of whiskeys, and in front of a Rothschild, Bendor would repeat, "I cannot bear those bloody Jews." It is a bit of irony that a few years later with the Nazi regime in power, Stephanie would become Adolf Hitler's "dear Princess." SS Reichsführer Heinrich Himmler solved her "Jewish problem" by making Stephanie an "honorary Aryan." Beginning in 1932, she worked in London as an agent for Nazi intelligence, serving as a liaison between British pro-Nazis and powerful men and women in London society and politics: Bendor, the Prince of Wales, London *Daily Mail* owner Lord Rothermere, Lady Margot Asquith, Lady Ethel Snowden, and Lady Edith Londonderry. In 1937, Stephanie was instrumental in arranging meetings between Hitler and Edward Wood, Lord Halifax, and the Duke of Windsor— the uncrowned King Edward VIII—and his bride, the American divorcée Wallis Simpson. All three were rabid anti-Communists, feared Soviet Russia, and preached an accommodation with Nazi Germany—in their view, an essential European rampart against the Communist hordes.

THE DISSOLUTION OF CHANEL and the duke's fairy-tale love affair was slow but inescapable. Chanel treasured her free spirit. She searched for true love, and when she thought she had it, it turned out to be an impossible love. It was impossible because Chanel was her own woman, and after nearly five years with Bendor, she was simply bored with the Duke's lifestyle. He, in turn,

Serge Lifar, as Vestris, in a costume designed by Chanel, with
Marie-Laure de Noailles at the "Bal du Tricentenaire de Racine,"
hosted by the Count de Beaumont, June 1939. Lifar was one
of Luftwaffe chief Hermann Göring's favorite ballet masters.
Terrified when Paris was liberated, Lifar hid from French resistance
fighters in Chanel's wardrobe at her apartment on the rue Cambon.

was no longer so keen on being part of hers. Bendor began to
dread spending time with her clever Parisian friends—the jokes
and sly asides of Cocteau, Diaghilev, and his lover, Serge Lifar,
were way over his head. But the egocentric Duke continued to
cling to Coco despite their bad-tempered shouting matches over
his frequent infidelities. Eventually, Churchill reminded Bendor
of his royal obligations—the need for him to have an heir and the
fact that Chanel would never be accepted at Court.

ALL THIS TIME, Chanel and Bendor apparently never realized that the French police and the Sûreté were closely monitoring
their comings and goings. One report told how:

The Duke makes frequent trips to France; [and] to the Château de Woolsack (at Mimizan, Landes). When in Paris the Duke stays at Chanel's apartment. The former demimondaine [Chanel] has excellent relations in political and diplomatic circles. The Duke of Westminster, who is divorced, takes a great interest in the "petites mains" [Chanel's little hands—artisan employees who sew dresses, buttons, etc.] of the House of Chanel. During last summer a number of [Chanel's employees] passed their vacations at the Château de Woolsack, where they were offered a princely table and lodging. It goes on every year.

Vera Bate divorced her American husband in 1929 and then married Alberto Lombardi, an Italian calvary officer. She now became an Italian citizen. The French Sûreté expanded its investigations to include Vera and her new husband. Reports documented their telephone conversations, travel, and relations with Chanel and Bendor. In 1930, Vera left Chanel to work for a competitor, the Paris fashion house Molyneux. Then suddenly, Vera moved to Rome with her husband, now a colonel in the Italian cavalry. The Sûreté suspected him of working for the Italian military intelligence service.

THE YEARS SLIPPED BY. Bendor could not stop seeking new conquests, and he could not stop wanting to possess Chanel. Later, Chanel would proclaim: "I never tried to get him. If one is titled, rich, very rich, one becomes fair game, a quarry: a hare, a fox. Those English ladies are great hunters; they are forever hunting. I have never imagined thinking, here is a man I want; I'll get him—where is my gun?"

The summer of 1929 brought their affair to its inevitable conclusion. Chanel and Misia Sert had agreed to join Bendor aboard the *Flying Cloud*. It must have been wonderfully irreverent irony—his crew of forty, amid the massive furniture, great canopied beds, and extravagance, contrasted with the two intimate and caustic Parisian women who could play mischievous imps, giggling and taking drugs together. The revelry ended abruptly when out of the blue, a telegram arrived from Venice, announcing that Diaghilev was near death.

When the *Flying Cloud* reached Venice, Misia and Chanel

rushed to the Grand Hôtel des Bains on the Lido to find Diaghilev desperately ill and being cared for by his lovers, the dancers Boris Kochno and Serge Lifar. Diaghilev was terrified of dying. Their visit seemed to lift his spirits. Leaving Misia to look after him, Chanel returned to Bendor. Misia approached a Roman Catholic priest to grant absolution to Diaghilev. At first, the priest refused, as the dancer was Russian Orthodox. Beset by Misia's fury, the cleric relented, and this Dostoyevsky-like character—a magician in the art of the ballet, the man who promoted Michel Fokine, Nijinsky, Léonide Massine, and George Balanchine—passed away.

Misia was crushed. She later claimed, "A piece of me went with him." Lifar and Kochno couldn't bear their master's death; it seemed a desperate moment. Chanel, driven by a presentiment, returned to Venice, where she and Misia arranged a mass followed by a burial service. Dressed in white, Misia, Chanel, Lifar, and Kochno accompanied Diaghilev's coffin mounted on a gondola through the canals of Venice and to the impresario's gravesite on the burial island of San Michele.

Bendor insisted Chanel return aboard his schooner. But the romance was spent, the passion long gone. Bendor could not resist his impulses. Like the hunter he was, he had to pursue other women—and Chanel found that intolerable. They quarreled continually. It may be one of Chanel's myths—one of the many that surround her years with Bendor—but nevertheless the anecdote is a touching final souvenir. The story has the couple arguing aboard the *Flying Cloud* anchored off Villefranche on the Côte d'Azur. The Duke had then gone ashore. One legend has it that he returned to Chanel with a breathtaking emerald, and, under a perfect moon, he slipped the stone into the hollow of Chanel's palm. Without a thought she let the precious gem fall into the sea.

AFTER BEING THE LOVER of the richest man in the United Kingdom, Chanel returned briefly to Pierre Reverdy—the pure Mediterranean and tortured poet. With his swarthy complexion and thick black hair, Reverdy may well have been a latent image of Gabrielle's lost love, the father she hardly knew. Unlike the duke, Reverdy was a mate—his origins being very much like hers. When he showed signs of boredom at living at the rue du Faubourg-Saint-Honoré apartment, Chanel found a studio apartment for him nearby. But Reverdy wouldn't allow himself to be captured. He soon fled again to Solesmes, only to return a few weeks later to Chanel, and to briefly carouse with Cocteau, Max Jacob (the Jewish poet converted to Catholicism), Blaise Cendrars, Léger, and Braque.

Reverdy now preferred American jazz musicians, solidly installed in Paris, to Chanel's friends. Coco scorned nights out: "the bad food, bad booze, and the idiots that repeat the same stories, time after time, just to say something." She seldom joined in Reverdy's nightlife, preferring to be in bed early so she could rise early for work.

Ultimately, Chanel lured Pierre to La Pausa—hoping a change in climate and the beauty of her Mediterranean hideaway would work some magic on their romance.

It was during visits to La Pausa that Reverdy helped Chanel compile a series of maxims that would years later be published in *Vogue*. Earlier, she had written articles for Parisian women's reviews: *Le Miroir du monde, Les Femmes et le sport,* and *Le Nouveau Luxe.* Now, in middle age, she wanted to do something literary— just as she had wanted to sing and play the piano as a young woman. The maxims included: "Our homes are our prisons; one finds liberty in their decoration." "One can get used to ugliness— never neglect." "Real generosity is to accept ungratefulness." The material was a bit like Reverdy's cut-and-dried poetry.

Back in Paris, Reverdy was again captivated but also repelled by the glitter of wealth that surrounded Chanel. Despite his hatred for Paris elite society, he accepted Chanel's money and seemed to enjoy embarrassing her—bursting in on dinner parties and then fleeing. Finally, as much as she loved Reverdy, Chanel realized he could never fit into her world. Forever friends and sometimes lovers, the pair agreed it was time for them to part. He left a touching few lines for Chanel: "I love you and I leave you/I need to walk on/perhaps we'll meet again/exchange memories, talk about other times/then, you'll come back to me/and we'll laugh." (Later, Reverdy, as an armed French partisan during the occupation, would arrest Chanel's wartime colleague, French Baron Louis de Vaufreland, during the liberation of Paris and send him to prison for collaboration with the Nazis.)

Among the Paris elite, the breakup with Reverdy did not have the same gravity as Chanel's split from Bendor. "Imagine," wrote Chanel's biographers. "The little peasant out of her provincial rut refusing to marry the Duke of Westminster." But as a child, Chanel had dreamed of escaping the prison of convent life. With hard work and an intuitive sense of good taste, feminine charm, and stubborn, rebellious, ambition, Chanel left poverty behind and entered a world of silks, satins, precious jewels, immense wealth, and notoriety. She was on a velvet roll as she set out to do without Bendor. "One must not let oneself be forgotten, one must stay on the toboggan. The toboggan is what people who are talked about ride on. One must get a front seat and not let oneself be put out of it."

Bendor fell in love again. He brought his fiancée, Loelia (pronounced "Leelia") Ponsonby, almost half his age and the well-bred daughter of the king's treasurer to Paris, in the spring of 1930 to meet Chanel. One had to wonder if Bendor was being deliberately cruel—or simply callous toward Loelia's feelings. Either way, Bendor insisted that Chanel speak with her and tell him if the lady was suitable. While the duke wandered around the rue du Faubourg-Saint-Honoré house that he knew so well, a sophisticated and elegant Chanel appeared bejeweled and dressed in a navy blue suit with a white blouse, making the twenty-eight-year-old Loelia feel "gawky and dowdy." Loelia remembered Chanel as

> small, dark and simian . . . the personification of her own fashion . . . hung with every sort of necklace and bracelet which rattled as she moved. Her sitting room was lavish and she sat in a large armchair, a pair of tall Coromandel screens making an effective background. I perched, rather at a disadvantage; on a stool at her feet . . . I doubt that I or my tweed suit passed the test. For something to say I told her that Mrs. George Keppel had given me a Chanel necklace as a Christmas present. Immediately she asked me to describe the necklace.
>
> "No," she said coldly, "that necklace certainly doesn't come from my establishment."

Some biographers claim that Bendor came to Paris to see Chanel a few days after his wedding to Loelia.

IN THE FALL of 1929 the American stock market crashed. U.S. securities worldwide soon showed a massive loss of $26 billion. In America, Great Britain, and on the Continent losses wiped out great fortunes. In Germany, political violence, general strikes, fear of Bolshevism, and hyperinflation eventually destroyed political stability, leading to the ascent of Adolf Hitler and the Nazi party. Fearing Hitler and German aggression the French began building the Maginot Line along a part of the French-German border.

Grand Duke Dmitri married a rich young woman from New York, and Bendor at fifty still longed for a son. Nevertheless, Bendor remained Coco's on-and-off lover, acting the spoiled, pampered, and sexually demanding self-indulgent "sport."

THE WALL STREET CRASH of Black Tuesday, on October 29, 1929, wrecked American industry and commerce and ushered in the Great Depression. Soon the bells tolled for Germany's Weimar Republic as American loans and investments to the German government and industry came to an end. In France, the early tremors of a coming economic slowdown were apparent.

Dincklage and his German half-Jewish wife, Maximiliane (called "Catsy"), now lived part time on France's sun-drenched Côte d'Azur. For the Dincklage couple it was a sublime moment as they savored their good fortune, an assignment in France far from the German economic turmoil and the chaos of Berlin.

Dincklage had earned this plum posting at a moment when nearly 6 million Germans were out of work. Coming from a family steeped in military tradition helped, but ten years of undercover work as a military intelligence officer had won him the friendship of General Walther von Brauchitsch, the man Hitler would later choose to be commander in chief of the German army, the Wehrmacht.

Because Dincklage spoke impeccable French and English, his cover story as a fun-loving, sun-worshiping tennis man and sometime independent German merchant was easily accepted. Having a flirtatious beautiful wife with Jewish blood helped, and the couple mixed easily with the locals and a growing colony of German refugees. In 1930 the town records of Sanary-sur-Mer show

Maximiliane von Dincklage receiving a residence permit from the Sanary Préfecture de Police along with a host of Italians and Germans. Thomas Mann, Aldous Huxley, and English writer Sybille Bedford, a German and Catsy's half sister, were in residence. Later, Sanary became a refuge for a growing number of German intellectuals and Jews who fled Germany and Hitler's Brown Shirt thugs.

When at Sanary, the Dincklages lived a life of pleasure on the bountiful Mediterranean coast, with abundant sunshine, fresh fish, and local wine. As the author Marta Feuchtwanger, a German expatriate in Sanary in the early thirties, wrote: "We were by the sea. From the cliff you could see deep blue bays and an island some way off. There was also a private beach . . . the size of a handkerchief. The rocks were covered with a dense brush: rosemary, sage and thyme. The scent . . . was intoxicating."

At Sanary-sur-Mer the only disturbance might have been from the clacking of the metal *boules* as the locals and their guests played at *pétanque,* or the sounds of a wind-blown sea crashing against the shore. Sun, surf, fun, and good company, "arrosés" with a delightful local wine, were guaranteed pastimes at this haven a few kilometers from where the French war fleet lay at anchor in the harbor of Toulon, the headquarters of the French Mediterranean ships. The fleet and French naval headquarters at Toulon would become Dincklage's principal target for the next few years; and Dincklage was financed through the German Embassy in Berlin from funds drawn from the coffers of the German military intelligence service and delivered via couriers. The flow of money paid Dincklage's agents, bribed corrupt officials, and supported their lifestyle. Spatz and Catsy's masters in Berlin were paying the Dincklages to build an espionage operation and to recruit a web of secret agents paid or blackmailed into penetrating the secrets of the French navy at their Toulon base, where secret plans and codebooks were stored. After settling in at Sanary and scouting out the Toulon naval base and fleet, Spatz and Catsy went about seeking potential recruits, men and women prepared to betray France.

The Dincklages were not the first Abwehr agents to be assigned to France. The French Ministry of the Interior, Sûreté générale, reported that eight years earlier three German military intelligence agents (no first names were given), Herr von Brink-mann, Count von Brennkendorf, and Major Roll had arrived in France each bankrolled with 500,000 French francs. Their mission, according to a source in the Polish army high command, was to organize an espionage network in Paris to penetrate the French army high command and obtain French military war plans. No record was found that the three spies were arrested.

Dincklage was the perfect man to head the Abwehr mission on the Côte d'Azur. His Berlin masters had picked a man with credentials and a pedigree. Dincklage was, after all, the grandson and son of senior military officers who had served German emperors in two wars. His mother, Lorry, was English-born. Her brother, Dincklage's uncle, was an admiral active in German naval affairs. From his early life he had been steeped in the social graces of old Europe. From 1914 to 1918 he had been tested in the world war and in the trenches of the Russian front. Dincklage, in another time and place, would have been the ideal recruit for the CIA or the British secret service, MI6.

Maximiliane had a Jewish mother, affording her the possibility of playing the role of an anti-Nazi German. It was good cover for an espionage assignment in France. And Maximiliane had solid credentials, too. A 1929 German Registry document tells of Dincklage's 1927 marriage to Maximiliane, the daughter of a Jewish mother and an aristocratic father, a lieutenant colonel in the German army. The report claims Dincklage retired in 1929 as a major from military service—but this was a cover story invented by his Abwehr bosses in Berlin. Dincklage simply swapped a cavalry officer's dress for the civilian garb of a clandestine intelligence officer. Indeed, French military intelligence prior to World War II documented "Dincklage, alias Spatz . . . from 1920 an officer of the German military intelligence service known as 'Abwehr.'"

It would take some time for the Sûreté, French military intelligence and counterintelligence, the Deuxième Bureau (often written in French as 2ème Bureau), to realize the extent of Dincklage's clandestine work on the Côte d'Azur. A 1934 secret Sûreté document headed "Suspected Germans at Sanary" describes how Dincklage (then special attaché at the German Embassy in Paris) carried out operations in the South of France: "living in a number of villas at the Mediterranean resort village of Sanary-sur-Mer, 13

Maximiliane von Schoenebeck, "Catsy,"
the wife of Baron von Dincklage,
sometime in 1930 when she spied for
Germany near the French naval base
at Toulon, France.

kilometers from Toulon; but settled at Villa Petite Casa for many years." The report goes on to say: "The Dincklage couple kept the villa even during their absences from the Côte d'Azur."

The Dincklages' cover at Sanary included an active social life. They befriended their neighbors, including the English pacifist writer Aldous Huxley and his wife, Maria. Sybille Bedford, Catsy's half sister, told of their adventures in diary entries from 1932, when, together with Catsy, Dincklage played at the casino and dined with Aldous and Maria Huxley. "There were Huxley picnics at sundown on beach or olive grove or cliff . . . we ate fried rabbit, zucchini flowers, and drank jugs of iced punch—white wine, lemon, rum—made by Aldous himself."

Among the Dincklages' friends at Sanary were French naval commissioner Charles Coton and his Jewish fiancée, Alida Léa Salomon. Coton described Sanary as "a small agreeable port filled with artists, writers, painters and sculptors. There was a passionate intellectual ambiance." Everyone met at the two port cafes. "We danced at the Marine, and we talked at the Nautique." Coton later

French naval lieutenant Charles Coton
and his wife, Alida (Léa), in the mid-
1930s. The couple were part of the
Dincklage-Abwehr ring that spied
for Germany at the French naval
base at Toulon, France.

wrote how he found Dincklage to be distinguished: "The Baron, known as Spatz, was an excellent tennis player and we played often. From what I knew they had left Germany because the regime didn't please them and because it had created some problems for them for racial reasons, his wife was Jewish . . . Rightly or wrongly, I don't know, the noise around Sanary was that he was a German spy, and that was one of the reasons he lived there since it was so close to the port of Toulon. In my case, he never spoke to me about military matters."

Coton's disingenuous remark was a pure lie. In 1933, French counterintelligence agents were already tracking Coton suspecting the naval officer was one of Dincklage's agents at the Toulon naval base. Later, Coton's spying was confirmed and he would become the Dincklage courier, traveling between Toulon and Paris.

IN 1930, Dincklage's Berlin masters pulled him out of Sanary and gave him temporary duty as a diplomat at the German Embassy at Warsaw. There, he was befriended by Bernard du Ples-

six, a fellow diplomat stationed at the French Embassy. Author
Francine du Plessix Gray, daughter of Bernard and his wife, Tatiana, remembered her parents befriending Dincklage in Warsaw.
Plessix Gray writes that her father and mother found Dincklage
"a charming Chargé d'affaires at the German embassy." However, there is no record in the German foreign affairs archives of
Dincklage being chargé d'affaires—the diplomatic term for the
assignment of an officer as a temporary replacement for an absent
ambassador.

Yet there is no doubt that Spatz was in Warsaw through 1931.
Despite the diplomatic dinners and balls, the city was torn with
intrigue and beset by an economic crisis after the collapse of the
Austrian Credit-Anstalt, the German Danat-Bank, and the official closure of all German banks. The financial crisis pushed Polish politics to the right, led by General Józef Pilsudski. In 1931,
the shift in political sentiment toward the far right was even more
pronounced in Germany where multimillionaires Alfred Hugen-
berg, Emil Kirdorf, Fritz Thyssen, and Kurt von Schröder agreed
to lend financial support to the eight-hundred-strong Nazi party
of Adolf Hitler.

FRANKLIN DELANO ROOSEVELT was elected the thirty-
second President of the United States in 1932. That same year
Dincklage shed his diplomatic role in Warsaw to return to clandestine work at Sanary, where Catsy had remained during his
absence.

Chanel was nearing fifty. In middle age she remained ever fas-
cinating, seductive, and ambitious—"attracting men and women
of the arts." Times were hard in France. Rich Americans were a
disappearing breed. On the Côte d'Azur, a quarter of the luxury
hotels closed. Still, between 1931 and 1935, the House of Chanel
prospered—almost doubling business: employing 2,440 women
in 1931 and nearly 4,000 by 1935, selling 28,000 dresses that year
in Europe, the Near East, and America. In Britain, Chanel made
her mark as English debutantes adopted her new designs for cotton evening dresses in piqué, lace, and organdy with innovative
zippers.

America beckoned.

FOUR

A HOLLYWOOD DIVERTISSEMENT

God makes stars. I just produce them.

—SAMUEL GOLDWYN

O NE SUMMER DAY in 1930 in Monte Carlo, Grand Duke Dmitri introduced Chanel to Samuel Goldwyn, who wanted her to design clothes for his stars—Joan Blondell, Madge Evans, and Gloria Swanson. At the height of the American economic depression, with 13 million citizens out of work, Goldwyn offered Chanel a million dollars (about $14 million in today's money) if she would spend a few weeks in Hollywood. Goldwyn's offer came at a time when American, French, and German fashion journals were celebrating Chanel couture. *Vogue* magazine had gone so far as to hire no less than four top fashion photographers—Cecil Beaton, Edward Steichen, Horst, and Hoyningen-Huene—to capture her creations.

It was the right moment for Chanel to leave Paris, to try something new. Her major competitor, Elsa Schiaparelli, was displaying her creations practically under Coco's nose on the Place Vendôme around the corner from the Chanel atelier on the rue Cambon. "The Italian Wizard" was bent on "clipping Chanel's wings . . . with her sudden flash of fantasy, surrealism, and extravagance that marked the 1930s." Art and photography were major fashion influences, and Schiaparelli had made a mark working with Salvador Dalí to create surreal sweaters and leg-of-lamb felt hats.

Hollywood would be challenging, but a trip to America would

be a break from Paris and far from the shadow of Schiaparelli—Chanel was sure of her own skill and talent. She was, after all, a long-established and star purveyor of clothes, jewelry, and perfume, "the best-selling fragrance in the world." Chanel had taken women "out of fussy clothes and hats . . . modeling them into jersey sportswear, with nautical details and beach pajamas—ideas she claimed she had stolen from Bendor and other men's wear."

But the fashion business was lagging, hurt by the impact of the economic crisis in Europe. Goldwyn offered more than money. He was a publicity genius who might get the House of Chanel a piece of the American ready-to-wear garment trade—without the Chanel Paris label, of course.

Later, Chanel would say, "Hollywood is the capital of bad taste. It was like an evening at the Folies Bergères. Once it is agreed that the girls were beautiful in their feathers there is not much to add—and when everything is super: super sex, super production it all looks alike—and it's vulgar." But Chanel couldn't refuse the package: a cool million, along with Goldwyn's well-oiled public relations expertise.

Despite her declared distaste for Jews, Chanel signed up for a trial with Goldwyn, born Schmuel Gelbfisz—once an inhabitant of the Warsaw ghetto. One author tells how Goldwyn did his best to keep Jews away from Chanel. Indeed, she was on good behavior, saying at the time: "There are great Jews, Israelites and there are youpins . . ." (a pejorative French slur for Jews).

The mass-produced "talkies" of the time were quickly outdated and often no longer in synch with the rapidly changing fashions of the day. Knee-length garments and unisex fashions went out overnight and long slinky gowns came in the next day—or so it seemed. "What looked young last year looks old this season as longer fuller skirts, a higher waistline looked right, smart and becoming." Something had to change. Goldwyn, a master at image building, now created another Hollywood fantasy. His stars were to be dressed by Chanel and his "women [moviegoers] would be able to see in our pictures the latest in Paris fashions."

CHANEL DECIDED that Marie Sophie Godebska, her aging Polish "Misia," had to come along to Hollywood, if nothing else to charm Goldwyn in his native Polish. And Misia needed a break.

Her troubles were a sordid Paris story of debauchery in the libertine late 1920s. She and her husband, José-Maria Sert, had been in love with a nineteen-year-old delectable Georgian princess and novice sculptress: Roussadana Mdivani, known as Roussy. Exceedingly beautiful and manipulative, Roussy had come to Paris with her refugee parents and was studying art when the fifty-year-old José fell for the teenager. Then Cupid struck again when Misia, too, fell for her charms. Paris tongues began to talk: "An inseparable trio . . . a sinister threesome . . . they drug her—use her." Roussy's "Tatar charm had captivated the Sert couple." Chanel had warned her friend to stop playing with fire. Instead, Misia gave José-Maria tacit approval to share Roussy's bed. Now Paris rumors spread about how Misia was intimate with Roussy—and how Chanel was intimate with Misia. Of the latter, Misia's biographers stated, "Coco and Misia were seen together so constantly and their relations were so highly charged that it was said they were lovers."

Homosexual and heterosexual affairs were common among Chanel's clique, as was the use of morphine, cocaine, and other drugs. The Serts; Cocteau and his new lover, French film actor Jean Marais; Serge Lifar; Étienne de Beaumont; painter Christian Bérard; and artist and editor Paul Iribe were all substance abusers. Indeed, by 1935 Chanel herself would be dependent on morphine-based sedol. Inconstant and whimsical, she paid the medical expenses to wean Cocteau off the drug, and yet in a magazine interview, she described him as "a snobbish little pederast who did nothing all his life but steal from people."

ALTHOUGH BOTH WERE fervent Catholics, José-Maria Sert divorced Misia in a civil court proceeding. The middle-aged José ran off with then-twenty-two-year-old Roussy after arranging a civil marriage in The Hague. Misia was devastated.

To the beat of Goldwyn's star-making drums, Chanel took a heartbroken Misia and a battalion of models, assistants, and seamstresses to the New World in the spring of 1931 aboard the Norddeutsche Lloyd SS *Europa*. Embarking from Calais, the luxury liner sailed the great circle route at 27.5 knots, landing in New York five days later. The ship's manifest noted Chanel's birth date as 1889 instead of 1883. She had somehow arranged to shave six years off her life; it would not be the last time she would lie about her age.

At a suite in the Hotel Pierre overlooking Central Park on Fifth Avenue, Chanel spoke to the press, in the words of the *New York Times,* "not as an animated picture star but as a shrewd businesswoman." Dressed in a simple rose-red jersey sport ensemble with a white knit blouse and a very Chanel collar and cuffs of white piqué, "a slight, charming brunette with bobbed hair told reporters [through an interpreter] long hair would be coming back into general fashion soon. If a few smart women wear their hair long the rest will follow."

Astute as ever, charming, and very French, she subtly tried to sell her costume jewelry: "a long string of pearls were looped several times about her throat and she wore a bracelet of multicolored semi-precious stones. She likes costume jewelry, she explained, with many eloquent gestures . . . She likes to wear plenty of it with daytime dresses, but thinks very little jewelry should be worn with formal costumes."

TO THE *NEW YORK TIMES* REPORTER, Chanel seemed "rather bewildered at the scores of interviewers and reception committee members who crowded into her suite." But rather than bewildered, she was sick. She had come down with influenza, but that didn't deter her from spraying the reporters and guests with a little atomizer of an as-yet-unnamed—or rather, unnumbered—new scent. She revealed to her guests that she never went to the movies; that real perfume is mysterious; and that men who wear perfume are disgusting. She later suggested, with no explanation: "If blonde, use blue perfume."

Chanel soon set out for the West Coast. Goldwyn had made all the arrangements for her triumphant arrival in Hollywood. There would be a special white railroad car to whisk his star to sunny California, a gala reception for the Chanel party on the Los Angeles train platform with Greta Garbo on site to peck her cheek, and then a soiree on the studio lot, where Chanel would meet the Hollywood headliners of the day. As the flashbulbs burst, Chanel was sweet-talked and kissed by Erich von Stroheim, Claudette Colbert, and Katharine Hepburn, who was filming *Little Women.*

With Ina Claire, when Chanel worked in Hollywood dressing
Goldwyn's stars, 1931.

In the background, three thousand walk-on faces looked on from
gigantic shooting stages.

It was all very grand and probably very dull for Chanel, but
the newshounds were entranced and gushing. Chanel's biographer, *Paris Match* editor Pierre Galante, wrote how they tasted
real Champagne, caviar, and "gawked at Paris mannequins and
laughed at French wit." The press cabled fulsome dispatches about
Chanel's entourage and her introduction to Garbo: "Two Queens
Meet," they proclaimed. While Polish-speaking Misia soothed an
obsequious Goldwyn—calling Sam "Mother"—Chanel learned
the ways of Hollywood. According to Galante, "The star actors
and actresses had to be pious, docile and smiling or be banished—
with millions of Americans out of work, the studios had imposed
a strict code of morality and good conduct—divorce was forbidden and famous names were photographed for the newsreels and
movie magazines in simple homes, visiting their church or pas-
tor." Hollywood casting decreed: "actors [were] strong as police-
men, pure as Boy Scouts and temperate as Quakers; yet despite
the American 'Code of Decency' that studio detectives tried to
enforce, behind the layers of veils, debauchery, drug abuse and
orgies were a way of life."

Gloria Swanson costumed by Chanel,
in the 1931 film *Tonight or Never.*

Robert Greig and Gloria Swanson, dressed by Chanel, in the film
Tonight or Never.

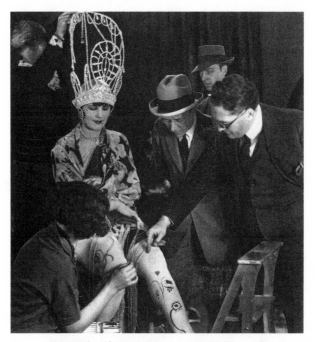

Paul Iribe (far right) in 1924 as Hollywood
director of the film *Changing Husbands*. Iribe and
Chanel fell in love in 1931 when he helped
manage her affairs. He was the director of her
right-wing publication *Le Témoin* that carried his
extraordinary illustrations of Chanel. Iribe
died with Chanel at his side in 1935.

Coco soaked up and reveled in the behind-the-scenes technical
details of making films—the huge soundstages, lighting techniques, and makeup. She designed costumes while her workers
dressed the actors, just as she had dressed the principals of many
ballet-operas in Paris. Her assistants turned their hands to creating an exuberant fluff the technicians could exploit. She knew her
business, but she also knew her limitations. "I never was a dressmaker; I am in admiration of those who can sew; I never learned;
I stick my fingers."

Chanel had hoped to apply her rigorous standards, and the London *Sunday Express* correspondent in Hollywood described lounge
pajamas as "bad taste and no lady should be seen dead in them."
Yet in 1931's *Tonight or Never*, the third Hollywood film Chanel
gowned, the first scenes show Gloria Swanson in lounge pajamas.
Chanel and her staff admired the Hollywood dressers even if they

Chanel designed costumes for Jean Renoir's 1939
masterpiece, *Rules of the Game*, featuring
Mila Parély (right) and Nora Gregor.

thought their costuming kitschy. It was obvious from the beginning that Chanel's Hollywood adventure was bound to fail. She
told biographer Charles-Roux: "The Hollywood atmosphere was
infantile; one day we were entertained by a famous actor who
had painted all the trees in his garden blue in our honor . . . I
laughed at it but it affected Misia. Erich von Stroheim impressed
me only because he was taking a personal revenge—a Prussian
persecuting Jewish inferiors and Hollywood was mostly Jewish.
These Jews from Central Europe found the actor [von Stroheim]
a familiar nightmare."

IN THE END, Chanel saw herself as too refined for the studio glitter of Hollywood, the lavish façades, the tastes of the
moguls and their coteries of actors and actresses, and the clash
of egos among the silver-screen divas. Her narrow jersey tailored

From left: Madge Evans, Ina Claire, and Joan Blondel in the 1932 film
The Greeks Had a Word for Them. Chanel designed the actresses' wardrobe.

suits with white collars and cuffs were not glamorous enough. Her vision lacked the flagrant sexiness sought by the players and movie directors to enhance their films. The discreet elegance of Chanel's costumes seemed bland on cinema screens. Diffidently, Chanel said: "I only like 'cop' movies." In fact, her costumes drew little comment, and the films she worked on were not successful.

Before sailing home Chanel returned to New York. The big city amused her. There she met with the two most important fashion editors in America: Carmel Snow of *Harper's Bazaar* and Margaret Case of *Vogue*—women who would dictate what American women would wear for years to come.

Chanel needed more. She visited Saks Fifth Avenue, Lord & Taylor, Bloomingdale's, and Macy's. But the store that really fascinated her was the flagship of ready-to-wear, New York's S. Klein, On the Square—located at Manhattan's Union Square.

There Chanel discovered Klein's self-service methods: women of all professions and ethnic origins trying one garment after the other under the surveillance of gum-chewing salesgirls and surrounded by signage warning, DO NOT STEAL! OUR DETECTIVES ARE WATCHING! DO NOT STICK GUM UNDER THE WASHROOM SINKS!

It was an America unknown to Chanel as she surveyed the thousands of dresses cut like French clothes—only the fabrics were different. The big money was made from copying and a massive investment in advertising and promotion. It was Chanel's lifetime lesson in mass merchandising.

After barely a month in America, Chanel sailed home on the French ocean liner SS *Paris,* along with a host of Americans including Franklin D. Roosevelt's mother. Coco's short American adventure was sweet and sour. She deposited a handsome fee in her bank account, and the publicity gave her a leg up over her competitors in the American market, even if her Hollywood sojourn was less than a triumph. After all the ballyhoo and PR hype, Chanel dressed Gloria Swanson for Goldwyn's *Tonight or Never,* the Goldwyn Girls in the musical comedy *Palmy Days,* and the three lead actresses, Ina Claire, Joan Blondell, and Madge Evans, in *The Greeks Had a Word for Them.* According to *The New Yorker* Chanel left Hollywood in a "huff." The magazine claimed the movie tycoons thought Chanel's costumes weren't sensational enough. "Chanel made a lady look like a lady," but "Hollywood wants a lady to look like two ladies."

FIVE

EXIT PAUL, ENTER SPATZ

"Struggling with the devil . . . who wears the deceitful face
of hope and despair."

—T. S. ELIOT, "ASH WEDNESDAY"

RETURNING FROM HOLLYWOOD, Chanel craved an
immediate change of scenery and went to London for "a bath
of nobility." Bendor, still under her spell, lent Chanel, rent free, a
nine-bedroom eighteenth-century house with ornate plaster ceil-
ings, cornices, and pine paneling at 9 Audley Street to be the
headquarters for her growing business in the United Kingdom.
He spent more than £8,000 to redecorate the house to her taste,
and lent her 39 Grosvenor Square for an exhibition of her designs
to raise money for the Royal British Legion. Five to six hundred
people came every day to see Chanel's dresses, even though none
were for sale. She was welcomed by the Churchills, including
debonair young Randolph, who escorted her to the opening of the
Legion's exhibition.

Chanel was beginning to show her age. Her face had hardened,
her neck was taut; overwork and incessant Camel cigarettes along
with middle age left their mark. Vain and slightly cross-eyed, she
refused to wear glasses in public. (In a rare photograph by Roger
Shall, we see Chanel wearing spectacles while watching one of
her fashion shows from the steps of rue Cambon, sometime in
the 1930s.) Yet fashion icon Diana Vreeland thought Chanel in the
1930s was "bright, a dark golden color—wide face with a snorting
nose, just like a little bull, and deep Dubonnet red cheeks." No

matter her looks, Chanel was now a queen enjoying her power; aggressive in speech, chattering, and scoffing: "I am timid. Timid people talk a great deal because they can't stand silence. I am always ready to bring out any idiocy at all just to fill up silence. I go on, I go on from one thing to another so that there will be no chance for silence. I talk vehemently. I know I can be unbearable."

Age had not weakened Chanel's taste for making money. In 1931, Janet Flanner wrote in a *New Yorker* profile how "each year [Chanel] tries not only to beat her competitors but to beat herself . . . Her last annual chiffre d'affaires [turnover] was publicly quoted [not by her] as being one hundred and twenty million Francs, or close to four and a half million dollars" ($60 million now). Flanner's reporting encountered obstacles: "Because she sensibly never talks, never gives interviews, or admits anything, and because she cannily distributes her money in a variety of banks in several countries, it is impossible accurately to approximate the fortune Chanel has amassed. But London City rumors it at some three millions of pounds [around $230 million in today's money] which in France, and for a woman, is enormous."

More definite figures lacking, perhaps the closest estimate of her financial genius is contained in a statement accredited to the banking house of Rothschild, a European establishment discerning enough to have made a fortune even out of the battle of Waterloo. "Mademoiselle Chanel," they are reported as solemnly saying, "knows how to make a safe twenty-percent."

CHANEL COULDN'T COUNT without using her fingers, but she was sure the Wertheimer brothers were cheating her out of her share of profits from the sale of her perfumes. She increasingly resented the deal she had made in 1924, when the Wertheimers took control of Société des Parfums Chanel—the company that owned her fragrance and cosmetic businesses. For the next twenty-five or so years her litany became: "I signed something in 1924. I let myself be swindled." Her accountants tried to assure her that the accounts of Société des Parfums Chanel were in order and that the penury of dividends was not due to chicanery but rather to the massive investment necessary to make Chanel No. 5 a world brand. But she was convinced that she was being robbed by pirates—Jewish pirates.

Suzanne and Otto Abetz with René de Chambrun
(in the middle), seen here walking away from a hospital in
Versailles in September 1941 after visiting Pierre Laval when
the minister was recovering from the attempt on his life.

She hired a young French-American attorney, René de Chambrun, to fight the Wertheimers. A direct descendant of the Lafayette family, Chambrun had dual U.S.-French citizenship. In 1930,
Chanel asked him to initiate a series of lawsuits aimed at harass-
ing the Wertheimers—a feeble effort to regain control of the
company. The trials would drag on for years, and Chanel would
lose. Chambrun would be her friend and attorney for the next
fifteen years and throughout World War II. An accused Nazi collaborator, Chambrun would play a major role in Chanel's wartime
adventures during the German occupation.

CHANEL'S CREATIVITY never waned. She abandoned the
tweeds, the sportswear, and the *garçonne* look, championing feminine dresses for afternoon wear. She appeared at her sumptuous evening parties in vaporous combinations of tulle and lace.

Despite the world economic crisis, Chanel launched a collection of costume jewelry inspired by Bendor's gifts of real jewels. It was a tribute to her ingenuity, the good taste of Étienne de Beaumont, Count Fulco della Verdura, and Parisian artisans she hired. Years earlier, Beaumont, a French aristocrat of the highest order, had invited her to come to his opulent Paris soirees, but some of the high-society women in attendance had slighted her. Later, she told the painter Marie Laurencin: "All those bluebloods, they turned their noses up at me, but I'll have them groveling at my feet." In fact, while ridiculing these women, she envied them.

Beaumont and Fulco della Verdura soon launched a line of dazzling Chanel costume jewelry. Out of the vault came some of her lovers' glittering gifts. The gems were removed from their settings and used to design a line of Chanel jewelry, including a copy of a Russian antique necklace with multiple strands of pearls set off with a rhinestone star medallion; clusters of sapphire-blue glass and turquoise studs attached to gold metallic chains; an enamel cuff in black or white studded with glass stones; and an Indian bib of red beehives, green glass balls, green leaves, and pearls imitating the rare rubies and emeralds of a Bendor gift. The line was a smashing success. Chanel now instructed wealthy society women: "It's disgusting to walk around with millions around the neck because one happens to be rich. I only like fake jewelry . . . because it's provocative." When the costume jewelry sold well, she brought out a line of real jewels in diamonds, diamond broaches, necklaces, bracelets, and hair clips.

A D O L F   H I T L E R , founder and leader of Germany's Nazi Party, became German chancellor in January 1933. He moved swiftly to consolidate his power, to become "dictator" in March of that year, and to fill key posts with devoted Nazi Party followers. Hermann Göring, on the führer's orders, created a Nazi secret police, the Gestapo, and later a modern German air force, the Luftwaffe. Germany's next most powerful man was a thirty-six-year-old "relentless Jew baiter and burner of books" Joseph Goebbels—the master propagandist for the Nazi Party. Goebbels now became the Reich Minister for Public Enlightenment and Propaganda, giving one man control of the communications media: radio, press, publishing, cinema, and other arts.

In early 1935, Hitler appointed Admiral Wilhelm Canaris to head the Abwehr, the German military espionage service. Canaris cooperated with his Nazi bosses—proposing that Jews be forced to wear a yellow star as a means of identification. Later, Himmler's SS organization under Walter Schellenberg swallowed the Abwehr.

One of the first appointments Goebbels made was to name Abwehr master spy Baron Hans Günther von Dincklage as a "special attaché" at the German Embassy in Paris. Operating under diplomatic immunity, Dincklage set about building a Nazi propaganda and espionage network in France. He would retain his diplomatic status until after World War II.

The French intelligence and police establishments knew about Dincklage and had been collecting information since 1919 about his work as Abwehr agent F-8680, operating on the Riviera since 1929. Their reports told of how Dincklage, returning from Warsaw, Poland, joined Catsy to employ their good looks and charm in recruiting new agents to penetrate the French naval establishment at Toulon, France, and Bizerte, Tunisia. By 1932 the Dincklages were settled at "La Petite Casa" in Sanary-sur-Mer.

Writing about Dincklage's power of attraction, Catsy's half sister Sybille Bedford ventured, "Spatz Dincklage's secret charm appeared nonchalant . . . and he had a beauty that pleased both women and men." Catsy soon seduced Spatz's tennis partner, French naval officer Charles Coton, into a long-term intimate relationship. Later she would set her sights on French naval engineer Pierre Gaillard, who spied for the Dincklages at the strategic French naval base at Cap Blanc, Bizerte, Tunisia. The two naval officers became the backbone of the Dincklage espionage network in the Mediterranean, and Coton became the Dincklages' secret courier between Sanary-sur-Mer, Toulon, and Paris.

WITH HITLER INSTALLED as Reich chancellor, Dincklage took up official duties at the German Embassy in October 1933—he was now driving a gray two-seater Chrysler roadster, and he and Catsy were settled in an apartment in one of Paris's chic neighborhoods. It was a new adventure for Dincklage. He now had offices at the German Embassy on the rue Huysmans. Under diplomatic cover, Dincklage went about building a black

A handsome Baron von Dincklage, ca. 1935,
at the German Embassy in Paris when
he worked with the Gestapo.

propaganda campaign and espionage operation financed by Berlin. The embassy provided direct and protected communication to and from his masters in Berlin, and the diplomatic courier service handled the voluminous reports and news clippings that all spies must pouch to headquarters. It didn't take long for the Dincklages to settle in. Within weeks of arriving in Paris, two Berlin moving vans delivered furniture to an apartment. Their German maid (an Abwehr-trained agent), Lucie Braun, joined the couple. She was issued a French identity card stating that she worked for an accredited diplomat at the German Embassy.

French police and military intelligence observed the Dincklages' new lifestyle: two apartments located in very chic and expensive sections of Paris—hardly affordable to the Austrian refugee that Dincklage sometimes claimed to be. In 1934 the Sûreté of the Ministry of the Interior labeled Dincklage a Nazi propagandist with agents buried in the German office of tourism (located on the avenue de l'Opéra). Dincklage had also planted German engineers as technicians in French factories in Paris suburbs to collect industrial intelligence.

By 1934 the Berlin Nazi machine issued orders to have Abwehr units work hand in hand with the Gestapo and the SS. Abwehr agents, like the Dincklages, were commanded to maintain close relations with all Nazi organizations involved in espionage and counterespionage. In a final order, demanding cooperation between Hitler's police and intelligence services, Abwehr agents were told to recruit and train individuals who would collaborate with the Gestapo in espionage activities. As part of this consolidation, German citizens of the Reich living overseas were commanded by Berlin and local consulates to join Nazi cells. In Paris, Dincklage, now labeled by French police as "directing a German police service," was also involved with the first Nazi cell in France. His group met every week at 9 p.m. at 53, boulevard Malesherbes. In 1934 the Dincklages' maid, Lucie Braun, was listed as the 239th member of the Paris cell, among 441 members.

The French military counterintelligence service (Deuxième Bureau) had by now accumulated a background file on Dincklage and his wife. The agency was informed of the couple's living habits and operations in Paris and at Sanary-sur-Mer. "Dincklage's wife, Maximiliane, [was] the daughter of ex-Colonel of German cavalry von Schoenebeck and Melanie Herz. The couple lived at 64, rue Pergolèse, rented for 18,000 Francs a month [the equivalent of $19,000 in 2010}." The report supplies endless detail: "Dincklage is traveling continually; his wife is often in Sanary at the villa La Petite Casa. In Paris the couple is visited at all hours of the day and night by Charles Coton and Georges Gaillard" as the Dincklages "continually seek out the company of French naval officers."

French authorities now decided to damage the Dincklage operations. Rather than outraging Hitler by expelling a German couple with diplomatic accreditation on grounds of espionage, French counterintelligence turned to the press. On November 27, 1934, Inter Press (a newswire service) issued a startling report about Dincklage and his underground network. The story was released about the same time Winston Churchill was warning the British Parliament about the "menace" of Hermann Göring's Luftwaffe air force. The Inter Press dispatch revealed how: "Baron von Dincklage, Hitler's agent in Paris, has been replaced . . . he was denounced in his own embassy as a member of the Hitler secret police . . . now he is involved in special missions in Tunisia— then under French mandate. One of Dincklage's close friends (Charles Coton) is an administrator of a French naval unit stationed at the French naval base at Bizerte, Tunisia. Coton comes frequently to Paris. On the 16–17 November [1934] Coton came to the Dincklage apartment with three suitcases which he claimed belonged to the Dincklage couple . . . Then a few days later the Vietnamese valet of the Dincklages' friend Georges Gaillard came to the Dincklage apartment with a box of keys to open the suitcases; when the Dincklages returned to their apartment they took two of the suitcases away—[they may have then traveled to London]." It turned out that French official Pierre Gaillard was one of Maximiliane's lovers. The report named other members of the Dincklage espionage network in France: Madame Christa von Bodenhausen (her lover was a French naval officer); German newsman Hanck; and Krug von Nidda, a notorious Nazi and later German ambassador at Vichy during the occupation. Ernest Dehnicks of the German Consulate General was also a Dincklage agent. Finally, the report confirmed "the German tourist office at 50, avenue de l'Opéra, Paris is suspected of acting against the national interest"—a French government euphemism for spying.

IN 1934 Chanel moved into a suite at the Ritz with a wood-burning fireplace and an austere bedroom. The Ritz was synonymous with good taste, refinement, and comfort, and renowned for offering a fine menu of French haute cuisine. Chanel's Ritz apartment overlooked the Place Vendôme, around the corner from the rue Cambon, where she created a four-room apartment above her workrooms. The space was decorated with objects and furniture she treasured: the Coromandel screens from Boy Capel, crystal chandeliers, Oriental tables, and a pair of bronze animals. From the Ritz's back entrance Chanel could cross the street to her salon and apartment, which allowed her to avoid the despised Schiaparelli's boutique on the Place Vendôme.

Chanel was in love with a dark, handsome Basque: the exceptionally creative illustrator and designer Paul Iribe, her same age. Born Paul Iribarnegaray, Iribe had made a hit in Hollywood directing one film and as an art director for Cecil B. DeMille. In France he was the popular illustrator of a book of erotica based on Paul Poiret's fashions. A writer and illustrator for *Vogue,* a designer of fabrics, furniture, and rugs, and an interior designer for wealthy clients, Iribe attracted Chanel with his provocative wit and multiple talents.

Using Chanel's money, Iribe revived a monthly newssheet, *Le Témoin,* and turned it into a violent ultranationalist weekly. According to one biographer, Iribe was an elitist bourgeois supercharged with an irrational fear of foreigners. Reading his issues of *Le Témoin,* one would think France was the eternal victim of some vast international conspiracy. The magazine was a timid echo of France's Fascist and anti-Semitic press, publications that supported French storm troopers named the "hooded ones"—La Cagoule—and groups promoting law and order in Italy and Germany. Biographer Charles-Roux believed Chanel's launching of *Le Témoin* with Iribe as editor and art director marked her transition from political indifference to a view of the future modeled on the opinions of Iribe—mixed in with ideas and prejudices absorbed during her peasant and Catholic upbringing. In the February 24, 1933, edition of the magazine, Iribe had the brass to draw Chanel as a martyred Marianne in her Phrygian bonnet—her naked body held by a collection of evil-looking men with obvious Jewish features. France, according to Iribe in *Le Témoin,* was suffering from a conspiracy managed by "enemies within" called "Samuel," or "Levy," the "alien" like Léon Blum, and "Judeo-Masonic Mafia," the USSR, and "red rabbles." His extreme political views aside, however, Iribe's artwork in *Le Témoin* was breathtaking.

No man before Iribe had raised Chanel's political awareness, and she brought him into her professional life to share the power she had always guarded assiduously for herself. Chanel was once again "happy" and in love. Iribe had become her confidential agent, her "knight," and Chanel asked him to work in conjunction with René de Chambrun on the Wertheimer case. Rumors of a marriage swirled about the city.

In August 1935, Chanel and Iribe invited a houseful of guests to La Pausa. Photographs of the event show a glorious summer afternoon, one of those golden days on the Riviera when a light breeze from the hills above joined with the salt air of the Mediterranean to create an intoxicating atmosphere. Chanel's guests that afternoon looked as if they had stepped out of a sketch printed in a fashion magazine featuring her summer modes: espadrilles, a French sailor's horizontally striped T-shirt, and casual pants made of jersey fabrics—an idea borrowed from the Duke of Westmin-

With Hitler in power, violent Nazi persecutions of
Jews raged in Germany. In 1935 the anti-Semitic
Paul Iribe, Chanel's lover, published in *Le Témoin*
this prostrate Marianne (representing France) with
Chanel's features. Hitler holds Chanel (searching for
a heartbeat) as men and a woman with Jewish traits
look on. The caption reads: "Wait, she still lives." The
publication, edited by Iribe, was financed by Chanel.

ster's crew on the *Flying Cloud*. Iribe, whom French writer Colette
depicted as a "very interesting demon," arrived at La Pausa from
Paris.

The next day—a splendid September afternoon—Chanel relaxed in the shadows of an ancient olive tree, its green leaves ruffled by a breeze. She watched Paul Iribe play an informal match
on her tennis court, delighting in her lover's athletic prowess. Her
Great Dane, Gigot, lolled beside her. Suddenly, Chanel's world
came crashing down. Suddenly, Iribe collapsed on the court before
her eyes, his face ashen. Later, horrified, she watched stretcher
bearers carry his body away. Paul Iribe, another "man of her life"
whom the gossip columnists were sure would wed Chanel, was
dead. She was "devastated."

A long winter of grief followed. From that moment on and

until the end of her life, Chanel injected herself with a dose of morphine-based sedol before going to bed. "I need it to hold on," she would say. As she had after Boy Capel's death, she sank into a void, using the sedative to calm her nerves.

Chanel's grand-niece, Gabrielle Palasse Labrunie, remembers a song her aunt repeatedly sang in heavily accented English during one summer's visit to La Pausa. The words were, "My baby has a heart of stone . . . not human, but she's my own . . . To the day I die I'll be loving my woman." Madame Labrunie thought the sad poetry was a cameo of Chanel's life.

Coco had lost her drive and energy. Without Iribe, she had no emotional attachment; she was entering her years of discontent. She longed to get away from the Parisian carousel. In London, always a refuge, she attended the Royal Ascot annual race with Randolph Churchill. The London *Daily Mail* quoted her: "Your Queen succeeds in a very difficult task. In an age where successive bizarre and extravagant fashions—not always in perfect taste— are sweeping the world, she maintains a queenly grace and distinction which are conservative without being old-fashioned."

BY THE SUMMER OF 1934, Hitler's campaign of terror seemed to know no end. In Austria, Nazis had murdered Chancellor Engelbert Dollfuss; in Berlin and Bavaria, Hitler personally supervised the murder of Ernst Röhm's Brown Shirt thugs—now his political opponents. To celebrate his gaining total power, Hitler's organizers brought two hundred thousand party officials with twenty-one thousand flags to a packed Nuremberg Nazi rally. A frenzied crowd heard their führer shout, "We are strong and will get stronger."

That same year, Hitler turned his attention to the anti-Nazi, Swiss-educated, liberal king of Yugoslavia, Alexander—a staunch ally of France and a thorn in Hitler's grand plan for Europe. In the summer of 1934, Dincklage traveled to Yugoslavia. He was tracked by the French Deuxième Bureau to the capital city of Belgrade, barely three months before a Bulgarian nationalist shot King Alexander dead as he landed at Marseille port to begin a state visit to France. French intelligence agents then revealed: "Dincklage . . . former attaché at German Embassy Paris was this summer in Yugoslavia for business." Dincklage wrote his former

Paris Embassy colleagues, "Business in Yugoslavia is tough like everywhere else."

Three months later, André François-Poncet, French ambassador to Berlin, wrote to Sir Eric Phipps at the British Embassy in Berlin: "The Germans are by no means as innocent in this assassination business as they would have us believe" and that Göring was somehow involved while he was visiting Belgrade.

In March 1935, Hitler brushed aside the Versailles Treaty. Repudiating it two years later, he ordered compulsory military services—trebling the numerical strength of the German military machine. French intelligence services now received permission to strike at the growing German espionage and black propaganda operation, which was spreading false and deceiving information in France. Dincklage was singled out as the principal target.

"*Gestapo über alles*" (Gestapo above all) were the words used for a dramatic headline in the September 4, 1935, issue of the Paris weekly *Vendémiaire*. The exposé (obviously the work of French counterintelligence) was spread over three columns. An additional long report followed in the September 11 issue of the paper. Both stories featured Dincklage's work as a Gestapo agent (at the time, the French did not differentiate between Abwehr and Gestapo) and as a special attaché at the German Embassy. In five thousand words, *Vendémiaire* unmasked the work of Nazi and Gestapo agents in France. The editors revealed that Dincklage was a Gestapo officer somehow linked to the assassination of King Alexander of Yugoslavia and that he had visited the Berlin Gestapo in September 1934 and delivered to "a Gestapo officer named Diehls a list containing the addresses of German exiles in France." Further, he had offered to provide the Nazis lists of former German Communists in France. Later, it was revealed that Rudolph Diehls was a close friend of Hermann Göring, who appointed him to a high Nazi post after he was dismissed as head of the Gestapo and replaced by Himmler.

The newspaper story is a close copy of an October 1934 report authored by French Army Headquarters. It notes that Dincklage received 100,000 francs a month (equivalent to about $105,000 today) to finance "his corrupt activities." *Vendémiaire* went on to document Dincklage's movements as a German agent on special missions to the Côte d'Azur, in Paris, and in the Balkans.

In a mission to Tunis, Dincklage employed dissident Muslims to launch a violent propaganda attack on the French colonial regime.

As France was preparing for war with Germany, French authorities—most likely the Deuxième Bureau—allowed author Paul Allard to publish almost the same story as the one that appeared in the weekly *Vendémiaire*. Allard's postwar book, *How Hitler Spied on France,* told how Goebbels's propaganda agent in Paris, Dincklage, urged his Berlin masters to supply him with favorable anecdotes about the domestic life of the families of SS officers. Dincklage explained to his bosses that the stories could be placed in French publications sympathetic to the Nazis.

DURING HITLER'S 1935 NUREMBERG RALLY, the Nazis enacted the Nuremberg Laws, a series of laws aimed at Jews. Overnight, Maximiliane von Dincklage, now considered a Jew under Nazi law, was deprived of her citizenship. It was the fulfillment of Nazi racial philosopher Alfred Rosenberg's wish that Germany's "master race," which he labeled as a homogeneous Aryan-Nordic civilization, be protected against supposed "racial threats" from the "Jewish-Semitic race." Among other things, the law prohibited marriage between Jews and Aryans. Dincklage must have known the decree was imminent. Three months earlier he had divorced his wife of fifteen years at Düsseldorf.

The newly single Dincklage spent the summer near Toulon in the apartment of his English mistress and her sister. With the release of the *Vendémiaire* news articles, Dincklage hurriedly moved to London. There, in a temporary haven at a Mayfair Court apartment on Strasson Street, he wrote to the German ambassador in Paris. The letter makes a feeble attempt to get the ambassador to protest to French authorities about the publication of the *Vendémiaire* series. His appeal didn't work, and the ambassador asked his aide-de-camp to reply to his former attaché. Here are excerpts from the exchange of letters:

To the Honorable Ambassador,
I have just now obtained from a French business . . . the Vendemiaire 4. Sept. 35. In my estimation, the author of the enclosed document . . . must certainly be paid by anti-German sources . . . The day before the assassination of the King of

Yugoslavia [I was] in Tunis . . . [you] must write . . . the authorities that [the information is presented] is untrue and completely unfounded. I am currently in the process of building a . . . [illegible] and this announcement could be a disadvantage to me. I faithfully request that Herr Koester . . . [tell] the French authorities in a truthful manner [in order] to clarify the errors . . . Much of my work, my many trips to France, and . . . my time at the embassy . . . have produced . . . good results for Germany and France. I express my respect and high regard, Mr. Ambassador, and remain your loyal . . .

[signed] Dincklage

The German Embassy in Paris responded:

Paris, the 13 September 1935
Dear Mr. Dincklage,
The Ambassador instructed me to thank you for your kind words. He doesn't believe an intervention in the matter which you explained is currently [illegible]: the rumors that were spreading earlier have abated, and undertaking measures to correct the rumors, whether in Quai d'Orsay [location of the French Foreign Ministry] or among the local press, would only cause old legends to take on new meanings and concern to spread. However, should the rumors emerge again[,] the Ambassador will take the opportunity to raise the issue of your concerns with the local foreign office.

With many greetings I am, Ever your loyal correspondent.

[signed] Fühn

PRIOR TO DINCKLAGE'S DEPARTURE for England, a 1935 secret Deuxième Bureau report revealed how his maid, a member of a Nazi cell in Paris, was now operating from the Dincklage base in Sanary-sur-Mer: "A woman whom Dincklage claims to be his secretary named Lucie Braun, also of the personnel of the German Embassy in Paris . . . [is] suspected of working against the national interest." The bureau believed that prior to Dincklage's departure for London, Lucie Braun lived near Toulon at Sanary where there was a large German community. The report adds that on February 9, 1935, Dincklage was visited by his seventy-two-year-old uncle William Kutter, a rear admiral of the German navy living at Darmstadt. Kutter arrived directly from Strasbourg (France) and remained in Sanary at La Petite Casa until the end of February 1935. The admiral was questioned at the Toulon rail station as to the reason for his visit. He told French agents he had come to Toulon as a tourist, but he did not reveal he was going to the Dincklage villa at Sanary.

NEWLY REELECTED PRESIDENT Franklin Roosevelt now proclaimed American neutrality and appealed to Hitler and Mussolini to settle European problems amicably. Still, Winston Churchill found time to cable Chanel. On December 2, 1935, he wrote from London: "I fear I shall not be an evening in Paris when I pass through on the 10th of December, but I shall be returning towards the end of January, and look forward indeed to seeing you then. I will give you two or three days notice by telegram from Majorca where I propose to winter. How delightful to see you again. Herewith my debt."

There is no explanation of Churchill's reference to "my debt." However, it is doubtful that he ever went to Majorca that winter of 1935. In the coming months Churchill would become embroiled in the political fortunes of Great Britain. With the death of King George V of England, his son Edward, Churchill's close friend, succeeded to the throne. Churchill would expend great political capital trying to protect his sovereign and close friend from the wrath of the British parliament, which opposed Edward's plan to marry the American divorcée Mrs. Wallis Simpson.

AS THE GERMAN GENERAL STAFF was hard at work on a plan to invade France, including the seizure of parts of North Africa, Dincklage was organizing an espionage network at French naval bases in Tunisia and a black propaganda operation among the North African Muslims. His former agent in Toulon, Charles Coton, had already left Sanary for an assignment at the French naval base at Bizerte, where he would again act as Dincklage's principal agent.

French authorities were eager to expel Dincklage. A 1938 Deux-ième Bureau report tells, "Since leaving the German Embassy [Dincklage] has been active in anti-French propaganda in North

"Spatz" von Dincklage and Hélène Dessoffy, his lover, on a
small boat off the French Riviera about 1938. Dessoffy was an
unwitting member of Dincklage's espionage operation
at the French naval base in Toulon.

Africa. He has been on missions to North Africa [including]
Tunisia—[but] after close surveillance Dincklage has not committed a punishable crime; he is, however, a dangerous subject."

By November 1938 Dincklage had taken a new lover and
agent. French counterintelligence identified her as "Madame
'Sophie' or 'Dessoffy'" (later identified as Baronne Hélène Dessoffy). A French agent in Bayonne reported, "Madame de Sophie
or Dessoffy and de Dinkelake [sic] travel frequently between Paris
and Toulon. She is the go-between for procuring radio sets 'Aga
Baltic' on behalf of a certain Dinklage [sic] who is supposed to
be an agent of [the company] 'Aga Baltic' in Toulon . . . The two
are suspected of espionage against France." In a report labeled
"Urgent Secret," French authorities warned all agents that "Baron
Dincklage, living at villa Colibri, Antibes [one of his accommodation addresses at the time] and carrying a German diplomatic
passport (ooo. 968 D.1880) arrived by the steamer, El Biar, at
Tunis without a visa and was asked to leave the Régence [Tuni-

sian territory] immediately. Dincklage was traveling with French Baronne Dessoffy, Hélène, born in Poitiers, 15 December 1900, domiciled at Paris, 70 avenue de Versailles . . . The couple is now at the Majestic Hotel in Tunis. They occupy adjoining rooms with communicating doors." The report detailed how Dessoffy had a telephone conversation with a friend, the naval officer M. Verdaveine, stationed at the French naval base at Bizerte. Dessoffy told the man, "I want to travel in southern Tunisia." Verdaveine then advised her not to travel—and definitely not with the German Dincklage.

Dincklage was somehow warned off. The report continues, "The couple left Tunis at 10:00 hrs on the steamer for Marseille . . . We have ordered the S.E.T. [unidentified French service] to determine the relations between Verdaveine and Dessoffy Hélène."

A year before the outbreak of World War II, the French War Ministry issued a secret instruction ordering that Dincklage be put under close surveillance. The Ministry was unequivocal: "Even if no direct proof exists to indict Dincklage he should be expelled immediately from France."

AND WHAT OF CATSY? The French reported in 1938:

> Despite being separated, Dincklage and wife are on good terms with each other and he sees her in Antibes, Sanary and Toulon . . . Mme Dincklage [the French apparently did not know of the 1935 divorce] arrived August 9, 1938, at Antibes . . . she left there September 13 and returned to the villa "Huxley," where she has stayed before. She is now the lover of Pierre Gaillard.

In 1939, the French police would report:

> Baronne Dincklage, known to the Sûreté, is living at Ollioles (Var) at a property belonging to one of her friends, the Comtesse [sic] Dessoffy; also known to the Sûreté (Fichier Central: Sûreté files). Baronne Dincklage's lover is twenty-seven-year-old Pierre Gaillard, an engineer and son of the founder and manager of a company manufacturing cable nets (used in the national defense against enemy submarines and erected at strategic points). Gaillard is presently in Oran [an important and strategic French naval

base in Algeria]. Mme Dincklage often corresponds with him; and we fear that Gaillard is constantly charmed by Mme Dincklage; and may unwillingly commit an indiscretion causing harm to the nation's defenses . . . ,

By late 1938, Dincklage knew war with France was imminent. Still, according to his watchers: "He is seen in Toulon . . . and also visits the shores of Lac Leman." (The lake borders the French city of Thonon-les-Bains. A regular boat service connects to the Swiss cities of Lausanne and Geneva and their array of banks.) "His lifestyle at Antibes is modest . . . [Dincklage] receives visitors day and night. Certain [guests] come by automobile; their license plates are . . ." Finally, French authorities ordered all agents to "watch postal, telephone and telegraph communications made by Mme Dincklage, 12, rue des Sablons, Paris and Mme la Comtesse Dessoffy de Cserneck [*sic*]." The Deuxième Bureau now requested the head of the Sûreté Nationale to identify the owners of the automobiles licensed in France (autos seen in front of the Dincklage home) and to do the necessary to "immediately expel Dincklage; if it is not possible to indict him for spying." French counterintelligence services told its agents: "Baron Hans Gunther Dincklage is considered as a very dangerous agent against France" and ordered its agents to seek information about "the relations between Dessoffy and Dincklage." Another report added a caveat: "Despite her foreign contacts [Dessoffy] is incapable of betraying France. Nevertheless, we advise French officers to exercise great discretion in their relations with the Dessoffys and the Dincklage woman."

WORLD WAR II was weeks away when French authorities warned of the Dincklages' clandestine intelligence work in France. The report is a summary beginning in 1931: the Dincklage couple "had divorced; and Dincklage was supplying his masters in Berlin with information about German refugees in France and intelligence on the national defense works." Maximiliane von Dincklage "is the daughter of a German Army Colonel in the Imperial Army of the Kaiser . . . she supports the monarchy" (meaning, autocratic rule).

In August 1939 France mobilized for war. Dincklage fled

to Switzerland. French military intelligence ordered "Baronne Dincklage confined to a fixed residence." In December of that year, French authorities issued a mandate: "[Maximiliane von Dincklage's] presence in France represents a danger. [Agent] 6.000 asks [Agent] 6.610 to take all measures to intern this foreigner."

Months before the Nazi invasion of France, Catsy, along with some other Germans living in France, was interned at Gurs, a French concentration camp located in the Basses-Pyrénées.

WHEN QUESTIONED ABOUT Dincklage at the liberation of Paris, Chanel would say, "I have known him for twenty years." It may be another Chanel exaggeration, and there is no firsthand information about when or where Chanel first met Dincklage. Her grand-niece, Gabrielle Palasse Labrunie, who knew Dincklage well, told the author that she was sure Chanel and Dincklage met in England well before the war. Some anecdotal evidence suggests the couple met in Paris when Dincklage was at the German Embassy and was known to attend evenings hosted by a number of Chanel's acquaintances and friends, many of whom were members of a pro-German clique in Paris in the 1930s. Among them were Marie-Louise Bousquet, Baroness Philippe de Rothschild, Duchess Antoinette d'Harcourt, and Marie-Laure de Noailles. Pierre Lazareff, who wrote about Chanel and the crème of Paris society, reported that in 1933, when Dincklage arrived at the German Embassy in Paris, this clique of bluebloods had been active in a Paris-based "führer's social brigade" sponsored by Dincklage's close friend, the "charming blond, blue and starry eyed" Otto Abetz, who would amuse his listeners with stories of Adolf Hitler. Abetz assured his listeners that Jews were pushing France toward war, but that France need not fear aggression.

Despite Chanel's mythmaking and her inventions about tennis-playing, English-speaking Dincklage—whom she and her biographers cast as more English than German—Chanel and her friends knew about Dincklage's Nazi connections and his espionage work in France. It would have been impossible to miss the gossip in elite circles based on the articles in the weekly newspaper *Vendémiaire,* or in the 1939 Allard book.

And Then the War Came

Medieval children playing nasty medieval games.

—Pablo Picasso

From her window at the Hôtel Ritz overlooking the Place Vendôme, Chanel watched demonstrators marching toward the nearby Place de la Concorde. It was February 6, 1934, and the beginning of her troubles. In an explosion of protests, French right-wing organizations with ties to Italy and Germany mixed with small groups of Communists to overthrow the government.

Paris Herald newsman William L. Shirer was in the Place de la Concorde that Tuesday afternoon in 1934. He watched Mobile Guards slashing away with their sabers in the Tuileries Garden as mobs attacked the police with stones and bricks. Shirer retreated to the third-floor balcony of the nearby Hôtel de Crillon overlooking the Place de la Concorde. There he watched right-wing youths attempting to break through to the Parliament building across the river Seine. They were driven off by mounted steel-helmeted Mobile Guards.

As night fell a large group of right-wing World War I veterans paraded into the Place de la Concorde behind a mass of tricolored flags. They were headed for the Concorde Bridge, which was already jammed with people. Shirer wrote, "If they get across the bridge . . . they'll kill every deputy in the Chamber [the French House of Representatives]." Deadly rifle fire stopped the mob.

On the Crillon balcony a woman suddenly slumped to the floor with a bullet hole in her forehead, barely twenty feet away from where Shirer stood.

"Shooting came from the bridge and the far side of the Seine . . . automatic rifle fire, and nearby the Crillon smoke poured out of the Ministry of Marine building. As the fire brigade brought their hoses to fight the blaze, the mob got closer and slashed at the hoses." Shirer went down to the lobby to phone the *Herald* and discovered several wounded lying there, receiving first aid.

About midnight the Mobile Guards got the upper hand. The police were in control. Shirer managed to write a couple of columns before deadline in which he reported the official figures: sixteen dead, several hundred wounded. The next day the government resigned.

IN THE MONTHS that followed left-wing demonstrations raged as Communist and Socialist groups fought with the Fascist Right for power. Barely two years later a Popular Front French government led by the first Jewish prime minister, Léon Blum, provoked industrial protests. Workers, backed by some newly elected Socialists and Communists, struck for higher wages and benefits.

The violence terrified Chanel. The unrest left the lovely Place Vendôme choked with tear gas and burning rubbish. The streets behind the Ritz—her neighborhood—were stained with blood. Chanel and her friends were panic-stricken. What was on the horizon as the chaotic years of the Great Depression gripped France? What was to happen to her twenty-five hundred employees— many of them leftists?

Worse was to come. On May 1, 1936, thousands of workers celebrating May Day marched along the tree-lined boulevards of Paris under gigantic red banners singing the anthem of international socialism, "The Internationale." Chanel must have felt the excitement—heard the workers singing and seen the banners from the French windows of her Ritz suite. David Seymour, a news photographer, captured their grim faces as they chanted, "It's our last fight!"—words from the marching song—and clutched poster sketches bearing the faces and names of France's humanists and artists: Honoré Daumier, Molière, Voltaire, Émile Zola, and a gaunt-faced Paul Signac.

For Chanel and for the privileged of Europe—indeed, for much of the French middle class that had toiled and saved for years—the 1936 strikes that closed French industry were scandalous and heralded the coming of Bolshevism. The French elections of April 26, 1936, brought a Popular Front parliamentary coalition of Communists and Socialists to power. A month later Léon Blum's coalition took over.

Emboldened by their victory at the polls, labor unions began a general strike in Le Havre on May 26, accompanied by factory occupations to prevent lockouts, which quickly spread to Paris. By June, the Ritz boutiques surrounding the hotel's elevator had closed, their owners having declared bankruptcy.

Chanel's salesgirls at the rue Cambon boutique and the "little hands" seamstresses who manned her ateliers followed suit. Some four thousand of her workers went on strike. When, early one June morning, Chanel's personal accountant, Madame Renard, discovered she had been barred from her office, she slipped away and entered the Ritz through the back entrance, taking the elevator to Chanel's suite of rooms. In a trembling voice, Renard told a sleepy Chanel that her little hands had locked her out. Startled, Chanel wondered if her workers had gone crazy. She later remarked, "I tell you in 1936 they were mad." Madame Renard thought the city was in the hands of thieves. She begged the designer to leave Paris. Chanel declared that her little hands and saleswomen were infected by an American invention—"le sit-down!"

The seamstresses, the artisans, meant business. That same morning they tacked a hastily written sign on the Chanel employee entrance: OCCUPIED. They crossed their arms and planted themselves in the workrooms and boutique—and waited. For Chanel, it was a stab in the back. Her workforce—"my girls" (*mes filles*), including her first hands and senior staff—had, as she saw it, "betrayed" her despite her generosity. She offered good pay for a day's labor and vacations (for most, unpaid). Manon, one of Chanel's top artisans, had proclaimed when returning from a vacation at Chanel's retreat: "The first time I saw the sea was at Mimizan."

All Paris seemed to be on strike. As Prime Minister Blum

Chanel's employees struck and closed her business, 1936. A delegation of her workers gathers in front of the rue Cambon employee entrance—the same entrance used by Chanel employees today.

pleaded for calm, shopgirls at Au Printemps and Les Galeries Lafayette—the Macy's and Bloomingdale's of Paris—answered by pushing "shrilly protesting, gesticulating shoppers and patrons out the doors." It was a French version of the American sit-down strike, and "[the girls] danced in the aisles and picnicked in the elevators." Shirer reported on it, "the good humor of the strikers a sinister sign." Sinister indeed: *L'Écho de Paris* told how salesgirls on the boulevard Haussmann were striking: walking out or locked in and laughing. Chanel and her clients, the elite of Paris, feared a civil war.

It was just as Chanel's former lover, Bendor, had predicted: the Bolsheviks and the Jews wanted to rule Europe and promote war between Britain and Germany. Bendor, the richest landowner in Great Britain and the man whom Chanel's grand-niece, Gabrielle Palasse Labrunie, called "Uncle Benny," wanted England to back Hitler and Mussolini against Russian Communism. The keystone to peace in the world was Anglo-German friendship, the duke insisted. Indeed, Germany should attack Russia, the country that threatened the West.

Blum's Socialist-Communist parliamentary bloc terrified the wealthy. Eighty-five percent of French voters had supported Blum's Front Populaire. The haves were terrified of a Communist take-over of Europe. The price of gold soared as the rich rushed to buy it up. In Paris, some of the well-to-do sent their treasures to Swiss banks. Others packed up and fled to the security of their country homes. They ordered their *mécanicien* (Chanel's word for a chauffeur) to load their Rolls-Royce and Delaunay limousines (she owned both) with precious works of art, jewels, and silverware. Those who remained double-locked their doors, loaded their shotguns, and filled their bathtubs with water. They feared that utility services might be cut. It was as if the sans-culottes, the revolutionaries of 1789 who worshiped the guillotine, were loose again on Parisian streets.

Chanel's workforce would not be bent. Seamstresses are by nature meticulous, focused creatures, so Chanel was facing a band of defiant women struggling for increased wages and hoping for a paid vacation for the first time in their lives. A group of them can be seen assembled in front of the Chanel boutique at 31, rue Cambon, and at the workshop entrance at 29, rue Cambon, posing for news photographers. Nameless in the photo captions, the ladies are clad in smart dresses and tailored women's suits. One striker, dressed in a Chanel outfit, timidly waves to the camera. Another smiles and shows a determined fist. Still another holds up the traditional strikers' collection box. One and all are smiling but stand solid and resolute.

Days of recriminations followed. Chanel's rue Cambon boutique and workshop remained shut. Chanel decided to try a new stratagem: if the women wanted Communism, she would give it to them. She offered to turn over her fashion business to her workers as long as she was appointed to run the business. The offer was refused.

In the end Blum and the French labor movement won a major battle. In the first week of June, Blum signed a pact forever known as Les Accords de Matignon (from the Hôtel Matignon, the offi-cial residence of the French prime minister), and French workers were granted a forty-hour workweek, paid vacations, collective bargaining rights, and compulsory schooling to age fourteen.

July and August slipped away. As the leaves of Paris's chestnut trees turned from green to rusty brown, most of the city returned to work. Chanel's advisors begged her to concede, to be reasonable, and to think about the fall collections. She hesitated. It was against her very essence to capitulate. Still, her prestige was involved. Large sums of money were tied up in overhead, fabrics, and machines. Business came first. Finally, she came around. The workshops hummed again, the massive street-level shutters on the rue Cambon boutique were raised, and the crème de Paris returned to be served by genteel Chanel employees.

ELSA SCHIAPARELLI'S NOVEL DESIGNS, her audacious, shocking pinks from Salvador Dalí's palette, and her use of art by Christian Bérard and Jean Cocteau to make dresses and accessories were now the talk of Paris. (The artists were all Chanel's friends.) Playwright Anita Loos, author of *Gentlemen Prefer Blondes,* and Wallis Simpson, the Duchess of Windsor, wore her creations; Marlene Dietrich donned her Russian furs. Her use of new materials resembling today's plastic drew clients into her Place Vendôme boutique—right under Chanel's nose. "Schiap," as Paris called her, was delightfully excessive with an evening dress composed of a skirt printed with a life-sized lobster and a bodice scattered with a few green motifs to represent parsley. Her handbag was in the form of a telephone; one skirt had pockets with flaps that looked like lips. Shocking pink was in, and Chanel's sober, refined look was overwhelmed. Some critics thought Chanel had lost her touch when she returned from Hollywood. Even before the strikes, she was sliding from her perch as France's first lady of fashion, and her diatribes on matters of fashion were now challenged.

Born of a noble Italian family, educated in Paris, London, and New York, Schiap was a stark contrast to Chanel, whose first boutique had been financed twenty years earlier by her lovers, "because two gentlemen were outbidding each other for my hot little body." Chanel the orphan, raised in a convent, couldn't stomach the woman she called "L'Italienne" (an insult in chic Paris).

Schiap's pretensions were simply "enraging." Schiap, in turn, called Chanel "the hat maker," infuriating her further.

Chanel believed that Schiaparelli was simply "that Italian artist who makes clothes." Schiaparelli didn't just "irritate" her; she "enraged" her. But Schiap wasn't Chanel's only serious threat. Mainbocher, the fashion house founded by Main Rousseau Bocher, the former editor of *Vogue* who had turned designer, and the houses of Madeleine Vionnet and Germaine Krebs, later Madame Grès, all became Chanel's fierce rivals. Yet it was Schiaparelli who prematurely announced, "Chanel is finished."

In public, Chanel shrugged off l'Italienne and the others. On the arms of her friends Christian Bérard, Étienne de Beaumont, and ex-beau Grand Duke Dmitri Pavlovich, Chanel dominated the galas, parties, dinners, and press conferences surrounding the Paris Exposition Internationale des Arts et Techniques held in the summer of 1937. Reporters thought she had never been so radiant and pretty as she posed for photographers and chatted with journalists.

Misia Sert, her soul sister, knew that behind the smiles, Coco was seriously wounded. She had suffered the death of her lover and business partner, Paul Iribe, two years before. She had been beaten down by the strikes of 1936. And now other couturiers were getting the attention that was rightfully hers. She tried her hand at doing costumes for Cocteau's *Œdipe Roi*—swathing the performers, including the young rising star, Jean Marais, in bandages. The result was hideous, and the press didn't spare Chanel: "Wrapped in bandages, the actors looked like ambulant mummies or victims of some terrible accident." The costumes were booed as being heavy and outmoded.

In the months that followed, Chanel disappeared from the rue Cambon. She retreated first to La Pausa and then to Lausanne, Switzerland, where her secret bank accounts held her share of the earnings from the worldwide sales of Chanel No. 5 perfume. She seemed to have lost interest in the business. Biographer Pierre Galante ventured otherwise: "Coco's supremacy was threatened." Still, Chanel believed, despite the success of Elsa Schiaparelli, that her work had not yet seen its day—the momentary infatuation with the extravagant Italian would be short-lived: the Chanel style was far from dead.

Misia Sert, Chanel's lifetime friend, in a gown by Chanel, 1937.

On January 21, 1936, forty-two-year-old Edward, Prince of Wales, Chanel's good friend David, ascended to the throne of Great Britain as HRH Prince Edward VIII. The uneasy reign of the still-uncrowned king saw Hitler snatching the Rhineland, occupied by France since 1918, and Mussolini's armies in Africa capture the Ethiopian capital of Addis Ababa. On June 9, 1936, more than a million workers went on strike in Spain, marking the beginning of the Spanish Civil War that would bring Spanish general Francisco Franco and a Fascist government backed by Adolf Hitler to power.

Edward was determined to marry an American divorcée, Wallis Simpson, who was being described in the French press as the *putain royale,* or royal whore. The British Parliament was as deter-

The Duke of Windsor and his bride, the former Wallis
Simpson, greeted by Adolf Hitler on a nonofficial
visit to Berchtesgaden, Germany, 1936.

mined to block the marriage. On the night of December 11, 1936,
the uncrowned Edward VIII told the world in a BBC broadcast
that he had abdicated. His forty-one-year-old brother Albert now
became king and emperor of Great Britain. He would reign over
the British Empire as George VI.

Winston Churchill, soon to be a member of Neville Chamberlain's government, was a regular visitor to Paris throughout 1936.
Some three months before Edward's abdication, he and Randolph
dined with Chanel and Jean Cocteau in Chanel's suite at the Ritz.
Churchill still hoped their mutual friend David could be swayed
to give up marrying Wallis Simpson.

Cocteau remembered the dinner very well. He wrote in his
journal how Winston had gotten drunk, burst into tears, and
sobbing in Chanel's arms, exclaimed, "A king cannot abdicate." A
few months later, Churchill would help his king and friend David
edit his abdication speech. Barely eight months later the exiled

Edward, now Duke of Windsor, and his bride, Wallis Simpson, a loyal Chanel customer, stayed in a Ritz apartment not far from Chanel's suite after returning from a visit with Hitler at Berchtesgaden, the führer's Bavarian retreat.

MOST FRENCH BELIEVED war could be averted. Neville Chamberlain, prime minister of Britain, was sure Hitler could be "contained." In September 1938, Chamberlain returned from Munich waving a copy of his signed agreement with the führer— telling a crowd in front of Number 10 Downing Street, "I believe it is peace in our time."

Chanel showed a gold lamé evening dress with a short jacket for the 1938 collections. British *Vogue* magazine wrote, "Sex appeal is the prime motif of the Paris collection and sex appeal is no longer a subtle appeal." As Europe teetered between war and peace during 1938–1939, business picked up. The Ritz boutiques by the elevator were thriving, selling Van Cleef jewels, tortoise-shell boxes, and other luxury goods. Chanel's boutiques were swarming with society women in search of smart suits and gowns, hats, jewelry, accessories, and, above all, that exotic Chanel No. 5 perfume.

At age fifty-five, Chanel was still beautiful and sexy, her silhouette stunning. She dressed with style and invention, and the photographers loved her. She was seen everywhere—in June 1938 with Spanish painter Salvador Dalí and French composer Georges Auric at Monte Carlo; later with dancer Serge Lifar and composer Igor Stravinsky at a Misia Sert dinner. At an after-theater meeting with French actor Louis Jouvet, she dressed in a sensational Chanel cut from a heavy white crepe fabric. Schiaparelli may have invented "shocking pink" for her 1938 collection, but Chanel trumped her. The Chanel collection of 1939 showed a series of Gypsy dresses that were copied in the United States and around Europe. As the fear of war gripped Europe in the spring of 1939, Chanel featured outfits in patriotic red, white, and blue.

During that torrid summer of 1939, the Hôtel Ritz was not a bad place to be. In the garden restaurant, Chanel and friends Jean Cocteau and Jean Marais could enjoy a classic Escoffier *salade Niçoise* caressed with olive oil and vinegar, or perhaps one of the famous chef's Oriental salads washed down with chilled Beaujolais, followed by an apple tart and coffee. Indeed, Monsieur

Ritz maintained a Swiss-run oasis of gentility where "militarists" debated "pacifists" in the Ritz's Psyche Salon.

Clare Boothe Luce, wife of *Time* and *Life* magazines' owner Henry Luce, toured Europe's capital cities in the beginning of 1940. At the Ritz in Paris, Luce mixed with a host of fashionable New Yorkers, including *Vogue* editor Margaret Case, who was there to cover the Paris collections. Luce was delighted to see that the Ritz hadn't lost its splendor: "The same smiling little manager at the reception desk, with his long cutaway coat that almost touched his heels . . . the same smoothly efficient and omniscient red-mustached concierge, and the gray distinguished Olivier, the great maître d'hôtel of Europe, bowing as always at the end of the corridor to the dining room." Luce thought they all looked "a little more solemn and pale than of yore." Nevertheless, she observed, "from the smell of fur and perfume, and the sounds of high bird-babble voices," the guests at the Ritz hadn't changed. She and Margaret Case had to put up with the horrid noise of jackhammers as workmen dug an extra bombproof cellar behind the hotel's garden wall. Case seemed put out, and Luce reassured her friend: "[Darling], I've noticed that bombs never make hits on people that live in the Claridges or the Ritz." With the coming of April, Luce observed: "The loveliest crystal-clear spring had come to Europe."

AT FIRST LIGHT, on September 1, 1939, German forces surged across the Polish border heading toward the cities of Lodz, Kraków, and Warsaw—as they had crossed the Czech border to seize Prague six months earlier. So it was that on the first Wednesday of September, Chanel woke up in the velvet opulence of the Ritz to learn that her country was at war with Germany. At first, nothing seemed to happen. The Brits dubbed the hiatus the "Phoney War"; the French called it a *drôle de guerre*; Berliners, *Sitzkrieg*—the opposite of blitzkrieg, the lightning blows that Hitler had dealt to Poland and would soon deliver to France and the Low Countries.

Chanel—once a penniless orphan, a rich man's paramour, and now the first lady of fashion—had made a fortune liberating women's bodies from corsets during the Great War of 1914–1918. Now, in the first days of World War II, self-made Chanel considered war to be men's business. The war was an opportunity for her to punish her employees for their strike action three years earlier. She fired some three thousand female workers: the artisans who cut her gowns; the little hands that stitched each creation from scratch; and the keepers of her salon. It was closure—the end of the fashion House of Chanel. It was Chanel getting even with the women who, three years earlier, demanded more pay and shorter hours; the women who had locked her out of her workshops and boutiques. It was payback for the massive strikes provoked, in her view, by the Jew Léon Blum's Socialist-Communist government of 1936. And Chanel was burnt out, convinced the world of fashion had ended with the war. "How could I suppose there would still be people who would buy dresses," she asked her friend Marcel Haedrich, chief editor of the French fashion magazine *Marie Claire*, after the war. "I was so stupid, such a dummy about life that it seemed impossible to me . . . well I made a mistake. Some people sold dresses all during the war. That will be a lesson to me. Whatever may happen hereafter I will go on making clothes. The only thing I still believe in."

Chanel believed Blum and Jewish liberal politicians were all Bolsheviks who threatened Europe. Her right-wing political beliefs had been sharpened over the years by her lovers—the men who had lifted her out of poverty and helped to launch her career as a successful Paris couturier.

Finally, Paul Iribe had fueled her fear of Jews. His anti-Semitism was so blatant that Edmonde Charles-Roux, a Chanel biographer, thought it was "disgusting." As for Bendor, the duke's anti-Semitic rants were notorious.

By the fall of 1939 Hitler and Stalin had crushed Poland. Later, Russia would rule Finland and northern Poland, while Italy menaced the Mediterranean Basin. In England, Chamberlain appointed Churchill to be First Lord of the Admiralty in a desperate bid to shore up the credibility of his appeasement-tainted government.

Chanel's ex-lover and friend, Bendor, was desperately trying to free his new mistress, a French woman who had tried to cross into Britain from France to join the duke only to be arrested as a suspected spy. In Rome Coco's old friend Vera Bate Lombardi was under surveillance by the Italian secret military police known as

SIM (Military Information Service). They believed she was a British agent because of her English aristocratic birth and frequent visits to the British Embassy in Rome—despite the fact that Italy had yet to declare war on England.

Sometime after 1929, Vera had joined her husband, Alberto, a member of the Fascist party, at his villa on via Barnaba Oriani in the exclusive Parioli quarter of Rome. Italian archives tell how Vera had taken Italian citizenship that year and, according to a letter from her husband to the Italian minister of justice, she had joined Mussolini's Fascist Party.

Vera led a leisurely life in Rome. With cavalry officer Alberto, she competed in numerous equestrian events and reveled in *la dolce vita*. She enjoyed her role as the wife of a senior Italian officer pledged to Mussolini. Alberto and his family were favorably known to Benito Mussolini and esteemed in Fascist circles; and Alberto was promoted to head a cavalry regiment. But Vera's very English habits and frequent attendance at British Embassy events made her suspect to the Fascist police and various intelligence services. In 1936, the chief of staff of the Italian Political Investigation Service sent the following report to the Italian Interior and War Offices:

> Mrs. Lombardi: the lively and quite mysterious life of Mrs. Lombardi, wife of Major of Cavalry Alberto from the Tor di Quinto Cavalry School, gives rise to suspicions . . . It seems she has relationships with some of Prince of Wales' friends and she has many acquaintances amongst the British political and financial circles . . . she has frequently worked for the Chanel fashion company whose owner was for many years the lover of the Duke of Westminster . . . This lady's mysterious and varied lifestyle makes us suspect she is in service for Great Britain without the knowledge of her husband, who is a highly respected person and sincere patriot . . . Lombardi frequently talks on the phone with London, it won't be difficult to monitor her calls coming from her place on via Oriani.

One week later, investigators were ordered to suspend tailing Vera "because she is a military officer's wife and because the

SIM had investigated Vera for some time, reviewing all her mail without any success." But Vera's problems with the Italian Fascist police and counterintelligence services were not over. For the next few years and throughout World War II, she would be suspected by the Italians of espionage for the British. Her later relations with Chanel during wartime would bring Vera to the attention of the British intelligence service MI6.

THE CONSTANT WAR NEWS and the air-raid drills grated on Chanel's nerves, and she fretted about nephew André Palasse. In 1939, André had been mobilized, leaving his wife and two daughters—Gabrielle, the oldest, who was named after "Auntie Coco," as she called her, and the younger, Hélène—at their property at Corbère in southern France. André was serving on the front at the Maginot Line fortifications that guarded the strategic border between France and Germany. From the time he was mobilized Chanel looked after his family's needs, keeping grand-niece Gabrielle with her as often as schooling allowed.

Often alone, Chanel missed being in love or feeling that she was in love—which was the same thing to her. There had been no serious romances since the death of Paul Iribe, and Chanel needed to feel that she was loved by a man, perhaps as compensation for her lonely childhood. Now as she waited to see what war would bring, she brooded over a long string of betraying lovers: Étienne Balsan, her first master; Boy Capel, her first serious love affair; Igor Stravinsky, the passing flirt; Dmitri, Grand Duke of Russia, a prized lover; the Duke of Westminster, her ultra-rich mentor. And still later: the poet Pierre Reverdy, who resembled her lost father. But most of all, she missed and mourned Iribe—a man whom she had trusted and admired. None of her suitors could commit to her completely, in large part because she refused to commit to them, or they had left to marry others. In the case of Iribe, who had crumbled before her eyes from a massive heart attack, she felt he had betrayed her by his death—just as her father's sudden disappearance forty years earlier had left her abandoned. Serge Lifar, the ballet master and Chanel's close friend, was shocked to hear Chanel say, "Oh, Iribe! He's finally dead, that one! He won't be seen anymore."

It was bravado. The men Chanel had loved were now either dead or out of reach. She told a number of authors, "There is nothing worse than solitude. Solitude can help a man realize himself; but it destroys a woman." She counseled women to "follow conventional standards if they want to be happy in life; otherwise . . . [they] will pay the terrible price of solitude."

Bitter in the midst of war, her heart empty, her hands idle, she wrote her brothers, Lucien and Alphonse, that their regular stipends were ending. "I've closed the business . . . and I fear living in misery . . . don't count on me anymore." It was a petty letter written in frustration. Though her income was cut with the closing of her fashion business, Chanel was still wealthy. Income flowed to her Swiss accounts from Chanel No. 5's worldwide revenues and from the sale of perfume and accessories at her boutiques on the rue Cambon, at Deauville, and at Biarritz. She could always be sure that women would want her perfume, and in wartime, sales of her fragrances in France, neutral Spain, and Switzerland would become a major source of income.

A challenge emerged. After firing her employees, Chanel wanted to leave everything nice and tidy, and do something else. Her poet lover Reverdy agreed. In 1939 he told Chanel, "war was a time to hide, lie low and keep quiet." But the French bureaucrats who regulated the fashion business—and the lords of high fashion, the Chambre syndicale de la haute couture—saw it otherwise. They were furious when she closed her mirrored salon on the rue Cambon and accused her of outright "treason." Her employees joined the French labor union, Confédération Générale du Travail (CGT), and the Chambre syndicale in an attempt to force her to stay open. It was a question of the prestige of Paris. Even the other couturier houses, her competitors, protested. What would Paris wartime galas in support of the soldiers be worth without Chanel?

In his book *L'Allure de Chanel,* author Paul Morand thought Chanel summed up her character: "Life is about combat and confusion and the idea thrills me and satisfies my profound taste for destruction." Despite closing her workshop, Chanel wasn't finished. The *New York Times* printed a dispatch to New York via Clipper Airmail and dated April 16, 1940:

In spite of repeated denials, rumors still persist here that the great Chanel will reopen her Paris house in the not too distant future. Be that as it may, she consented to design an evening gown to set off Van Cleef & Arpels's newest pin—a great flower like star, or perhaps a comet, trailing a long supple fringe of jewels in lieu of a tail. The star has a tremendous diamond center. Its rays—or petals—are made of ruby, emerald, jade and large pearls, finished in pear-shaped precious pendants. Chanel designed a rich-colored background for this regal bijou. She uses it casually to attach flattering triple shoulder straps of ruby-red velvet ribbon with streamers that trail to the floor in back and thus counterbalance the effect of the heavy jewel fringe. The dress itself is of heavy crinkled crepe in the tone of darkest "emerald jade." It is deeply décolleté and molds the figure in the inimitable Chanel manner. Glamorous finishing touches are a little head-dress of looped velvet ribbons and ruffled green suede gloves with ruby velvet ribbons tied in bows around the wrists to match their ribbon borders.

IN AN ATMOSPHERE of false gaiety, soldiers came home on leave during the so-called Phoney War, and Parisians tried their best to amuse them. Maurice Chevalier and Josephine Baker, the American diva (who would take French citizenship in 1937), were belting out songs at the Casino de Paris. The racecourses at Auteuil were packed. One could enjoy the chatter and laughter at Maxim's or the smoke-filled rooms of the Brasserie d'Alsace, where the best choucroute in Paris was still being served.

Meanwhile, desperate refugees, mostly working-class Jews, continued fleeing Germany and Eastern Europe, hoping to find freedom in England, France, and the United States. Paris had now become a safe harbor for professionals and craftsmen who feared Hitler's Germany and SS-run concentration camps. Some of those lucky enough to reach France found work as artisans and seamstresses at Parisian couturier houses. When war broke out, there were 120,000 refugees in France, the majority of them Jews.

That first winter of war gave Parisians a real taste of deprivation amid dreadful cold spells. The average Parisian lived a somber life, ill-tempered and irked by food and fuel rationing. Fathers, young husbands, and brothers were away at war and some sixteen thousand children were sent to the country. The air-raid drills were a constant annoyance, and the occasional real firebombing of a factory in the Paris suburbs sounded a deadly note.

For those lucky enough to be guests at the Ritz that winter of 1939–1940, the hotel remained an island of wartime luxury. Despite shortages of food and qualified staff, the Ritz was a mecca for the rich. Private chauffeurs had been mobilized. The wealthy had closed their Neuilly villas and moved into Ritz suites. Downstairs they could enjoy a smoke in the Psyche Salon, dinner in the Grill Room, and a drink at the Ritz bar. Chanel and her guests went on enjoying the Ritz's fine cuisine. One luncheon menu offered pheasant soup, medallions of veal, and a baked apple washed down with a glass or two of a Premier Cru classé— Pauillac Château Latour 1929.

Jean Cocteau and his partner Jean Marais lived in an apartment a short walk from the Ritz at Chanel's expense. They dined frequently at Chanel's table. The handsome Marais, not yet a French movie idol, had been called up to serve in the air force. He knowingly assured Chanel that a real war was out of the question. Marais ventured, drolly, that Hitler was bluffing; that the armor used to protect the German tanks that had crushed Poland was papier-mâché. The Phoney War would soon end. Hitler's offer of peace was sincere. Marais was certain a peace deal was in the works.

Parisian newspapers announced that Chanel and Cocteau would soon marry. The reports amused the openly homosexual Cocteau and Marais. Chanel was less amused but didn't deny the stories.

The Ritz was a convenient place to hold court. The Duke and Duchess of Windsor, as well as Arletty, the music hall actress and film comedienne, had suites there. The American business consultant Charles Bedaux and his wife, Fern—intimate friends of leading Nazis in Berlin—occupied three apartments near Chanel's. The war didn't stop the duke and duchess from giving a black-tie dinner, which was suspended temporarily because of an air-raid alert.

Noël Coward, a frequent Ritz guest at the time, observed that when the air-raid sirens screeched along the hotel's hallways, Chanel was forced to flee her luxury suite and to find shelter in the hotel's basement. During one such alert, Coward spotted Chanel with her maids in tow, rushing for the cellar. According to Coward, her attendants, Germaine and Jeanne, trailed their boss into the shelter carrying her gas mask on a pillow. This bit of farce is probably one of Noël Coward's piffles.

MOST FRENCH FAMILIES knew nothing about the luxuries of the Ritz. They ate meat only twice a week. Even Parisian households in the better neighborhoods tightened their belts. Pastry stores were forced to close three days a week. Butter was restricted and meat in short supply, while liquor stores were forbidden to sell spirits but could offer wine and beer. Even the privileged who dined in restaurants had to get by with one meat course in a two-course meal. As winter ended, fuel for autos was rationed, and 5.5 million French farmers and farm workers were ordered to stay on the land and keep out of the cities. (No one explained how this was to be enforced.)

It was worse for the average German. While Dr. Goebbels broadcasted in "suave radio tones" about Germany's historic rights to lebensraum (literally: living space) and sang the praises of Hitler's genius, the German *Arbeiter* (worker) plodded to his job in wooden-soled shoes, clutching black bread and margarine wrapped in newspaper. Tobacconists could sell only two cigars or ten cigarettes daily to male customers and none to females. The restaurants' normal ration of beer was cut by 60 percent, while 40 percent of their wine reserves would go to the army. Later, dancing would be forbidden and "German Hausfrauen driven to desperation by the pleading of sallow, hungry children because the state had cut the spinach ration to one-half pound a person."

The Reich's propaganda machine churned on. As Germany perfected its plans to overrun the Low Countries and France, Hitler urged peace negotiations. His pronouncements were carried in lively headlines in Paris newspapers. *Paris-Soir,* the popular Radio Cité, and the BBC all spoke of diplomacy at work. French men believed politicians would find some neat political compromise to end the war.

For Parisians sipping chicory-laden coffee in their local cafe, there was a certainty that no matter what happened, Paris would be spared. They held an unshakable conviction that the devastating war losses of World War I had made another all-out war with Germany inconceivable. A million and a half men, one-tenth of metropolitan France's male population, had been sacrificed in 1914–1918. Wasn't the Great War the war to end all wars? Four million men had come home wounded: blind, limbless, with broken faces—Les Gueules Cassées. Could it be that across the Rhine the Germans had forgotten their dead and wounded? Had the horrors of World War I been blanked out?

The French writer Jean Guéhenno, gravely wounded in 1915, thought, "I will never believe that people are made for war." French men lived "a delicious illusion"—convinced that if the Germans did come again, they wouldn't get across the Seine River as they had in 1914. They couldn't possibly penetrate the impregnable defenses built since 1930 by André Maginot: a formidable cluster of reinforced concrete artillery positions, machine-gun pillboxes, and tank traps called the Maginot Line, where Chanel's nephew André Palasse served. It had cost taxpayers 3 billion francs, and it had been constantly upgraded. It would stop Les Boches.

Jean-Paul Sartre, who manned a post on the Maginot Line, believed, "There will be no fighting, that it will be a modern war, without massacres as modern painting is without subject, music without melody, physics without matter." He spent his days on the Line sending weather balloons into the air and watching them float away through his army-issued binoculars. He wrote, "What they do with this information is their affair." Everyone hoped that a quick, diplomatic settlement was on the way.

The French military command lived in a fool's paradise.

A few men—Charles de Gaulle and his fellow officers—knew the "futuristic fortifications" were "foolish" and a "dangerous distraction," and in the end they did prove a "pitiful irrelevance." West of the Maginot defense line, the 400-kilometer border between France and Belgium was largely unprotected against Hitler's coming blitzkrieg.

The French and British staff officers couldn't agree about the vulnerability of their line of defense in northern France. They argued over troop dispositions and strategy. When the Duke of Windsor visited French front-line positions, he was struck by the political feuds. The French generals, he reported to London, "were more actively hostile to each other than to the Germans." Intelligence reports revealed the incessant quarrels among the French and British high commands and the weaknesses in France's defense. A disaster was in the making. And Hitler was revising his plans of attack at that very moment.

Winston Churchill visited Paris frequently that winter and spring of 1940 but never grasped how badly the war was being managed. More than once, he saw Chanel at the Ritz. The future prime minister of Britain had been beguiled by Coco since 1925, when the two had met often at the home of the Duke of Westminster and later at Bendor's hunting parties in France and on the Côte d'Azur. The war had spoiled everything. The good times were now memories. Days when Churchill lingered on evenings in Chanel's rooms, drank too much, and wept in Chanel's arms were bygone memories.

On his Paris visits Churchill wanted to know everything. After meeting Chanel, he would then interview Hans-Franz Elmiger, the Swiss manager of the Ritz, probing him about conditions in Paris, the attitude of Ritz employees, and the morale of Parisians. Did Churchill bring Chanel news of Bendor—now a powerful nuisance in wartime England, with his pro-German and anti-Semitic pronouncements? Did he assure Chanel that the Allies could defend France? Churchill could not believe otherwise. His love of France was too great to see her flaws. His experiences with the French officer corps—the valiant Frenchmen that he, the Prince of Wales, and Bendor had known twenty-five years earlier on the Western Front in World War I—made him believe France could not be defeated. Later—too late—he realized how the political intrigues in the French high command had rotted the will to win.

CLARE BOOTHE LUCE prefaced her book *Europe in the Spring* with the words of an English wit: "Hitler and his cohorts may send death to me and you. For it's just the sort of silly thing that silly man would do." As the green shoots of poppies appeared in Flanders Field, *Time* magazine editors wrote: "Last week long-dreaded World War II was six months old . . . as spring breathed sweetly on Europe . . . as the first storks returned to Belfort . . . the wings of war rustled more and more ominously. Somewhere on the Rhine the Germans were reported massing pontoon bridges . . . the German people expect a vast Nazi offensive to begin soon."

They were off by four weeks. The Rhine offensive would have to wait. Hitler had a different surprise for Europe. In the first week of April 1940, Chanel must have been startled as other Parisians were with the news that the führer's warships had bombarded Danish and Norwegian ports. German secret agents simultaneously triggered a Nazi putsch in the Norwegian capital of Oslo. King Haakon VII, the royal family, and the government fled to London. All of Norway and Denmark were occupied.

In London, Neville Chamberlain resigned. Churchill was called to King George VI, the forty-five-year-old younger brother of the Duke of Windsor. Churchill reassured his king that Parliament would vote for him to direct Britain's life-or-death struggle for as many years as it took.

AS HITLER SWALLOWED Norway and Denmark, Parisians began packing. Ritz manager Elmiger vowed to stay open despite operating with only twenty-four employees, a quarter of the usual staff. The sisters Germaine and Jeanne, Chanel's two chambermaids, decided it was time to get out of Paris. They abandoned their mistress for their home village, while Chanel went about trying to replace the chauffeur she had lost to the military.

WHILE EUROPE HELD ITS BREATH, the handsome now forty-four-year-old Dincklage was at work in neutral Switzerland. He had fled there when Britain and France declared war on Germany. Posing as a businessman, Dincklage's mission was to collect military intelligence on Swiss defenses. He was to advise the German high command in Berlin on whether the Swiss would fight if Germany attacked France. Dincklage wasn't alone; he was backed up by his former spy chief, Major (later Lieutenant Colonel) Alexander Waag, a veteran Abwehr intelligence group leader now stationed at the German Embassy in Bern. Driving a Fiat Topolino with French license plates, Dincklage first spent several weeks in Ruvigliana near Lugano in the Italian Ticino at the Villa Colinetta owned by Dr. Leonardo Dicken, an old acquaintance and retired German official. Dr. Dicken's villa may have served as an early mail drop where Dincklage could receive correspondence. But French counterintelligence had already issued orders to its agents and to the various post and telegraph services that all communications from Maximiliane von Dincklage (Catsy had retained her married name) and from the baron's new mistress, Hélène Dessoffy, be opened and monitored.

In Switzerland, Dincklage must have learned that his former wife and Abwehr agent, Catsy, now age forty, and Dessoffy were under French surveillance. Dessoffy, the daughter of a high-ranking naval officer, had become Dincklage's mistress and a friend to Catsy in the mid-1930s. With the coming of war, she had been interrogated by French counterespionage agents at her home near the French naval base at Toulon. Earlier, before war was declared, Dincklage and Hélène had been expelled from Tunisia for spying. They had been discovered by French counterintelligence trying to penetrate the French naval base at Bizerte. Dincklage had deserted Hélène to return to Berlin before beginning his espionage assignment in Switzerland.

Edmonde Charles-Roux recalled how, just before the declaration of war, Hélène's husband, Jacques, had been "devastated" to learn that his wife was to be tried for espionage. Indeed, with all mail from Germany being screened by French counterintelligence officers, Dincklage may have unwittingly caused the arrests of Hélène and Maximiliane by writing to the two women earlier from Berlin.

Moving from one Swiss canton to another, Dincklage eluded detection until he checked into the Clinica di Viarnetto at Pregrassona, near Lugano, claiming he suffered from a nervous disease. (It was a classic ruse used by German agents "to avoid police control.") His efforts to operate covertly failed. Neither Waag in Bern nor their Abwehr handlers in Berlin had counted on the efficiency of the Swiss intelligence apparatus, which was just as effective as the German Gestapo. It turned out that Dr. Dicken was suspected by Swiss counterintelligence of being the chief Gestapo agent in Lugano, and the Swiss had already tagged Dincklage as a spy in 1933—perhaps when he was stationed in Warsaw. Dincklage then moved to Davos and finally landed at the Hôtel de la Paix at Lausanne—somehow managing not to fill in a registration card. Within a few days, the local police were tipped off, and his presence at the hotel was transmitted to the senior Swiss intelligence officer in Lausanne, Colonel J. Jacquillard.

A Swiss police officer now called on Dincklage at his hotel and took his diplomatic passport for examination. The document turned out to have been issued in Paris in 1935 and was valid until April 1940. The Swiss were now more than curious, which prompted the Bern headquarters of the Swiss intelligence service to open a formal investigation. When questioned later by Swiss officers, Dincklage was outraged. He told a Swiss police inspector named Decosterd that he had an English-born mother and had left France because he "wasn't enthusiastic about returning to Germany." The baron was furthermore so offended that he fumed to Decosterd, "You ought to investigate some of the clients at the bar of the Lausanne Palace Hôtel," observing that they looked pretty suspicious.

If anything was fishy, it was that Dincklage now kept company with women of "ill repute, addicted to morphine and suspected of spying for Germany." What's more, Swiss counterintelligence discovered that the suave former German diplomat had a Union Bank of Switzerland (UBS) account with a substantial balance of 18,000 Swiss francs (about $63,000 in today's money). When the Swiss contacted French sources, they learned that in France Dincklage had been a notorious womanizer who also had led clandestine operations in Spain and Tunisia and that he and Catsy ran an espionage network in France before and after their divorce. Dincklage used his good looks and charming personality to recruit French women to spy against targets on the Côte d'Azur. Hélène Dessoffy had been his mistress, courier, and agent. Later, the Swiss discovered that a forty-year-old German princess named Adele von Ratibor Corvey was, like Dr. Leonardo Dicken, receiving letters from France as a mail drop for Dincklage.

Pushing ahead, Swiss authorities asked their French colleagues for more information and discovered that a Parisian court had issued an arrest warrant for the baron at the request of the French intelligence and police services: Dincklage was wanted for spying against France.

Still, Bern, where the Swiss intelligence services directed operations, had no tangible and documented proof that Dincklage had broken Swiss law or committed espionage. Dincklage managed to let others do the dangerous work of receiving and transmitting documents to Berlin. He still held a valid German diplomatic passport—and at this crucial moment in German-Swiss relations, Bern had no desire to provoke an incident.

Bern finally decided to politely ask him to leave the country. By November 1939, Dincklage had left his hotel and closed his UBS account. He somehow managed to move 18,000 Swiss francs out of the country, and then went skiing in Davos. Swiss counterintelligence finally discovered that Alexander Waag and Dincklage were running two agents for the Abwehr: Hans Riesser and his wife, Gilda Riesser (agent cover name 1001). Hans was arrested. When Swiss agents examined his German passport, they found the document didn't bear the obligatory "J" for Jew. Since Riesser was indeed Jewish, the Swiss concluded he must have been an agent. He would spend the next four years in a Swiss prison. His wife, Gilda, managed to get across the Swiss border to France, where she would later serve the Abwehr.

THE COUNTDOWN to the blitzkrieg of France was nearing zero hour when Dincklage and Major Waag left Switzerland for Berlin. They would soon show up in Paris seemingly from nowhere and back into the lives of people who had once befriended them.

On the night of Monday–Tuesday, May 10–11, 1940, Berlin was blacked out. Despite the curfew, a *Time* magazine correspondent reported that Adolf Hitler, Field Marshal Hermann Göring, and Dr. Joseph Goebbels were, unusually, all seen together that evening at a Berlin theater. When morning broke on Tuesday, German foreign minister Joachim von Ribbentrop, looking pale and bleary-eyed after a sleepless night, told newsmen at a hastily assembled 8 a.m. press conference, "England and France at last dropped the mask." Belgium and Holland had "plotted" against the Reich, he rasped. Everyone in the press room knew that the German war machine had finally struck against France and the small neutrals.

Minutes later all Europe heard the smooth radio voice of Dr. Goebbels as he announced that "Holland, Belgium, and Luxembourg had been taken under protection by the Reich." In banner headlines, Berlin newspapers announced, "Germany has become the protector of the endangered and oppressed continent." Broadcasting from the German Rundfunk in Berlin, William L. Shirer, now the CBS News correspondent in Berlin, broke the news to the United States that Hitler had "marched into" Holland and Belgium. Like a great scythe, an armada of tanks and mechanized infantry swept aside Dutch and Belgian troops as Panzer units maneuvered through the dense Ardennes forest to crush French border outposts. Above Rotterdam, German parachute units floated down to capture strategic points. Specially trained Wehrmacht troopers blasted open sectors of the Maginot Line. Hitler's orders to his army and navy were clear: "The hour for the decisive battle for the future of the German nation has come . . . The battle will decide the future of the German peoples for the next one-thousand years."

Holland and Belgium surrendered. As German armies approached the Channel, British and French troops began evacuating France at Dunkirk on the North Sea beaches. According to Shirer, "Most people here in Berlin think that Hitler will try now to conquer England—maybe he'll try to finish France first."

Panic seized Paris. Carmel Snow wrote in *Harper's Bazaar* that the city had already become "an empty city. The taxis disappeared. All the telephones were cut. You can walk for miles without seeing a child. Even the dogs—and you know how Parisians love their dogs—have been sent away." At the Ritz, manager Elmiger soon realized the situation was desperate. Chanel must have heard the tragedy unfold on French radio and on the BBC. From London came the news that four million French men, women, and children, along with Belgian refugees, were fleeing south before the German armies.

Chanel hesitated. Her nights were filled with terrifying shadows. She eased fretfully into sleep with a dose of morphine from the syringe she kept by her bedside. Alone now, she desperately searched for a reliable man to replace the chauffeur who had been mobilized. Did she try to call Westminster in London? A news blackout added to the anxiety. From her window on Place Vendôme, Chanel could see "clouds of black smoke darkening the sky—at three in the afternoon it was like nightfall as bits of charred paper covered the city's streets." People imagined the Germans were burning everything before them; but no—the

Germans were hours away. The black smoke came from the burning of oil storage tanks and cartons and paper as diplomatic missions and French ministries torched their documents.

Clare Boothe Luce was listening to jazz on the radio that day in Paris when she heard the music stop, and then a crackling, raspy announcement: "We are bringing you the message of Pius XII." In a trembling voice the new pontiff—he had just been elected pope in March 1939—pleaded for the Belgian people.

Few Parisians imagined how rapidly German organization, modern communications, and a blitzkrieg attack could overrun the French defenses. By June 10, 1940, the Allied armies had been routed. Ever the agile scavenger, Mussolini declared war on France.

ON JUNE 11, Paris was declared an open city. Chanel's friend, U.S. Ambassador William C. Bullitt, was seen at Notre Dame Cathedral weeping before the altar. Like most Parisians, Chanel was now desperate to get out of town. No one knew if Paris would be bombed or devastated by the Wehrmacht steamroller. Chanel made arrangements for Mme Angèle Aubert, her right hand for thirty-some years; her chief seamstress, Manon; and a handful of other employees to go to the Palasse residence at the château at Corbère, near Pau. She packed up and left her trunks with the Ritz porter. A newly found chauffeur-bodyguard refused to drive the blue Rolls-Royce through swelling crowds of refugees. A Cadillac was found, and Chanel left Paris driving south through desperate masses, leaving behind the ominous clouds of thick, black smoke. She knew where she wanted to be: with the Palasse family across the Pyrenees at Corbère, near where her first lover, Étienne Balsan, had retired and where she was sure she could find a momentary peace.

SEVEN

PARIS OCCUPIED—
CHANEL A REFUGEE

For a woman betrayal has no sense—one cannot betray
one's passions.

—GABRIELLE CHANEL

A N EERIE SILENCE descended over the Paris Chanel
had left behind. French ministries had burned their codebooks, locked their offices, and joined the stream of refugees fleeing south. Clouds of oily black smoke drifted over the slate-gray
Seine; churches, monuments, and parks were deserted; cafe life
was extinguished. All communications had been cut—as if some
dreadful cataclysmic event had suspended life.

William C. Bullitt, the American ambassador in Paris, cabled
President Franklin D. Roosevelt: "The airplane has proved to be
the decisive weapon of war . . . the French had nothing to oppose
[the Germans] but their courage . . . It was certain that Italy
would enter the war and Marshal Philippe Pétain would do his
utmost to come to terms immediately with Germany."

Seven weeks after German troops first entered France, the Nazi
swastika flew from the Eiffel Tower. A few days later, Adolf Hitler was in Paris as his Wehrmacht troopers goose-stepped trium-
phantly down the Champs-Élysées. CBS correspondent William L.
Shirer reported from Paris:

> The streets are utterly deserted, the stores closed, the protec-
> tive shutters down tight over all the windows—the emptiness of

the city got to you . . . I have the feeling that what I have seen here is the complete breakdown of French society: a collapse of the French Army, of Government, of the morale of the people. It is almost too tremendous to believe . . . Petain surrendering! What does it mean? And no one appeared to have the heart for an answer.

CHANEL'S TRIP from Paris to Corbère, located near Pau, was laborious and sometimes hair-raising as her chauffeur, Larcher, drove south—inching from town to town, seeking safe passage. Hitler's Panzer tanks were already in the French heartland, and dive-bombers strafed columns of refugees seeking shelter along the narrow tree-lined roads. The advancing German forces had forced millions of desperate citizens to take to the roads of northern France on foot in overloaded autos, trucks, and horse-drawn wagons. Their baggage, spare tires, and mattresses were piled every which way.

At Corbère, André Palasse's wife, Katharina, and children waited anxiously for news from Auntie Coco. The family had had no information from soldier Palasse for weeks. As the tragic hours of France's defeat slipped by, they feared the worst. For Chanel, the Palasse château would be a temporary haven, isolated in the foothills of the Pyrenees. It was near Doumy, the home of Étienne Balsan, and she could count on his help.

No one knew where the Germans would stop. French radio correspondents continued to tell how British and French troops were fleeing French soil at Dunkirk, headed for refuge in England. From Paris, CBS radio correspondent Eric Sevareid reported, "No American after tonight will be broadcasting directly to America, unless it is under supervision of men other than the French." A French government had assembled in Bordeaux from where Prime Minister Paul Reynaud and Charles de Gaulle hoped to fight on. But they failed. Eighty-four-year-old Marshal Philippe Pétain wanted the war stopped, and Reynaud resigned. General de Gaulle fled to London. Marshal Pétain now took over what was left of France and its vast overseas empire. By mid-June 1940, the hero of the World War I battle at Verdun had asked the Germans for an armistice. Soon he would establish a regime at Vichy bent on collaboration with the Nazis. "Collaborator," a mundane term, would become the most highly charged word in the political vocabulary of occupied France. A *Time* magazine correspondent observed: "The best the French could hope for was to be allowed to live in peace in Adolf Hitler's Europe."

AFTER CHANEL AND LARCHER crossed the river Garonne at Agen, they found the roads less encumbered. In the foothills of the Pyrenees, at Doumy, they turned east onto country roads to find the Palasse château at Corbère. Katharina (Dutch-born Katharina Palasse, née Vanderzee), Étienne Balsan and his wife, and Chanel's grand-nieces, fourteen-year-old Gabrielle and Hélène, twelve, were "wildly relieved" to see Chanel—their bene-factor for years. Grand-niece Gabrielle was Chanel's favorite, a vivacious child with a mind of her own. "Uncle Benny," the Duke of Westminster, had nicknamed her "Tiny" because she was so petite. The name stuck.

The family reunion at Corbère was full of drama and pathos. News of André arrived via the International Committee of the Red Cross: he was alive, captured in one of the Maginot Line forts along with some 300,000 other French troops who had been sent to prisoner-of-war camps in Germany. The Palasse family was relieved. Surely he would be home soon, Gabrielle Palasse Labrunie remembers thinking. "The war would be over, Papa would come home." A few days later Angèle Aubert, Manon, and some ten other Chanel employees arrived from Paris, joining a group of Chanel's friends, all refugees from the City of Light. Later, Marie-Louise Bousquet, an intimate friend of Misia Sert, arrived from nearby Pau. Life at the château was a break from the chaos of Paris. Food was plentiful, the property's vineyards produced delightful amber white *vin du pays,* and Marie, the Pa-lasses' cook, served the family's table well. From time to time a small group gathered. Katharina, Chanel, the Balsans, and Marie-Louise Bousquet dined together. The children ate earlier. Gabrielle Palasse Labrunie remembers: "At home, children were to be seen and not heard." Madame Aubert, Manon, and the other Chanel employees lived and dined in an annex to the château. But Tiny, Chanel's favorite, had breakfast with Auntie Coco in her room.

Chanel's favorite grand-niece, Gabrielle Palasse, seen here at eleven
or twelve years of age in the library of the Palasse home at Corbère
on the eve of World War II. During the war, Mlle Palasse met
Baron von Dincklage in Paris.

Just after noon on June 17, French radio interrupted its usual
broadcast. At the Palasse château that Monday and all over Europe
and Britain, people listened as Marshal Pétain announced France
was surrendering—asking Hitler for armistice terms. "You, the
French people, must follow me without reservation on the paths
of honor and national interest. I make a gift of myself to France
to lessen her misfortune. I think of the unhappy refugees on our
roads . . . for them I have only compassion . . . it is with a heavy
heart that I tell you that today we must stop fighting."

Chanel was aghast. She went to her room and wept. Gabrielle
remembered, "When she learned France had been defeated, Auntie
Coco was inconsolable for days. She called it a betrayal." After the
debacle of May–June 1940 and with the occupation of France it
was common for French men and women to believe they were
betrayed by corrupt politicians and military leaders. That feeling
would give way to confidence in French hero Marshal Philippe
Pétain when he took over the Vichy government.

In the weeks that followed, the family learned that General de
Gaulle had made a broadcast to France from the London BBC.

André Palasse, Chanel's nephew, in Paris before World
War II. He was captured on the Maginot Line in 1940
and interned in a German stalag. Chanel managed
to secure André's freedom by cooperating with
the German Abwehr spy organization.

Slowly and often clandestinely via pamphlets distributed by anti-
Nazis, French men and women heard of de Gaulle's June 18,
1940, appeal to French citizens everywhere: "France has lost a
battle but not a war. The flame of resistance must not die, will not
die . . ." But in 1940 few in France knew who the fifty-year-old
general was. Only later, through BBC broadcasts from London,
would they come to know of a Free French movement headed
by de Gaulle and based in London. In 1940 only a handful of
French officers joined de Gaulle's resistance movement. De Gaulle
made few friends when he tagged Marshal Pétain "the shipwreck
of France." A French soldier listening to de Gaulle's broadcast in a
cafe remarked, "This guy is breaking our balls."

Marshal Pétain stripped General de Gaulle, his former protégé, of all rank, removing him from the rolls of the army he had

served his entire adult life. De Gaulle was then sentenced to death for treason. For many French men and women the surrender was a relief; France would be spared the bloodletting of 1914–1918. With Pétain in power most French and European politicians believed "Better Hitler than Stalin"—and they hoped that Hitler would turn against the Soviet Union.

As the summer wound down, Chanel wanted to return to Paris where her perfume business needed her attention; after all, she said later, "The Germans weren't all gangsters."

ON JUNE 22, 1940, the Nazi propaganda machine offered radio listeners a minute-by-minute humiliating description of France's defeat, broadcasting the details of the signing of the armistice agreement. Indeed, twenty-two years earlier, at the same railroad siding in the Compiègne forest clearing at Rethondes, the French had taken Germany's surrender. On a breezy Saturday morning French General Charles Huntziger signed France's capitulation in front of ranking German officers, making France a vassal of Germany. Hitler, Göring, Ribbentrop, and Rudolf Hess were there as was Dincklage's mentor General Walther von Brauchitsch. William L. Shirer, covering the event for CBS News, told listeners in America of Hitler's look of "scorn, anger, hate, revenge, triumph."

In thirty-eight days, the leader of the Third Reich had achieved what the kaiser's German army had failed to gain in the four years of bloody war in 1914–1918 that had cost millions of lives. Hitler had realized a German dream: Paris was at his feet.

After the signing of the armistice at Rethondes Hitler drove to Paris. There, the world's newsreels captured the führer strutting up the steps of the Palais de Chaillot at the Trocadéro. The movie cameras panned slowly over the German conquests: the Eiffel Tower with its Nazi swastika floating in the breeze, the gardens of the Champ de Mars, and the nearly eight-hundred-year-old twin towers of Notre Dame Cathedral. If one could believe Nazi propaganda, Great Britain was to be next on the Reich führer's menu.

THE ARMISTICE DIVIDED France into *la zone occupée* and *zone non occupée* (or *zone libre*), terms the French would soon label *zone O* and *zone nono*. France's new masters created a line of demarcation between north and south—an absolute foreign boundary, a major barrier to the movement of people, and an impediment to business and commerce. Beginning in June 1940, French citizens would have to apply for a *laissez-passer* or *ausweis* to travel between zones. *Laissez-passer* were never issued automatically; they were a privilege closely supervised by the Gestapo. Even Pétain's ministers had to ask German permission to travel from Vichy to Paris. For the French people, the line of demarcation was a humiliating nightmare.

Sixteen days after France capitulated, Prime Minister Churchill, fearing the French fleet would fall into German hands, ordered a British fleet to sink French warships based at Mers-el-Kébir in Algeria where masses of French vessels lay at anchor. Thirteen hundred French sailors perished; scores were wounded. It was a national dishonor—seen as a treacherous act by a former ally. For Marshal Pétain and his Anglophobic ministers, it was an excuse to end diplomatic relations with Britain. Pétain now declared that the nation was to have a "National Revolution" dedicated to "Work, Family and Fatherland." Britain blockaded French ports as Hitler's war staff planned to cross the English Channel and crush England. The Battle for Britain had begun.

Vichy, Marshal Pétain's new headquarters, was now in the hands of men who wanted to share in a European "New Order" under Hitler. They were convinced that Germany would defeat Britain and create a powerful force against Communism and international Jewry. Soon, the Nazis forced Pétain to appoint the rabid anti-Communist and anti-Semite Pierre Laval as deputy prime minister. Barely three months after Pétain signed an armistice agreement with the Nazis, his Vichy ministers had prepared a first "Statute on Jews." Pétain not only approved the law but in his own hand added restrictions on Jews in unoccupied France: defining who were Jews and banning Jews from high public service positions (physicians and lawyers, for example) that might influence public opinion. The Statute became law on October 3, 1940, three weeks before the Germans issued a similar law in Paris and the occupied zone. The thesis that Pétain was manipulated by his anti-Semitic Vichy entourage was a myth.

If Vichy was now the seat of French power in the unoccupied

zone, Chanel wanted to go there. She was determined to return to Paris by way of Vichy. She knew Pierre Laval, now Pétain's senior minister, through his daughter, Josée Laval de Chambrun (the wife of Chanel's lawyer, René de Chambrun), and a handful of Vichy ministers' wives—former clients and friends in Paris and Deauville.

Near Corbère Chanel's chauffeur Larcher managed to find enough petrol to feed the gas-guzzling Cadillac, and what fuel the tank couldn't hold was poured into tin cans and stored in the trunk of the car. Accompanied by Marie-Louise Bousquet, Chanel set out for Vichy. Then fourteen, Gabrielle Palasse Labrunie recalled years later and with sadness Auntie Coco's departure in the limousine. She was struck by Marie-Louise, a chic Parisian society lady who nearly fell off her platform shoes as she walked along the château's cobblestone courtyard to the car. It would be more than a year before Tiny would receive a pass to travel to join Chanel in Paris. The Palasse family would now live out the next months without ever seeing a German. News from André finally arrived via a Swiss Red Cross postcard: he was alive but ill.

The girls continued being tutored by Madame Lefebvre, a French refugee from the north. Their days were spent studying for the French national diploma, the *brevet élémentaire*. Bedtime was 8 p.m. French country people rose with the sun and went to bed early. Later, agents for the German troops, garrisoned at Pau, would come to the château to requisition foodstuffs, rabbits, pigs, and chickens.

CHANEL REACHED VICHY in late July. Her chauffeur covered the 270 miles (434 kilometers) driving over country roads along the river Allier without event. With the French surrender, the area was now occupied by German tank battalions and infantry. Refugees were returning home, and German troops had orders to be on their best behavior.

VICHY HAD ONCE BEEN a sleepy watering place on the river Allier. Until the war old men came to gamble at the casino, drink the curative waters, and ogle the pretty hostesses and buy their favors. By July when Chanel arrived, the town swarmed with some 130,000 politicians, diplomats, prostitutes, and secret agents installed in hastily built cubicles in former gambling rooms or in unheated hotel rooms transformed into offices. Their archives, brought from Paris, were stuffed into bathtubs. And everywhere the walls were graced with the likeness of Marshal Pétain, sternly glaring down at the bureaucrats at work.

When Chanel and Marie-Louise arrived, the town had the air of a tawdry commercial fair, pulsing with energy—sexual and otherwise—where life went on in cabarets, nightclubs, and brothels that served the needs of the civil servants, politicians, and professional hangers-on. A friend of Chanel's from Paris, André-Louis Dubois, a senior French official, claimed Chanel met Misia Sert in Vichy. Dubois recalled that all three of the ladies lodged in his Vichy hotel room—and not in an attic chamber, as some of Chanel's biographers have reported. (As it happened his rooms were free because Dubois had just been told to leave Vichy when it was discovered that he had helped Jews obtain visas to travel to America.)

At Vichy, the ladies took their meals at the Hôtel du Parc. Chanel's biographers tell how she was shocked by the behavior of a woman dining nearby—laughing and drinking Champagne under a huge hat. For Chanel—and perhaps Misia, too—the merriment was out of place as the French mourned their defeat at the hands of their age-old enemy across the Rhine River. Chanel made a caustic remark: "Well it is the height of the season here!" Hearing this, a gentleman nearby took umbrage; he exclaimed, "What do you insinuate, Madame?" Chanel then backed away with, "I mean everyone is very gay here." The man's wife calmed him.

Chanel had a reason for stopping at Vichy, now the seat of French power. She was determined to move heaven and earth to get her nephew André back from captivity—if she didn't see Laval personally, she certainly sought the advice of powerful Vichy leaders.

It must have been heartbreaking for Chanel to learn that André was only one of millions of French soldiers being held in German prisoner-of-war camps called stalags, and as early as 1940 people in the know were sure the Nazis would use those prisoners as bargaining tools. If she were to get André back, it would have to be done through a powerful German official—and she returned to Paris determined to act.

THE PARIS CHANEL returned to was awash in black-and-red swastika banners strung on the Arc de Triomphe, the Eiffel Tower, above the Parliament and ministries, and above the Élysée Palace. For the next four years Parisians would endure the sights and sounds of the German invader. Daily, Wehrmacht troopers goose-stepped to martial music down the Champs-Élysées to the Place de la Concorde. The Ritz was now a sandbagged fortress. Its entrance was guarded by elite German troopers in gray-green *feld-grau* uniforms presenting arms to arriving Nazi dignitaries while officers shouted lusty "Heil Hitler"s with outstretched arms.

Crueler still was the huge banner the Nazis had stuck to the upper façade of the French National Assembly and hung on the Eiffel Tower. In bold, black Gothic letters it read: *Deutschland siegt*

Nazi führer Adolf Hitler on his only visit to Paris after France capitulated, June 1940.

To humiliate the French, the Germans raised
the Nazi swastika above the building of the French
Interior Ministry in occupied Paris, January 1940.

an allen Fronten (Germany everywhere victorious). The Nazi masters piled insults on injuries. They ordered a bust of Adolf Hitler
placed front and center of the rostrum, where the president of the
French Parliament presided.

Parisian streets were crowded with Wehrmacht soldiers and
Kriegsmarine sailors. They strolled along the Champs-Élysées, the
rue de Rivoli, and rue Royale, gawking in shop windows at luxury
goods that they had never seen in their lives. They snatched up
souvenirs, paid in French francs bought with inflated reichsmarks.
"Thanks to the artificial exchange rate everything was cheaper
for the invader." Formally correct, they would mumble a polite
"*danke schön, Fräulein*" to the shop tenders and wink at passing
demoiselles—some all too ready to flirt with the handsome Aryan
lads homesick and desperate for female company.

By the autumn of 1940 some 300,000 German officials and

soldiers occupied Paris and towns around the city. They took over villas and apartments, evicting French tenants and owners, opened their own whorehouses, and earmarked their preferred hotels, restaurants, and cafes. Most Parisians came to terms with the occupation. Many would hang Pétain's portrait on the walls of their offices and homes. The Germans owned France: the grand boulevards, the monuments, even the street kiosks on the city's corners were festooned with Nazi signage and posters, warning the locals in German and French to obey occupation edicts, rationing laws, and the rigorous curfews—or face punishment.

Everywhere, Mercedes saloon cars, bumper pennants flapping in the wind, and camouflaged Wehrmacht squad cars scooted about the nearly empty city streets. Nonofficial Parisians put their

A gathering of German officers, possibly at the Paris Opéra ca. 1940, shows a man who may be Dincklage (top row, second from the left) dressed as a Wehrmacht officer.

Correspondence from German Military Headquarters, Paris,
stating the Hôtel Ritz was reserved for senior German
officials. Among the foreigners allowed to reside
there is "Chanel Melle."

automobiles in storage, as rationing made it impossible to get
fuel, whether to heat homes or drive cars.

FOR DINCKLAGE, a German cavalry officer at age seventeen,
a veteran of the bloody campaigns on the World War I Russian
front, and a German military intelligence officer for over twenty
years, World War II was the realization of the German dream for
lebensraum—"the space Germany was entitled to by the laws of
history . . . [which] space would have to be taken from others."

On a crisp fall morning in 1940 bystanders on the avenue Kléber
might have noticed how a German Mercedes military staff car
abruptly pulled to the curb. A German officer exited and hailed
an old friend he had seen walking along the chic avenue. The

Name	Nationality	Room
CARTER Mr	(U.S.A.)	206
CHANEL Melle.	(FRANZ.)	227.228
CHANAY Mr	(Franz.)	226
COSSERAT	(Franz.)	230
DUBONNET Mr Mme	(Franz.)	261.262
DUBONNET Melle U.Nurse	(Franz.)	263
DONALSON Mme	(U.S.A.)	269
ERSKIN OF MAR Mr.Mme	(Engl.)	301
PAFRI Mr.	(Belg.)	302
GOSSELIN Mr Mme	(Franz.)	207.208
GONZALES DE PENA Mme	(ENGL.)	223.224
GUILLAUME Mme	(Franz.)	281
IBRAHIM S.A Pce.Pcesse Mohamed Ali	(Egyp.)	283.248
JASELMANN Mme	(Franz.)	214
KIRVAN Mr	(Juslw.)	292
KUNG Melle	(Fre nz.)	222
LANZA Prince	(Ital.)	306
LANE Mr.	(U.S.A.)	221
LAMOTTE Comtesse de	(Franz.)	207.208
MOISE Mr	(Belg.)	304.305
MALEVAL Mr	(Franz.)	205
MAEGHT Mr	(Franz.)	303
NELIS Mr	(Belg.)	202
PENA Mme GONZALES	(Engl.)	223.224
RIVAUD CTE Csse de	(Franz.)	234
ROLIN Baronne et Fille	(Belg.)	212
RITZ Mme	(Franz.)	266.268

A list of the few civilian occupants the Nazis allowed to room at the Hôtel Ritz. Chanel's name, room 227–228 is on line two: CHANEL Melle, (FRANZ.) 227.228.

uniformed German was forty-four-year-old Baron Hans Günther von Dincklage. He rushed to greet Madame Tatiana du Plessix, who with her husband had known Dincklage from his days on the Côte d'Azur and at the German Embassy in Warsaw. In that split second, Madame du Plessix discovered that the friendly Spatz was not the broken-down journalist he had pretended to be after he left Poland, but a seasoned German intelligence officer.

Spatz's presence startled Tatiana. "What are you doing here?" she asked.

"I am doing my work," he answered.

"And what is the nature of your work now?" Tatiana snapped.

"I'm in army intelligence."

"*Tu es un vrai salaud* [you are a real bastard]!" Tatiana burst out. "You posed as a down-and-out journalist; you won all our sympathy, you seduced my best friend, and now you tell me you were spying on us all the time!"

"*À la guerre comme à la guerre,*" Spatz answered, and proceeded to ask her to dinner.

"I was vaguely tempted to accept," Tatiana admitted later. She added, "He had posed as a victim of Hitler's racism, he had worn rags, he had ridden in a beat-up third-hand car . . . He had seduced Hélène Dessoffy into an affair because she had a house near France's biggest naval base, Toulon, and we had all fallen for the bastard's line."

Dincklage was back in France. The French Sûreté and Deux- ième Bureau knew of his movements in and out of Switzerland. They knew he had returned to Paris with the German occupa- tion authorities. For the next four years French counterintelligence agents in France and de Gaulle's Free French in London would be watching and reporting on their old adversary.

AT AGE FIFTY-SEVEN, Chanel was ready to fall in love again, and in 1940, a great romance unfolded as Dincklage, now a senior officer of the German occupation forces, stepped into her life to play the willing cavalier. It would be Chanel's last great love affair. There remains only one living eyewitness with intimate knowledge of the Chanel-Dincklage romance in the war years. Gabrielle Palasse Labrunie met Dincklage in occupied Paris in late 1941, when she was fifteen years old and visiting her Auntie Coco. She recalls, "Spatz was *sympa,* attractive, intelligent, well dressed, and congenial—smiled a lot and spoke fluent French and English . . . a handsome, well-bred man who became a friend." She saw how he captivated Chanel: "He was the pair of shoulders she needed to lean on and a man willing to help Chanel get André home."

For the next few years, Dincklage would manage Chanel's rela- tions with Nazi officialdom in Paris and Berlin, and he would be involved in arranging for the German High Command in Paris to grant Chanel permission to live in rooms on the seventh floor of the Cambon wing of the Hôtel Ritz. It was a convenient loca- tion, as the back entrance and exit of the hotel gave onto the rue

Cambon—a few yards from her boutique and the luxurious apartment she set up at 31, rue Cambon. The bizarre story of how, upon returning to Paris, a German general saw a distressed Chanel in the Ritz lobby and spontaneously ordered that she should be lodged at the hotel could only be another charming Chanel myth. Only Dincklage or some other senior German official could have made the complicated arrangements for her to have rooms in the Ritz's *Privatgast* section, reserved for friends of the Reich. One only needs to read the German diktat: "On orders from Berlin the Ritz was reserved exclusively for the temporary accommodation of high-ranking personalities. The Ritz Hotel occupies a supreme and exceptional place among the hotels requisitioned." In fact, only certain non-Germans (*Ausländer*) were privileged to stay at the Ritz during the occupation. Chanel's rooms (227–228) were near German collaborator Fern Bedaux (243, 244, 245); the pro-Nazi Dubonnet family (263) and Mme Marie-Louise Ritz (266, 268), wife of the hotel's founder, César Ritz, lodged on the same floor.

Everyone entering or leaving the Ritz had to be identified to sentries posted day and night at sandbagged entrances. Hitler's heir apparent and commander in chief of the Luftwaffe and head of all occupied territories, Hermann Göring, was installed in the Royal Suite. Other luxurious rooms were reserved for Nazi Foreign Minister Joachim von Ribbentrop; Albert Speer, Reich Minister of Armaments and War Production; Reich Minister of the Interior Dr. Wilhelm Frick; and a host of senior German generals.

For those allowed entry into the Ritz, the German High Command had "strict" orders about the dress of their compatriots: "No weapons of any sort were allowed inside the establishment" (an area near the entrance was set aside for depositing arms), and "manners had to be perfectly correct and no subaltern officer was allowed." Non-Germans had to be invited before entering the hotel.

What was it like in 1940 at the Ritz? A printed decorative menu for June 14, the day German officials occupied the hotel, survives. In this desperate moment for the French as hundreds of thousands of French families fled the German onslaught, the Ritz's first wartime Nazi guests were offered a sumptuous menu. Lunch included grapefruit—in wartime, a rare treat—and a main course of either *filet de sole au vin du Rhin* (sole cooked in a dry German wine, and an obvious flattering choice from the vanquished to the conqueror) or *poularde rôtie*, accompanied by potatoes *rissolées*, fresh peas, and asparagus with a hollandaise sauce. For dessert, there was an assortment of fresh fruit.

Later, when French families were near starvation, senior German officials and their guests would go on dining at the Ritz restaurant. One German officer in the early days of the occupation wrote: "In times like these, to eat well and eat a lot gives a feeling of power."

Cocteau, Serge Lifar (the Ukrainian-born ballet artist), and René de Chambrun were permitted by the Nazis to dine at the Ritz. They enjoyed a regular lunch and dinner there, often as Chanel's guest at "her" table—rubbing shoulders with the Nazi elite including frequent visitors from Berlin: Joseph Goebbels, Dincklage's former chief, and Hermann Göring, Lifar's patron and admirer. Lifar, the former lover of Sergei Diaghilev, founder of the Ballets Russes, lived part-time at the Ritz. Hitler had met Lifar on the führer's only trip to Paris, immediately after France's defeat. Göring then appointed Lifar head of the Paris Opéra corps de ballet. Chanel believed "the Germans are more cultivated than the French—they didn't give a damn what [men such as] Cocteau did because they knew that his work was a sham."

Another guest was Dincklage's protégé, Baron Louis de Vaufreland Piscatory.

The winter of 1940–1941 was bitterly cold—but not so at the Ritz. Chanel "was seen everywhere with . . . Spatz Dincklage." Writer Marcel Haedrich claims that Chanel told him, "I never saw the Germans, and it displeased them that a woman still not bad looking completely ignored them." Haedrich repeats yet another myth: "Chanel took the Metro. It didn't smell bad, the Germans feared epidemics and saw to it that Crésyl [a strong antiseptic] was spread everywhere." (Hardly possible; as the mistress of a German senior officer, Chanel would have had an automobile at her disposal.)

For the privileged few, Chanel and her entourage, wartime Paris was really no different than in peacetime. High society went on much as before: nightclubs and cabarets thrived. Dincklage dined often at Maxim's, where German officers and officials

Dining room of the Hôtel Ritz, 1939. During the "Phoney
War" the Paris elite dined in luxury from gourmet menus
prepared by the hotel's chefs.

nightly enjoyed the best of French haute cuisine. Chanel and
Dincklage were guests at Serge Lifar's opera and at his Nazi-
sponsored black-tie-and-tails evenings there. Lifar, Cocteau, and
Chanel were frequent guests at candlelight dinners (because of
the power shortages) at the Serts' apartment at 252, rue de Rivoli.
Jojo (Sert) amused his guests with tales of British and American
spies in Madrid. Sert was a frequent visitor to Madrid. In 1940 he
had arranged to acquire from the Franco government a diplomatic
post as the Spanish ambassador to the Vatican, but based in Paris.
The Serts and their friends relished the array of food shipped to
them via the diplomatic pouch from neutral Spain.

Chanel preferred hosting intimate dinners at her apartment
on the rue Cambon, where her treasured objects and her precious Coromandel screens were displayed. Meals were prepared
by her cook and served by her faithful maid Germaine, who had
returned to Paris. On those evenings with beau Dincklage, Cha-

A common sight during the Nazi occupation—starving Parisians searching
in the garbage for food and scraps, September 1942.

nel would sing and play the piano for her friends. Then, as the
guests amused themselves, she and Dincklage would cross the rue
Cambon to the back entrance of the Ritz to her third-floor apartment with its whitewashed Aubazine-like starkness.

Nazi collaborator Fern Bedaux, Chanel's neighbor at the Ritz,
reported to Count Joseph Ledebur-Wicheln, her Abwehr contact, how Dincklage (who Bedaux may not have known was an
Abwehr agent, too) visited Chanel every day. Bedaux also told
Ledebur that Chanel was a drug abuser.

Chanel's close friend, Paul Morand, who would dub her "the
exterminating angel of the nineteenth-century style," was an

important Vichy official during the occupation. He and his "pro-German" wife, Hélène, hosted Parisian soirees where Chanel dined with her small circle of friends: the omnipresent Cocteau, writer Marcel Jouhandeau, and his once-beautiful, eccentric, and erotic ballet dancer wife, Caryathis. Chanel's old friend and dance instructor prior to World War I, Caryathis was now an aged but intimate friend of André Gide.

But for a truly amusing evening, Chanel would dine with Dincklage's onetime intimate friend, Francophile Reich ambassador in Paris, Otto Abetz, and his beautiful French wife, Suzanne. Their sumptuous dinners at the ambassador's residence, the Hôtel de Beauharnais, 78, rue de Lille in Paris (behind what was then the Gare d'Orsay) were the envy of the crème de la crème of Paris and Nazi-occupation society. Abetz's salons were furnished with handsome paintings stolen from the Rothschild family apartments.

After Abetz, former lawyer and journalist Ferdinand de Brinon, now the Vichy ambassador to the German government in Paris, was the preferred host of the Paris elite, and Chanel dined often at Brinon's Parisian townhouse. Prize-winning author Ian Ousby, historian of the German World War II occupation, was brutal about Chanel's comportment at mealtime: "Coco Chanel . . . indulged in anti-Semitic diatribes" at the Abetz and Brinon dinners. An invitation to such an event was a passport to social intimacy with top Nazis. Pierre Laval's daughter, Josée, a longtime friend of Chanel's, and her husband, René de Chambrun, were regular guests of Abetz at the German Embassy evenings. René, nicknamed "Bunny," was noted for his cutting remark when his father-in-law, Laval, and Marshal Pétain came to power at Vichy, repeating Laval's words: "That's the way you overthrow a republic."

Josée raved when describing an Abetz evening: "Champagne flowed, and the German officers, dressed in white tie and splendid uniforms, spoke only French. Social life had returned with friends and our new guests, the Germans."

Josée was ebullient about a Christmas gala held in 1940 — the first year of the German occupation and a tense moment for Parisians. The Germans had just executed twenty-eight-year-old

Jacques Bonsergent at Mont Valérien outside the walls of Paris—
the first Parisian civilian to face a German firing squad. But for
Josée,

> in a blacked-out Paris there was gaiety. Abetz in a uniform half-
> civil and half-military [Abetz held the rank of an SS lieutenant-
> colonel] and his wife Suzanne turned about a magnificent buffet
> dinner while the overweight German Consul in Paris, General
> Rudolf Schleier, bowed low to the ladies, kissing their hands as
> did Luftwaffe General Hanesse, dressed in a white uniform—his
> chest covered with decorations. [Presumably, General Hanesse's
> decorations were awarded for killing the French.] The Cham-
> pagne flowed; the German officers, particularly the pilots, in eve-
> ning dress did honor to the ladies, moving like butterflies, and no
> one spoke German. It was a real French gala evening when speak-
> ing German was prohibited. The officers competed to be most
> erudite in the language of Rabelais [French sixteenth-century
> satirist] . . . No one thought about the war. We all thought that
> peace, a definitive peace, a German peace would win over the
> world with the approval of Stalin and Roosevelt . . . only England
> continued to face the Germans.

IN CONTRAST, the daily life of an average Parisian was one of
hardship during the coldest winter on record—and each succeed-
ing winter seemed colder. There would be no Champagne soirees
for them. Coal for fuel was rare, gas supplies paltry, and electricity
frequently cut off. Petrol for automobiles was sometimes available
on the black market, but most automobile engines were converted
to run on natural gas—two bottles on top of the cars. Some transformed their motorcars to burn charcoal. As the months of occupation passed, things got tighter and tighter.

Within weeks of the German arrival in Paris, everything
was snatched from the marketplace to be resold later for two to
three times its original price. Within months, the Germans had
imposed a regime of virtual starvation on the population. Field
Marshal Göring decreed that the French people would have to
subsist on 1,200 calories a day—half the number of calories the
average working man or woman needed to survive. The elderly
were rationed to 850 calories a day. The measures were staggering.

Every commodity was rationed. It was the old folks who suffered the most and risked serious illness or death from hypothermia or undernourishment when they couldn't keep their apartments warm in the long, cold, wet months of the war years. The American Hospital at Neuilly, still run by an American physician, and Otto Gresser, a Swiss manager, were able to supplement their patients' diets by arranging for a wealthy French landowner to sell the hospital potatoes for a reasonable price. The foodstuffs were then transported to the hospital kitchen by ambulance. Gresser tells about bartering wine for more potatoes: "We had 250 patients . . . The French authorities allowed each patient one-half a liter [a pint] of wine per day and soon we had more wine than the patients could drink. The farmers, however, couldn't get enough wine. We took 500 liters [almost a hundred gallons] of wine and bartered the wine for 5,000 kilos of fertilizer. One farmer gave us 10,000 kilos [about 22,000 pounds] of potatoes for the fertilizer . . . We gave 50 kilos of potatoes to each staff member and it was very important for them to feed their families."

By late 1941, meat—desperately needed to fend off malnutrition—was almost impossible to find except at outrageous prices. Gresser remembers that when 300 kilos of beef, bought on the black market, was delivered to the hospital in a big "borrowed" German car, suspicious German authorities asked to inspect the hospital kitchen. The staff then hid the meat in the hospital's garden.

Even the French staple, wine, was in short supply. In their book *Wine and War,* Don and Petie Kladstrup tell how wine production fell by half between 1939 and 1942. The Germans loved and knew about wines—particularly the wines of France. Their Weinführers managed to take away not only the best of the annual French production but also massive amounts of ordinary table wine for their armed forces. The Germans shipped more than 320 million bottles of wine to Germany each year at fixed prices.

Göring ordered the Weinführers to systematically ship even mediocre wine to Germany. The result was catastrophic. "The old and the ill needed wine," French doctors advised German and French authorities. "It is an excellent food . . . it is easily digested . . . and a vital source of vitamins and minerals."

EIGHT

DINCKLAGE MEETS HITLER; CHANEL BECOMES AN ABWEHR AGENT

À la guerre comme à la guerre.

—FRENCH PROVERB

IN EARLY 1941, Dincklage left Chanel in Paris. He traveled to Berlin with Baron Louis de Vaufreland. The two men had met in prewar Paris when Dincklage was "the lover of Madame Esnault Pelterie," the wife of a prewar French aviation pioneer.

In Berlin, Dincklage was singularly honored. He was received personally by Adolf Hitler and Joseph Goebbels, Hitler's propaganda minister and Dincklage's chief when Spatz was at the German Embassy in Paris in 1934. The text of a French counterintelligence report of Dincklage's meeting with the führer tells about his role as a senior French clandestine agent: "Von D [Dincklage] lived before the war in Paris at rue des Sablons. He said he was Swedish but in reality is German . . . in Berlin he had an audience with Hitler and Goebbels. He is also very close to [German army commander] von Brauchitsch."

Dincklage must have found Berlin in a triumphant mood that winter of 1941. German armies had by now run over Western Europe, and Hitler's Wehrmacht was on its way to conquering Yugoslavia and Greece. Secretly, Hitler was preparing to attack the Soviet Union in the coming spring.

French document
(certified reproduction)
revealing French
Abwehr agent
Vaufreland was "an
intimate friend of
Chanel."

le 8.10.41.   N°1526/112

R E N S E I G N E M E N T

Destinataire:6000

Source:0.2084b du 3.10.41

Baron Louis de VAUFRELAND,domicilié 74 faubourg St
Honorée à Paris,ancienne adresse:4 rue Rigeard,pretend
avoir refusé des propositions de la Gestapo.
Peu scupuleux,ami intime de Mme CHANEL,il est connu à
l'"Union Artistique"
Serait actuellement à Vichy et partira bientôt pour
l'Allemagne sous le couvert d'affaires industrielles.

NOTA: D'après 112bis,de VAUFRELAND aurait toujours un
appartement qui lui serait reservé au "RITZ".

We know nothing of what Vaufreland did in Berlin during
the trip with Dincklage. However, a document in the archives
of the Bureau Central de Renseignements et d'Action (BCRA),
de Gaulle's counterintelligence service in London, tells how after
Berlin, "Louis de Vaufreland was sent to Tunisia, posing as an
Alsatian and using the alias, de Richmond." Though Vaufre-

Dincklage's protégé, Baron Louis
de Vaufreland, was a trusted German
agent who went to Madrid with Chanel
in 1941 and later introduced Chanel
to senior Nazi officials in Paris.

land's trip is clouded in secrecy, it could hardly have been coincidental that Tunisia had been Dincklage's old Abwehr hunting grounds when he worked among Muslims. The report went on: "D [Dincklage] is [now] on very bad terms with Abetz . . . he claims Abetz stole 200 million French francs [about $90 million in 2010]. This colossal sum was shared with Pierre Laval; for it was Laval who arranged that the Yugoslavian French-owned Bor mines be turned over to Nazi Germany."

Being received by Hitler was, indeed, an honor for an Abwehr officer, and Dincklage returned to Paris under orders to work directly for Berlin. Dincklage had become an influential and senior officer of the Abwehr. Meanwhile, Vaufreland had earned the title of a *V-Mann,* meaning that he was now a trusted Abwehr agent, code name "Piscatory," Agent No. F-7667. (*V-Mann* is also an appellation for trusted Gestapo agents.)

Dincklage now arranged to have Vaufreland meet Chanel. Their first meeting took place so casually that Chanel might not

Police intelligence report showing Chanel's
Abwehr agent number and code name.

have immediately realized that the coming adventure had been
set up by Dincklage.

EVER INVENTIVE and opportunistic, Chanel thought she
knew how to navigate through Nazi-occupied Paris and how to
arrange the release of her nephew André Palasse from a German
prisoner-of-war camp so he could safely be returned to her side. It
was an urgent matter. She had learned from Corbère that André
might have contracted tuberculosis. The Abwehr was well aware
of Chanel's anxiety over André's fate. They would help Chanel—
for a price. Chanel was the perfect target for recruitment by the
Germans: she needed something the Abwehr could supply, and
she had powerful connections in London, neutral Spain, and Paris.

Chanel and Dincklage paid a brief visit to La Pausa at Roque-
brune, free to travel between zones of occupation thanks to
Dincklage's authority. When they returned to Paris, a Chanel-
Vaufreland meeting was arranged at the Ritz.

Soon, Vaufreland had convinced Chanel that through his German friends, he could arrange André's freedom from the German
stalag and his return to Paris. Vaufreland also intimated that his
German friends could help her wrest control of the Chanel perfume business from the hands of the Wertheimers or their proxies.

Vaufreland and Chanel made an unlikely pair of agents. The
baron, who dressed like an effete dandy, was openly homosexual.
A London Free French report described Vaufreland at the time as
"a 39-year-old, blondish-red head, aristocrat-playboy (alias, Pes-
catori [sic]), Marquis d'Awyigo, de Richmond)." Another French
intelligence report called him a "pudgy homosexual of medium
height always impeccably dressed" and "an Abwehr agent being
run by Abwehr lieutenant Hermann Neubauer—[Vaufreland was]
in need of large sums of money, intelligent and well spoken and
fluent in English, German, Italian and Spanish . . . an extremely
dangerous German spy." The report goes on: "In 1940 Vaufreland
worked as a Gestapo agent in Morocco before joining the Paris
Abwehr." Later, another Free French report stated that by the time
Vaufreland met Chanel, he had been responsible for the arrest of a
team of French Gaullist resistance fighters in Casablanca.

Vaufreland's Abwehr boss, Neubauer, soon stepped into the

One of Chanel's Abwehr contacts was Sonderführer Albert Notterman, seen here after the war when he worked for the U.S. Army, 1947.

picture to close the deal with Chanel. Neubauer must have known Dincklage. His office, like Dincklage's, was located at the Abwehr-sequestered Hôtel Lutetia at 45, boulevard Raspail off of Saint-Germain-des-Prés. Like Dincklage, he dressed in civilian clothes and spoke excellent French.

Sometime in the spring of 1941, Neubauer met Chanel with Vaufreland at her boutique-office on the rue Cambon. There, Neubauer assured her he would help free André if Chanel would consent to helping Germany obtain "political" information at Madrid.

Chanel was delighted with the idea of a trip to Spain. According to Vaufreland's later testimony to a French judge, Chanel had "adroitly suggested she needed a visa to travel to Spain and make a trip to England, so she could give her important friends economic and political information."

With this, Vaufreland said, "Neubauer was won over."

SOMETIME IN 1941, the Abwehr enrolled Gabrielle Chanel in their Berlin registry as Agent F-7124, code name Westminster. One has to wonder: Who might have thought to use Bendor's ducal title for a code name? Was it Dincklage, acting behind the scenes, who slipped this reference to Chanel's former lover into her record? (After the war, Chanel denied she knew anything about these matters.)

Agent Neubauer now took matters in hand. Chanel and Vaufreland left Paris on a hot and muggy evening, August 5, 1941.

They traveled to Spain by train via the French border crossing at Hendaye. The night before, the Abwehr office in Paris cabled the German police at Hendaye: "Leaving Paris at 20:10 hours, August 5, 1941, arriving Hendaye, August 6 about 9:11 hours, [are]—the Baron Giscatory [*sic*] de Vaufreland, holding French passport No. 3284 delivered at Casablanca, and Gabrielle Chanel, holding French passport No. 18348, delivered in Paris. Treat these two passengers with consideration, accord them all facility and spare them any problems." The telegram is signed, "Abwehr Bureau Paris, No. 695 L/7.41 g IIIF." (Roman numeral three "F" refers to the Abwehr foreign counterintelligence service.)

The Spanish-speaking Vaufreland was well suited to his mission, with close family ties in Madrid through his aristocratic Spanish aunt. French and British files described the initiative as part of an ongoing German military intelligence effort to recruit new agents willing to serve Germany. The trip also suited Chanel's own interests. She expected to bring her nephew, André, home. And while in Madrid, she could improve the sales of Chanel No. 5 in the Spanish market.

In Madrid, Chanel moved into a Ritz suite, living in prewar luxury while Vaufreland stayed in the city with friends. Franco's World War II archives have all been destroyed, and it is impossible to reconstruct Chanel's activities in the Spanish capital during August and September 1941. We do have from British archives a report of an evening Chanel and Vaufreland spent with the British diplomat Brian Wallace and his wife. Wallace, whose code name was "Ramon," reported to London in detail a conversation he and his wife had with the couple at a Madrid dinner party. (Details of who hosted the party have not been uncovered. The British Embassy dispatch sent to London with the report of the conversation has not been found.) Wallace's attachment to the British Embassy dispatch, No. 347 of August 22, 1941, is reproduced below with the deletion of insignificant remarks:

MI, COPY. ENCLOSURE TO MADRID DISPATCH NO. 347 OF
22 AUGUST 1941

Memorandum by Mr. Brian Wallace
(Report on conversation with Mlle Chanel and Baron Luis [*sic*] Vaufreland.)

On Wednesday, August 13th, my wife and I attended a dinner
party amongst whom were Mlle Chanel and Baron Vaufreland
[*sic*] (a Frenchman). The following is the joint result of our conversations.

VAUFRELAND: We have both known him some years (though
not well) in Paris. He was a young man about town with strong
Rightist sympathies and alleged to have homosexual tenden-
cies. He was a liaison officer with the Grenadier Guards and the
Inniskilling Dragoons, and was evacuated from Dunkirk on June
2nd. He is half Spanish, and a nephew of the Duchess of Alma-
zan. He has come to Spain as a handyman for Mlle Chanel (with
whom he scraped an acquaintance recently in Paris). Personally
he is an unreliable person . . .

Both Vaufreland and Chanel warned us about the French Embassy
here, especially the Ambassador and his wife, whom they claimed
was "anti-British."

MLLE CHANEL: She talked for nearly three hours very frankly
about Paris, and impressed me deeply with her sincerity. She is a
friend of the P.M.'s and is obviously greatly attached to the Duke
of Westminster. She would like to go to England but cannot
bring herself to abandon France. Her stated reason for coming
here (or rather going to Portugal) is that she couldn't stand Paris
any longer and has to have a holiday. The main subject she talked
on was Parisians. Her chief points were as follows:

1. The Germans cannot understand the French and this
is making them hate the French to the point that she,
Mlle Chanel, is afraid of what will happen.

2. The French all the time "rigole" [laugh] and "fait des
blagues [tell jokes]." They are pinpricks, but they have
worked the Germans to a state of fury. So much has
been done in the Metro, twisting tickets into "V's," and
later in "H's" (for Hitler), scribbling on walls etc. that
the Germans have threatened to close the Metro.

3. The French affect extreme gaiety. "Why," the Germans ask, "when you have lost the war are you so gay?"
"Why," the Parisians retort, "when you have won the
war are you so sad?"

4. In the occupied zone the people are not pro-British; only anti-German.

5. France is slowly being transformed into two countries. Those in the un-occupied zone seem to think that those in the occupied zone are there at their own wish.

6. Very few Frenchmen realize that they have lost the war. "You wait until we have got rid of these swine," they say, and, "If you point out that France has been defeated they accuse you of being anti-French and talk vaguely of rising and English help."

7. The Germans are bitterly anti-French but generally rather pro-English (in that they have a great admiration for all that is British).

8. The Germans hate and fear Churchill and divide England into Churchill and the rest. The latter they are convinced want peace; the former to exterminate Germany.

9. There is great lack of coordination among the Germans particularly between the civil and the military authorities, who hate one another and delight in undoing the other's arrangements. They are all frightened, they are all wretched, and the watchers are themselves watched.

10. There is a separate [German] commercial organization and this is extremely active—Chanel gives a particularly grave warning about this: "They are buying themselves into every business, covering it up in many ways so that when peace comes it is going to be extremely difficult to weed all the German interests out."

11. Summing up, Chanel said that France even now doesn't know what hit her. She is still in a daze, but has already come to sufficiently move her eyes and see what is going on around her. Soon she will recover the use of her limbs and then the trouble will start. They have tried passing the whole thing over, but it is still there. There is perplexity and mounting impotent rage among the Germans and a growing realization of their true position among the French.

Sgd: BRIAN WALLACE, 21st August 1941

Note: They were both leaving for Lisbon for about two weeks on Wednesday the 20th.

CHANEL AND VAUFRELAND never went to Portugal. They returned to Paris sometime in the late fall or early winter of 1941. There, Chanel discovered that André Palasse had been returned to France—safely, but ailing. And by then the French intelligence services in London had noted in their files that Vaufreland was "an intimate friend of Chanel's."

With André free, Chanel now concentrated on her perfume business. She would use her status as an Aryan French citizen to get back what she believed "was stolen" from her by the Wertheimers.

For the next twelve months Vaufreland would assist Chanel in her efforts to convince the Nazis that Chanel's No. 5 perfume business, sold to the Jewish Wertheimer family in 1924, rightfully belonged in Chanel's hands. Vaufreland arranged for Chanel to meet the senior Nazi official who administered the laws concerning the "Aryanization" of Jewish property. Chanel's principal biographer in France, Edmonde Charles-Roux, described Chanel's efforts to recover her perfume franchise: "Now it was [Chanel's] turn to play the exploited . . . and the Wertheimer clan would see what she was made of. She was Aryan and they weren't. She was in France and they were in the United States. Emigrants . . . Jews. In the eyes of the occupying power, in short, she alone existed."

NINE

CHECKMATED BY THE
WERTHEIMERS

War or peace she lived . . . entrenched in her fortress.

—MARCEL HAEDRICH, *COCO CHANEL:*
HER LIFE, HER SECRETS

As 1941 CAME TO A CLOSE, momentous news swept Europe.

Japanese forces had attacked Pearl Harbor and within days Germany declared war on the United States. Winston Churchill was soon on his way to Washington to meet President Franklin Roosevelt. The two men mapped out an initial strategy to defeat Germany and Japan during this first American Christmas at war.

In France, General de Gaulle's Resistance networks began recruiting clandestine groups of domestic freedom fighters to sabotage German works and kill Nazis. The Germans called them "terrorists." They would be remorselessly pursued and, when rounded up, their members were sometimes turned to work for the Nazis, tortured, or executed, and in some cases deported to extermination camps.

WHEN CHANEL AND VAUFRELAND returned from Madrid in the early fall of 1941 Paris residents had lived through fourteen months of occupation. The German curfew enveloped Paris in evenings of silence. In a 1941 essay, Jean-Paul Sartre contrasted earlier "years with the chattering of Republican politics" to the present "Republic of Silence." In the face of German occupation, much of the French public willingly abdicated their republican rights and accepted the allegedly benevolent dictatorship of Marshal Philippe Pétain. And most Frenchmen believed the old marshal had saved the nation from a greater catastrophe.

Meanwhile, in Nazi Germany one of Hitler's favorite SS leaders, Reinhard Heydrich, became the führer's architect for the Nazi Final Solution. Heydrich's assistant, Adolf Eichmann, set to work in the summer of 1941 to design methods for the physical extermination of Jews. In January 1942, at a conference at the Wannsee lake resort located outside Berlin, Heydrich and Eichmann laid down the modalities for implementing the Final Solution.

At Vichy, in unoccupied France, Jews had already been banned from holding any position that might influence public opinion. Soon, they would be excluded from commerce and industry, their businesses and property confiscated. In Paris and throughout occupied France, non-French Jews—immigrants—were arrested and sent to deportation camps. Then all Jews in France would soon suffer the same fate: arrest and deportation to, and extermination in, SS-run concentration camps.

The war was moving toward a dramatic conclusion in Europe. With the Axis powers now controlling Greece, Yugoslavia, and parts of North Africa, German Panzers launched a surprise attack across Russian borders on June 22, 1941. Later they would fail to defeat Stalin's Red Army at Leningrad, Moscow, and Stalingrad.

In France, de Gaulle's emerging Free French and Communist resistance fighters began attacking German soldiers and sailors at Bordeaux and Nantes. There German troopers were shot on the streets; while in Paris, a German naval officer was shot while waiting for a subway train.

Retaliation was swift. Across the country, French hostages were shot by Wehrmacht firing squads.

Nazi terror now mandated that all Jews older than six years of age wear a yellow Star of David with *Juive* or *Juif* stitched in black across it. The symbol was to be displayed over the heart on all clothing. Some eighty thousand Jews in Paris alone are known to have obeyed the law. The penalties for disobedience were harsh. (Homosexuals, Roma, political prisoners, and others were forced to wear different-colored triangles.) Then, from the summer of

1942 Parisians watched as Jews and Jewish refugees were arrested, destined for deportation. Hitler had ordered the complete destruction of the Jewish race.

IN THE MIDDLE of this mayhem, Nazi Holocaust master Adolf Eichmann hesitated over the question of deporting French children younger than sixteen years of age. Vichy chief Pierre Laval stepped up. He sanctioned a telegram to Eichmann, who was then managing the Holocaust from Berlin. The telegram read: "Laval has proposed that children below the age of sixteen be included in the deportation of Jewish families from the free zone. The fate of Jewish children in the occupied zone does not interest him." For many French, the European refugee Jews in France, indeed all Jews, had "ruined the good order of things." Many citizens extolled the anti-Semitic laws being enforced by French administrators, French police, and the Nazis. One educated French woman, when seeing pictures of Jews being deported, remarked to the author, "But they are not French, they are Jews."

Chanel must have known about the round-up of Paris Jews. John Updike noted in the September 1998 issue of *The New Yorker* that "all the available evidence points to Chanel's total indifference to the fate of her Jewish neighbors—or indeed the lesser deprivations and humiliations suffered by the vast majority of Parisians." Updike reported that, at age fifty-eight, Chanel was seemingly "happy" living with her German lover. "Happy, in a world in which mountains of misfortune were rising around them . . . in the Jewish quarter, a fifteen-minute walk from the Ritz."

Chanel had no doubt that the Nazis meant business when it came to applying anti-Semitic laws against Jews and Aryanizing Jewish businesses and property. She had told Misia Sert around Christmas 1941 that with the Nazis in power she hoped to gain control of the firm now in the hands of the Wertheimer family, which had fled to the United States. Chanel and Dincklage must have calculated that if Hitler prevailed—and most of the world believed he would—Chanel would control an Aryanized Chanel No. 5 perfume company. The rewards to her would be immeasurable. As did many Germans and Englishmen, including Bendor, Duke of Westminster, Chanel and Dincklage must have hoped for a negotiated Anglo-German deal to end hostilities. They had profited from prewar trade with Germany, and they wanted commerce with Germany restored. They saw a deal with Hitler as an opportunity to reunite the German and English aristocracies. Few could forget how Hitler had promised to restore Chanel's intimate friend, Edward, former king of the British Empire, now Duke of Windsor, to the British throne as king with his wife beside him. Indeed, if trade could be restored, Germany and Britain would become an international economic steamroller and Chanel's stake in her No. 5 fragrance would become priceless.

Chanel was reassured; the Abwehr had fulfilled its promise to free her nephew, André, who was now with his daughter Gabrielle in Paris being treated at Chanel's expense for tuberculosis. Later, he would be cared for in Switzerland.

As promised, Vaufreland now contacted his friend, a German official named Prince Ernst Ratibor-Corvey (also a friend of Dincklage). Ratibor-Corvey advised Vaufreland to arrange an appointment for Chanel with Dr. Kurt Blanke, who operated out of the Gestapo offices at the Hôtel Majestic where Blanke and his coworkers administered Nazi laws providing for the confiscation of Jewish property. Chanel sought Blanke's help to Aryanize La Société des Parfums Chanel in her favor.

With the occupation of France, the forty-year-old Blanke, a German lawyer and Nazi, had been appointed by Berlin to head the Paris office responsible for *Entjudung,* "the elimination of Jewish influence." Until 1944 he played a key role in seizing Jewish assets—transferring Jewish-owned businesses and property into Aryan hands.

Chanel and Blanke met at the Hôtel Majestic sometime in the early winter of 1941–1942. After speaking with him, Chanel believed she was one step closer to defeating the Wertheimers and getting full control of the Societé des Parfums Chanel. But she had woefully underestimated the foresight and shrewdness of the Wertheimer brothers. They had long ago devised a plan to save their business if the Nazis came to power in France.

As early as 1936, with Hitler in power in Germany, the Wertheimer brothers believed that Germany intended to swallow Europe. The Jews of Europe were doomed. The Nazi invasion of the Rhineland that year confirmed their fears: war was inevitable. Kristallnacht, November 9–10, 1938—a night of attacks on Jews and Jewish property in Germany and Austria—convinced them that Hitler was determined to wipe out the Jewish race.

At the end of World War I, when aviation was still in its infancy, the Wertheimers had entered into business with Félix Amiot, an aviation pioneer, becoming a minority shareholder in the Amiot aviation company. By 1934 Amiot was supplying bombers to the French air force, and the 370, the 350, and the 340 bomber aircraft were catching the eyes of German Luftwaffe engineers. In an effort to open the American market, Pierre Wertheimer traveled to New Orleans in 1939 to negotiate setting up an Amiot plant to assemble planes in the United States, but France's declaration of war and the United States' declared neutrality ended the project. Pierre returned to France to join his older brother Paul in organizing the emigration of the Wertheimer clan from France to America.

In an August 1939 report the French Deuxième Bureau described how forty-three-year-old Félix Amiot, the president of SECM, a mechanical engineering firm that had manufactured bombers for the French air force since 1925, had received 50 million French francs (the 2010 equivalent of about $22 million) from the Wertheimers via a bank transfer from their account at the bank Manheimer Mendelsohn in France. There is no record of how these 50 million francs were invested. However, in the months to come, Amiot used his influence with Hitler's right-hand man and commander in chief of the Luftwaffe, Reich Marshal Hermann Göring, to shield the Wertheimers' businesses in France.

WITH GERMAN TROOPS streaming across France's borders, the Wertheimers took refuge in the Chevreuse valley about 20 miles southwest of Paris. Just before fleeing, with German armies threatening Paris, Pierre Wertheimer and Amiot met at Pierre's Paris apartment. Journalists Bruno Abescat and Yves Stavrides quote Amiot: "We said goodbye. Pierre asked me to help save what was possible and to look after his son Jacques who was in the military." Félix Amiot, the forty-three-year-old Norman from a wealthy Cherbourg family, and the Wertheimers now made a secret pact: Amiot would take control of the French company La Société des Parfums Chanel, and hold the business in trust for the

Wertheimers. (After the war the Wertheimers regained control of the French company but only after a legal battle with Amiot.)

Paul and Pierre then assembled their families and fled to Brazil through Spain. Many months later, after obtaining U.S. visas for his family, Pierre and his wife, Germaine, sailed to New York aboard the SS *Argentina*. They reached Manhattan in the first week of August 1940. Paul, his wife, Madeleine, and their children Antoine and Mathilde, followed, landing in New York a few weeks later.

The Wertheimers found a welcome refuge in the United States. Their money, unlimited resources, and their established reputation as reliable entrepreneurs guaranteed success in America. Paul and Pierre went about building a new life for their families: Paul in a handsome six-story brownstone at 35 West Seventy-fifth Street just off Central Park West, and Pierre at 784 Park Avenue. The brothers soon launched a new Bourjois perfume, Courage, designed to pull at the heartstrings of a sympathetic American public. After all, there were many Americans and a growing refugee population nostalgic for Paris and for France. They flocked to cinemas to see Humphrey Bogart and Ingrid Bergman in the hit film *Casablanca* and put the 1941 ballad "The Last Time I Saw Paris" on the hit parade.

Sales of Courage soared. Later, the Wertheimers' Hoboken, New Jersey, plant began production of the distinctive Chanel No. 5. The perfume was a success in North and South American markets. Later still, the Wertheimers exploited the lucrative U.S. domestic and overseas military post exchanges, known as PXs, to sell Chanel No. 5.

From 1940 the Wertheimers became one of the earliest supporters of General Charles de Gaulle's Free French and Jewish causes in New York. Their success infuriated Chanel.

SOMETIME IN MID-AUGUST 1940 a German frontier guard watched "a big-boned, jagged-faced, giant of a man" advancing in a line of travelers to get police clearance at the Hendaye border crossing between Spain and France. When the German control officer examined the man's passport, he learned that the bearer, Don Armando Guevaray Sotto Mayor, measured an impressive two meters in height (six feet, eight inches). After

For posterity, H. Gregory Thomas places a Bourjois perfume sample in a vault at the 1939 World's Fair in New York. With the German occupation of Paris, Thomas, acting as a secret agent for the Wertheimer perfume barons, slipped into Paris as "Don Armando Guevaray Sotto Mayor" to steal the Chanel No. 5 perfume formula so the Bourjois firm could manufacture Chanel No. 5 perfume in the United States. After the war Thomas became president and then chairman of the Wertheimer firm.

a tiresome series of questions and a minute search of the man's luggage, Don Sotto Mayor was waved through police and customs. He then boarded the Hendaye–Paris train for the 500-mile (800-kilometer) trip to the Gare d'Austerlitz on Paris's Left Bank.

Besides his height, the only thing out of the ordinary about Don Sotto Mayor was his identity. On that hot August day, the man en route to Paris was not actually Don Sotto Mayor but Herbert Gregory Thomas, a thirty-three-year-old American citizen and the son of Herbert Thomas of Brooklyn, New York, and Amanda Caskie of Boone County, Missouri. A vice president of the Wertheimer's Bourjois perfume company in New York, Thomas had assumed the Don Sotto Mayor persona to carry out a series of secret missions in Europe for the Wertheimer family.

Thomas had been educated in Switzerland. He graduated from Corpus Christi College, Cambridge, and held advanced law degrees from the Sorbonne in Paris and the University of Salamanca in Spain. He had practiced international law in Paris, Geneva, and The Hague before moving to New York to work for the Guerlain fragrance enterprise. In 1939, he joined the Wertheimer-owned perfume manufacturing company, Bourjois, Inc.

On that August day when he was leaving for Europe, Thomas

met with the press at the Pan Am Clipper departure lounge at New York's Municipal Airport (renamed LaGuardia in 1947). He told a *New York Times* reporter that he had resigned from Bourjois, Inc., and was now working for the Toilet Goods Association in New York. He said he was going to Europe to study conditions relative to the supply and shipment of raw materials and essential oils from France, Italy, and Switzerland. But that was far from the truth. Thomas had a number of objectives. First, posing as Don Sotto Mayor, he was to retrieve the chemical formula needed to produce Chanel No. 5 perfume. Second, he had to secure the key ingredients—"natural aromatics" such as jasmine—so that the signature perfume could be manufactured on site in Hoboken. Third, Thomas was to help Félix Amiot get twenty-nine-year-old Jacques Wertheimer, Pierre's son, who was hiding in Bordeaux, out of France and to New York. Jacques had been mobilized in 1939. After France's defeat, he escaped from a German prisoner-of-war camp with the help of Félix Amiot.

In 1942, when he joined the Office of Strategic Services (OSS), the forerunner to the CIA, Thomas admitted to his employers that two years earlier he had still been working for the Wertheimers when they asked him to undertake a four-month undercover operation in France. For the rest of his life, Thomas said little about it.

Thomas's few close friends testified to his secretive nature. One, an OSS colleague, Peter M. F. Sichel, told this author: "Thomas was not an easy man to make friends with; he had a mystique surrounding him and his past. Still, he was a man with a common touch—an imposing and erudite man but never a snob."

The exact details of Thomas's covert activities for the Wertheimers remain secret—particularly how he managed to acquire the formula of the Chanel perfume—but he did get it to the Wertheimers in New York. Thomas left behind no details when he passed away in 1990 at age eighty-two; but Peter Sichel has filled in some blanks. Sichel, when based at the OSS's World War II headquarters in Algiers and later in Europe, knew of Thomas's OSS work in Portugal and Spain. Other information was revealed by investigative reporters Bruno Abescat and Yves Stavridès, writing in the French magazine *L'Express* in 2005, and by Véronique Maurus, writing in *Le Monde*. Abescat and Stavridès reported that Claude Lévy, the Wertheimers' lawyer and the former mayor of Orléans, France, told them: "The feats accomplished by Pierre and Paul's [Wertheimer] agent, Gregory Thomas, and his ability to get large quantities of jasmine out of France and to the United States, are out of a James Bond movie."

Sichel believes Thomas paid for his secret operations using "either Louis d'Or coins or English sovereigns" to pay agents and purchase supplies. Explaining OSS tradecraft during World War II, Sichel wrote: "The OSS used gold coins to finance missions in Europe and to buy foreign currency for OSS agent operations. I once smuggled Louis d'Or coins out of a European country, hidden in a shoe in my luggage. Though heavy, a big strong man like Gregory could easily have carried 500 Louis d'Or in his luggage." Today a gold Louis, depending on the date of the coin, could be valued at between $800 and $3,000 each. Sichel added that at the time, "French francs had no great value, and Gregory had access to currency in Switzerland . . . [The OSS] had arrangements in France during the occupation to pay French agents using French francs advanced in France by others. The OSS reimbursed them by depositing money into their accounts in Switzerland."

In a 1989 interview in *Forbes* magazine, Thomas had revealed he "bribed French gangsters" to help get Jacques to America. From other sources we know that Jacques left Lisbon aboard the American Export Lines on the 7,000-ton *Excalibur,* a transatlantic steamer bound for New York, on November 21, 1940. The *Excalibur*'s manifest curiously lists Jacques, a French citizen, as a "Hebrew."

Eventually, Thomas completed his mission for the Wertheimer brothers and returned to New York. A few months after Pearl Harbor, with the United States now at war, he was recruited as a senior officer into William J. "Wild Bill" Donovan's OSS spy organization and sent to Spain and Portugal as chief of station. (Thomas was in Madrid when Chanel arrived there in 1944 on a mission for SS Reichsführer Heinrich Himmler, but there is no reference to Chanel in Thomas's OSS files.) After the war the Wertheimer brothers made Gregory Thomas the president of Chanel, Inc., the United States parent company for the Chanel firm. Thomas remained at Chanel, Inc., for the next twenty-five years.

A MISSION FOR HIMMLER

She wanted to live a hidden life.

—EDMONDE CHARLES-ROUX, *L'IRRÉGULIÈRE*

O N MONDAY MORNING, November 9, 1942, most of France woke to headlines. One read: "Dirty Anglo-American Attack Against Our North Africa."

Chanel was stunned. Paris was reeling.

It had been a bold and secret operation. The front-page editorial in *Le Matin* offered a familiar scapegoat: "The Jews with their low blows will fail as will the English and Americans. When France is betrayed it strikes back—every Frenchman, all Europe, stands with France."

Another newspaper assured the reader, "Adolf Hitler" declared "We will fight to the end." Within a few hours a Paris radio announced how British and American troops, led by General Dwight D. Eisenhower, had stormed the beaches of Algeria and Morocco at dawn that Monday. The world learned later that the risky invasion dubbed Operation Torch was "President Franklin D. Roosevelt's baby."

With the beaches of Algeria and Morocco secure, Winston Churchill broadcast to Europe over the BBC: "Now this is not the end. It is not even the beginning of the end. But it is perhaps the end of the beginning." Though the Nazis forbade the French from listening to the BBC, clandestine radios everywhere were secretly tuned to the regular evening broadcasts: "This is London calling." Night after night, dry-toned BBC commentators told of the Allies' successes in North Africa, and how Pétain's right-hand man Admiral François Darlan had gone over to the Americans. The BBC didn't miss a chance to warn how *collabos* would be punished when France was liberated.

BBC threats and Churchill's brave words made many collaborators' stomachs churn. Chanel had already been labeled a "horizontal collaborator" along with French actress Arletty. In 1942, *Life* magazine published a blacklist of French citizens accused of collaborating with the Germans. Among the entries was Chanel's lawyer, René de Chambrun. The Free French knew that hanging on the walls of Chambrun's home was a group of valuable paintings stolen by the Nazis from the Schloss family and Rosenberg collections. The *Life* magazine article warned, "Some [collaborators] will be assassinated . . . others will be tried when France is free." The publication, read by millions of Americans, claimed that the Vichy leaders Marshal Philippe Pétain and René de Chambrun's father-in law, Pierre Laval, would be tried as collaborators and punished.

The *Life* report must have come as a shock to Chambrun, a direct descendant of Lafayette, an honorary citizen of the state of Delaware, and a man respected by the elite of Washington. Now he was condemned by General Charles de Gaulle's secret underground army in France. Chanel and other collaborators had to wonder what lay ahead.

On the Monday of the invasion, Chanel's friend Josée Laval Chambrun noted in her diary: "The Americans have attacked Algeria and Morocco. André Dubonnet woke us [Josée and husband René] with the news and wanted to know if it was true." Josée went to lunch at Fouquet's ultrachic restaurant on the Champs-Élysées that day and noted later: "Darlan and Juin [the commanders of French forces in North Africa] will also soon switch sides to support the Allies. I have the same sensation as in May and June 1940 when life was suspended [when the Germans invaded]. It's the end of an epoch."

René and Josée had reason to worry. From early in the occupation, Chanel's lawyer edited a confidential information sheet for Pierre Laval, explaining Vichy's anti-Semitic actions. He also represented U.S. companies with subsidiaries operating in Nazi

Germany. Chambrun didn't trouble to hide his enthusiasm for collaborating with Hitler's Reich. Until the North African Allied landings, he cohosted business luncheons at the Ritz, where Nazi and French *collabos* met to plan business ventures—political, economic, and financial cooperation as part of Hitler's European New Order.

At Christmas, the headlines blared again: "Gaullist Patriots Assassinate Admiral François Darlan in Algiers." German troops now occupied all of France. When they tried to seize the French fleet at Toulon, French sailors scuttled their ships in the harbor. France was now totally under the Nazi boot. Nazi thugs ruled at Vichy. Pétain was powerless.

By January 1943, Chambrun was so demoralized he confessed to friend Dr. Ernst Achenbach, Otto Abetz's right-hand man at the German Embassy in Paris: "It's tough, collaboration is."

THE WINTER OF 1943 was unbearable. As the temperature dropped, damp winds gripped Paris. The mood dipped with the thermometer. The freezing cold was made unbearable by near starvation as rations were cut for those unable to pay black-market prices. Everything was scarce: shoes, cloth, milk, cheese, butter, meat, and wine. Old folks were literally starving in their beds trying to keep warm and to make it through the day.

The image of the enemy, of proud and handsome Aryans swaggering along the Champs-Élysées flirting with pretty *demoiselles,* had been transformed into one of overbearing, arrogant, aging men too old to be conscripted to fight on the Russian front. The mood had turned from reluctant acceptance by ordinary Parisians to the grim fatalism of the occupied.

By year's end open hostility and resistance to the Germans was manifest. In the offices of a French law firm on the Champs-Élysées, employees now turned their backs to the tall windows when German troops paraded on the street below in a show of their disgust. Paris, once the center of culture and good taste, had become a dangerous outpost where angry men set out after the evening curfew to kill Germans and to punish known collaborators and black-market operators. A senior Nazi official reported to Berlin that as of early 1943, there was no denying a "general rejection of all things German" and a widely shared hope among the French for "an imminent collapse of Germany and an Allied victory in this year." German enlisted men and their officers "spent one Sunday a month practicing grenade throwing and rifle shooting at the Paris firing range." They knew they might have to defend their lives against an army of shadows sometime soon.

Dincklage and Chanel had to wonder if they could escape the wrath of Charles de Gaulle's resistance. His Free French fighters or the Communists in France were growing more violent toward collaborators. Chanel's relations with the Nazis, her fierce anti-Semitism, and her declaration, "France has got what she deserves," a remark she made at a lunch party on the Côte d'Azur in 1943, had been recorded in London by General de Gaulle's Free French intelligence service and by partisan resistance forces in France. Chanel, Jean Cocteau, and Serge Lifar were also marked for punishment.

Dincklage knew he was a marked man. British and French underground agents working in France and General de Gaulle's Free French in London had a record of his work for the Nazis on the Côte d'Azur and in Paris and Switzerland. His cooperation with the Gestapo, his naming of Jews in France, and his link to Adolf Hitler were on record. Inevitably, Dincklage and Chanel were slated for vengeance. They knew the curtain was slowly descending on their tidy world. Already, Dincklage's friend and Abwehr colleague, Nazi major Theodor Momm, was hinting that Dincklage should leave Paris. Momm wanted Dincklage to go to Turkey and work with Momm's brother at the Abwehr headquarters in Istanbul.

When Coco learned that Momm might arrange to separate her from Dincklage, she must have been devastated. Until Dincklage came along, Chanel, age sixty (she had lied about her age on her passport application, giving her birth date as 1893 instead of 1883), had not had a permanent male companion since the death of Paul Iribe in the summer of 1935. And though charmless, Momm may have hoped to replace Dincklage, but he was no alternative. Chanel would have moved heaven and earth to keep Spatz close to her.

Dincklage and Chanel had a plan. It called for Chanel to meet with her old friend, the British ambassador Sir Samuel Hoare, in Madrid. It was a repeat of her earlier mission to Madrid with Vau-

Abwehr major Theodor Momm, Dincklage's fellow German World War I officer. Chanel and Dincklage sent Momm to Berlin in 1943 to offer Chanel's services to SS general Walter Schellenberg.

freland, except this time it was for a cause she believed in. Chanel knew through Sir Samuel that she could communicate with the Duke of Westminster in London via the British Embassy's communication network in Madrid. She hoped with Bendor's help to inform Prime Minister Churchill that some senior German officials wanted Hitler removed from power and hostilities with Britain ended. Churchill must realize it would be a disaster if Germany fell into Soviet hands.

Dincklage would accompany Chanel to Madrid—there he would act as a link between Chanel and the German Embassy in Madrid and be available to communicate with Berlin from the embassy. He would also explore the possibility of contacting other Allied sources in Madrid.

IN THE EARLY WINTER OF 1943, Dincklage traveled to Berlin in the hope of convincing his Abwehr bosses that Chanel was a valuable and willing intermediary ready once again to cooperate with the Abwehr and travel to Madrid; she would use her high-level contacts to reach out to Westminster and Churchill through British ambassador Sir Samuel Hoare.

While in Berlin Dincklage must have seen evidence of Berlin's destruction by Allied bombers. His mother, Lorry, now seventy-seven and living in the countryside near the seaport of Kiel with her aunt, Baroness Weher-Rosenkranz, must have told her son how life was growing desperate in his homeland. The Kiel area was being devastated by Allied bombs. Dincklage returned to Paris convinced that Nazi Germany was doomed and confident his Abwehr bosses would look favorably on his offer to have Chanel serve their interests "among important persons in American and British circles."

Henry Gidel, an award-winning French historian and a biographer of Chanel's, wrote that Mademoiselle Chanel thought she could barter her friendship with Winston Churchill to persuade the Nazis that she and Dincklage had the contacts to broker a separate peace deal with Britain. Gidel believed Bendor, Duke of Westminster, well known for being pro-German along with many other senior British politicians and royals, feared that the Soviet Union would grab all of Europe. Bendor encouraged Chanel to act as emissary between Berlin and London. Gidel wrote: "It was established that Westminster was a determined partisan of a separate peace with Germany. It is certain that from the beginning Chanel's initiative (to carry a message from the Nazis to the British) was secretly supported by Bendor who had already tried to get his friend Churchill to accept his point of view"—a negotiated bilateral end to hostilities. Further: "Bendor believed that if Chanel had even a small chance of bringing the Germans or their intermediaries together with Churchill it was worth the effort."

Bendor was not the only member of the British establishment seeking to end hostilities between Britain and Germany. James Lonsdale-Bryans, British diplomat and Nazi sympathizer acting for the Foreign Office, traveled to Rome in 1940 to meet Ulrich von Hassell, the German ambassador to Italy. However, for reasons never explained his mission failed. According to a British Secret Service report (MI5), Lonsdale-Bryans "had the ear of several members of the British Parliament, including Lord Halifax."

IN NAZI GERMANY, Heinrich Himmler, Reich Minister of the Interior, chief of the SS and the Gestapo—the man Hitler picked to be "the supreme overseer of the Final Solution"—was secretly convinced Germany could not win the war. As early as fall 1942 Himmler tacitly allowed General Walter Schellenberg, then Himmler's head of SS intelligence, to secretly test how Swiss and Swedish representatives might be used to seek an end to hostilities with Britain. Himmler wanted Schellenberg to find "a way out of the raging sea of blood of SS mass murders." The Roman Catholic son of a piano builder, Schellenberg, thirty-three, was a former lawyer. He was described by the American journalist William L. Shirer as a "university-educated intellectual gangster." British historian Anthony Cave Brown called Schellenberg "the sixth most powerful man in the Reich, but not a Nazi tin god— a man able, quick and dangerous."

Schellenberg's postwar interrogators were a distinguished British group of "spy catchers"—Hugh Trevor-Roper, Helenus Patrick Milmo, Klop Ustinov, Sir Stuart Hampshire, and Roy Cameron—all having different opinions about the SS intelligence chief. A succinct résumé of Schellenberg's character, compiled by one of his captors and signed with a cryptic "MFIU 3 HDH," makes chilling reading:

> By all counts, [Schellenberg is] a low character without standards of loyalty and common decency—a man who under no circumstance could be trusted. A consummate actor. He can turn on the charm and when he does, the impression of being face to face with a nice harmless and quite ingenious young man is all but irresistible . . . [H]e looks people deep in the eyes as if he were trying to convey: "Look, what I am telling you here is from the depth of my heart." The real Schellenberg is an ice-cold, ever-calculating realist who leaves nothing to chance. In his weak moments, he knows how to regulate the impression he sees fit to give. Schellenberg knows what he wants, knows how to get there if need be over corpses. For Schellenberg, the words "friendship" and "loyalty" bear no meaning, nor does he expect them for others . . . Besides his manifold talents and his unabashed self-esteem, Schellenberg suffers from a bad case of inferiority complex.

With Himmler's approval and despite Hitler's unshakable dictum of total war—meaning either the destruction of the Reich or ultimate victory—Walter Schellenberg now harnessed his contacts in neutral countries to find a way out should Germany fail. Initially, he managed to obtain a promise from Swiss army commander in chief General Henri Guisan that Switzerland would remain neutral but would repel any invader. With Guisan's pledge in hand, Schellenberg convinced Himmler and the Nazi hierarchy not to invade their neighbor. With this move Schellenberg enhanced his relations with Bern and now pushed his contacts to open a dialogue with American OSS agents working for chief Allen Dulles in the Swiss capital. As proof of his good faith, Schellenberg released a number of Jews held in concentration camps to the Swiss.

THE YEAR 1943 began badly for Hitler. German forces were on the run after the siege of Stalingrad was broken by the Red Army. A declaration by Churchill, Roosevelt, and de Gaulle (with Stalin's agreement) proclaimed that the Allies would demand the unconditional surrender of the Axis powers. Soon, German and Italian forces would capitulate to the Allies in North Africa, and Eisenhower's GIs would take the lead invading Sicily. After Allied forces invaded the Italian mainland, Benito Mussolini was dismissed by King Victor Emmanuel III. In July 1943 Italy would surrender to the Allies. Later that year the king and his prime minister, General Pietro Badoglio, would declare war on Germany. Even the censored news in Paris couldn't hide the fragility of the German situation. The BBC evening broadcasts spared no details of how German cities were being massively bombed day after day. Nazi Germany was doomed.

In the early spring of 1943 Count Joseph von Ledebur-Wicheln, a senior Abwehr agent in Paris, received a telephone call from Berlin. Captain Erich Pheiffer, head of the Abwehr foreign espionage section in Berlin, was calling via a secure line. He wanted Count Ledebur to contact Baron Hans Günther von Dincklage.

Ledebur defected to the British Secret Service, MI6, in Madrid in 1944. He told his MI6 interrogators what happened after he talked with his boss, Captain Pheiffer: "Pheiffer told me Dincklage was offering the high-level contacts of Coco Chanel in London to assist the German intelligence service . . . Pheiffer asked me to investigate Dincklage's proposals."

Ledebur now summoned Dincklage to his office on the rue de Tilsitt, off the Champs-Élysées. During this first meeting, Dincklage explained to Ledebur how "Chanel was ready to cooperate with the Abwehr—to go to Madrid and Lisbon and con-

German Abwehr agent Count Joseph von Ledebur-Wicheln interviewed Dincklage in Paris about Dincklage's plan to use Chanel in Madrid, Spain, to contact Winston Churchill via the British Embassy there. Ledebur is seen here after he defected to the British MI6 in Spain, 1944.

tact important persons in American and British circles and later to England." But, Dincklage insisted, "The Abwehr had first to bring to France a young Italian woman Coco Chanel was attached to because of her lesbian vices. The woman was to accompany Chanel on her trips to the Iberian Peninsula and to London. Ledebur would have to arrange for the Abwehr to furnish passports and visas for Chanel, the girl and Dincklage."

At the time Dincklage offered no other details of the proposed mission to Madrid and London. (He may have told Ledebur that the woman, Vera Bate Lombardi, was a member of the British royal family and a childhood friend of Winston Churchill and the Duke of Westminster.) Ledebur then went about gathering additional information on Dincklage and Chanel. He questioned Fern Bedaux, wife of the Nazi agent Charles Bedaux, who was well known to Ledebur. Fern had a suite at the Ritz on the same floor as Chanel. She told Ledebur that Coco was a drug addict who "every evening received Dincklage in her rooms."

Ledebur needed more information before giving Captain Pheiffer an opinion. He turned to Dincklage's old Abwehr chief in France and Switzerland, Colonel Alexander Waag, who was still stationed in Paris. Ledebur learned from Waag that "Dincklage had been one of Waag's Abwehr agents before the war and had run Abwehr spy networks on the Côte d'Azur and Toulon, where

he lived with two beautiful English girls, the Joyce sisters—
one of whom was Dincklage's mistress." (We know nothing else
about the sisters.) According to Waag, "Dincklage was a marvelous professional agent who spoke English and French fluently
and furnished a number of reports about French fortifications and
warships at the Toulon French naval base. He (later) worked as a
diplomat at the German embassy in Paris."

In 1938 Dincklage was forced to close down his espionage work
in France "because he was burned by the French 2ème Bureau
intelligence services. Dincklage then left for Switzerland, where
he again worked under Colonel Waag running a German spy network there."

However, now (during the occupation) Waag said, "I couldn't
use Dincklage because he wanted too much money. He lacked a
sense of purpose." And in any case, "Dincklage was now directly
working for the Abwehr foreign services in Berlin . . . under cover
of being a purchasing officer for the German occupation purchasing organization in Paris." Waag said that in Paris, "Dincklage
was in contact with Major von Momm of the Berlin Abwehr."

Ledebur then consulted Abwehr archives. He learned "Dincklage had trouble with the Gestapo in 1940 apparently because his
wife was half Jewish." Finally Count Ledebur called on Dincklage
"at a sumptuously and luxuriously furnished apartment on the
avenue Foch." There, Ledebur discovered Dincklage had a butler
in uniform, golf clubs standing in the hall, and other luxuries
that impressed the visitor. The apartment was obviously one that
would be given only to a very senior Abwehr officer.

During their conversation at Dincklage's apartment, "Dincklage explained that a trip to Madrid offered many opportunities
for Chanel to put her many British and American friends there on
the [Abwehr] string." When pressed for details, Dincklage urged
Ledebur to meet Chanel. He added that "a first trip to Madrid
was needed to develop the project."

Without having time to meet Chanel, Ledebur told Dincklage
that Colonel Waag, his former boss, "opposed the Chanel trip to
Madrid." Ledebur then called Berlin to advise Captain Pheiffer, "I
didn't favor the Dincklage trip to Madrid. Pheiffer agreed."

For Ledebur, the case was closed. However, ironically many
weeks later, he learned from one of his contacts in Paris, Comtesse

Édith de Beaumont, that she had seen Dincklage at Hendaye, the French-Spanish border crossing:

> I [Ledebur] learned that at Hendaye in January 1944 Dincklage had a long conversation with the Gestapo chief [at] the border station . . . I was now intrigued. I knew Dincklage had hoped to obtain intelligence from the British and the Americans in Spain through Chanel's international connections. I then asked German military intelligence sources if they had issued a visa to Chanel or to Dincklage. I also enquired from the German passport service, the *Passerierschein Pruefstelle,* how Chanel and Dincklage could have traveled to Madrid.
>
> A few days later I was told by *Passerierschein Pruefstelle* (safe conduct pass control station) that the couple must have traveled under assumed names.

Ledebur may never have learned that Chanel's passage to Madrid had been arranged by the German SS security services in Paris on the orders of Berlin. He may have never known that the Gestapo officer Dincklage met at Hendaye was SS general Schellenberg's liaison officer in France, forty-nine-year-old SS captain Walter Kutschmann, the SS Border Police commissioner at Hendaye. (A secret postwar report prepared by the U.S. Political Advisor for Germany on Nazi war criminals tells how Kutschmann "had been selected by Schellenberg to assist Chanel in every way and to deliver a large sum of money to Mademoiselle Chanel in Madrid.")

ABOUT THE SAME TIME Dincklage met with Count Ledebur in Paris, members of Ribbentrop's foreign office staff in Berlin were secretly seeking ways to open negotiations with Britain. Himmler was not the only Nazi looking for an escape route. Indeed, Ribbentrop and staff were also "fishing for lines to the Western allies, as well as the Soviet Union." Simultaneously, Allen Dulles, OSS chief in Bern, Switzerland (and later first director of the CIA), and British agents were seeking meetings with reliable German sources. While in Turkey, Dincklage's Abwehr boss, Admiral Wilhelm Canaris, and German ambassador Fritz von Papen "were receiving peace overtures from American sources in 1943."

In the months ahead, the game of negotiating his exit strategy through mediation would become an imperative for Himmler. He and his colleagues had no doubt that they would be tried for criminal behavior at war's end if Germany had to accept unconditional surrender. Schellenberg was so concerned about Hitler's sanity that he now risked talking about the outcome of the war with his psychiatrist friend, William Bitter, at the University of Berlin.

Schellenberg was not alone in fearing that Germany was damned under Hitler. In 1943 a group of senior German Wehrmacht officers in Berlin and Paris—some connected with the Abwehr and led by Prince Claus von Stauffenberg—were hatching another plot among senior Wehrmacht officers to kill Hitler.

BY THE LATE SUMMER or early fall of 1943 Dincklage had heard nothing more from his contacts at the Abwehr in Berlin. In Paris Chanel and Dincklage now convinced World War I comrade-in-arms and friend Major Theodor Momm, a member of the Nazi party and an officer of the Berlin Abwehr, to travel to Berlin and seek other avenues to offer Chanel's services as a way of reaching the Duke of Westminster and other British nobles. Momm was to emphasize, as had Dincklage before him, that Chanel's close relationship with the Duke of Westminster and her long-standing friendship with Winston Churchill could be used to communicate to the highest levels in London.

Arriving in Berlin, Momm contacted German Foreign Office officials—but he failed to pique their interest. He then turned to an old friend, Dr. Walter Schieber, a Nazi state counselor and Reich SS-Brigadeführer. At the time Schieber was a senior advisor to Hitler's Minister of Armaments and War Production, Albert Speer. With Schieber's help Momm soon learned SS general Walter Schellenberg, Himmler's intelligence chief, might be interested. In a preliminary meeting with Schellenberg, the SS general "urged that Chanel be brought to Berlin." Dincklage immediately made preparations to travel to Berlin with Chanel.

IN THE FALL OF 1943, a trip to Berlin was not arduous, though it might have been dangerous if the traveler were unlucky enough to be caught up in one of the frequent air raids staged by

British bombers. Chanel and Dincklage had a choice: they could travel on the French-German railroad system or the regular German Alte Tante Ju (Old Aunt Ju) air service. ("Ju" stood for Junkers, the aircraft's manufacturer.) The plane flew daily between Berlin's Tempelhof airport and Paris's Le Bourget—where Lindbergh had landed in May 1927 in his history-setting New York–to–Paris flight.

A more comfortable route was by wagon-lit (sleeper) train from Paris's Gare du Nord to Berlin's Zoo Station—a service that ran daily. Chanel and party would leave Paris at 23:17 hours and arrive the next day in Berlin at 21:34, enjoying comfortable dining and sleeping facilities.

At Berlin's rail station, Schellenberg's trusted SS officers would meet Chanel, flanked by SS orderlies on hand to carry baggage. The party would then be conveyed to a side exit on Berlin's Jebensstrasse and shown to an SS limousine for a drive through the blacked-out streets of Berlin. The weather that fall and winter of 1943 was cold, the streets lined with snow banks. Chanel was certainly witness to how Berlin had been bombed out. Even the Kaiser Wilhelm Memorial Church had been gutted by British incendiary bombs.

The SS chauffeur would have taken the Ring Autobahn highway to reach the Berlin SS guesthouse at Wannsee, a lake resort in Berlin's western district. The area had not been touched by air raids. (In case of a raid, there was a bombproof shelter a few meters from the guesthouse.) In January 1942, the Wannsee facility had been used by SS general Reinhard Heydrich to hold his infamous conference to coordinate the plan for the destruction of European Jews.

Chanel was about to meet Himmler's right-hand man and an SS general. She was entering the halls of Nazi power.

A first meeting with Schellenberg would have taken place at Schellenberg's offices at the Reich Main Security Office at Berkaer Strasse at the corner of Sulzaer Strasse. The building had been a nursing home for the Jewish community until it was seized by the SS in 1941.

The story of the Chanel-Dincklage meeting with SS intelligence chief General Walter Schellenberg in Berlin is contained in a 1945 British Secret Service transcript of Schellenberg's state-

SS headquarters in Berlin where Chanel traveled, late 1943. Seen here, the building was once a Jewish hospice. Chanel, Dincklage, and Momm met at SS headquarters with SS general Walter Schellenberg when they arrived from Paris.

ments made during "harsh" interrogations lasting for months after he was arrested by the British. The sixty-page transcript reveals Schellenberg was ill and under stress: "I was finished after eight weeks in a lightless cell." Still, a check of historical records confirms the information he provided his interrogators is largely accurate. However, the date of Chanel's first visit with Schellenberg is recorded incorrectly. Chanel first met him in Berlin in December 1943 or January 1944—not in April, as stated in the transcript. The April date may refer to Chanel's return visit to Berlin after the Madrid mission had failed.

The following is what SS general Walter Schellenberg told his MI6 interrogators about Chanel's first visit to his Berlin SS headquarters:

In April 1944 Staatsrat Scheibe an SS Brigadefuhrer and Albert Speer's right-hand man in the Nazi Ministry of War Production and one Rittmeister Momm told Schellenberg of the existence of a certain Frau Chanel, a French subject and proprietress of the noted perfume factory. This woman was referred to as a person who knew Churchill sufficiently to undertake political negotiations with him. [She was] an enemy of Russia and desirous of

SS General Walter Schellenberg (center), Himmler's chief of SS intelligence, and SS colleagues (date unknown). Late in 1943 Schellenberg met with Chanel, Dincklage, and Momm in Berlin and approved the Modellhut mission to Spain in January 1944.

helping France and Germany, whose destinies she believed to be closely linked. Schellenberg urged that Chanel should be brought to Berlin, and she arrived in that city accompanied by a certain Herr Dincklage. (It is believed by Schellenberg that Dincklage may have had some working connection with the Abwehr and the SD but that he is unable to confirm this.)

Schellenberg made Chanel's acquaintance in the presence of Dincklage, Schieber, and Momm when it was agreed: a certain Frau Lombardi, a former British subject of good family then married to an Italian, should be released from an internment camp in Italy and sent to Madrid as an intermediary. Frau Lombardi was an old friend of Frau Chanel and had been interned with [her] husband for some political reasons connected with the latter and possibly [Pietro] Badoglio [then prime minister of Italy]. Lombardi's task would be to hand over a letter written by Chanel to the British Embassy officials in Madrid for onward transmission to Churchill. [The letter referred to by Schellenberg has never been found.] Dincklage was to act as a link between Lombardi in Madrid, Chanel in Paris, and Schellenberg in Berlin. (Chanel's mission to Madrid was given the code name Modellhut— German for model hat.)

IN ROME, Vera Lombardi knew nothing of what had transpired between Chanel and Schellenberg in Berlin. Edmonde Charles-Roux in her biography of Chanel writes that Chanel wrote to Vera to ask for her help in opening a business in Madrid and to tell her that the Germans would make arrangements to help Vera reach Chanel in Paris.

IN JULY 1943 Mussolini's bet that Fascism would bring a "New Order" to Europe had turned sour. In Rome Il Duce suddenly was replaced by Marshal Pietro Badoglio as head of the Italian government. Mussolini then escaped north to set up a rump Fascist government behind German lines north of the Po River.

During the early war years, Vera Lombardi, the woman who had brought Bendor, Duke of Westminster, and English aristocrats like Winston Churchill into Chanel's life, was living in Parioli, a chic residential quarter of Rome near the villa Borghese with her husband, Colonel Alberto Lombardi. He had been a Fascist Party member since 1929. Colonel Lombardi's family had been close to Mussolini for nearly two decades. His brother, Giuseppe, was head of the Italian naval intelligence service.

Despite having Italian citizenship through marriage and her connections to prominent Fascists, Vera's royal blood and her English ways and looks now made her a suspect. Indeed, from 1936 the Italian secret police attached to the Ministry of the Interior and the Military Information Service had been tracking Vera's visits to the British Embassy and her connections with the British community in Rome. She was suspected of being "a British informer."

Vera had been an informer, but there are no records of her being a British agent. When the police first suspected her of treachery against Italy she was writing her childhood friend Winston Churchill in London—then a member of Parliament—to tell him how popular Mussolini was in Italy. Her letter, "My Dear Winston, how I wish you were here . . . ," dated June 1935, urged

Churchill to work to have Great Britain make friends with the dictator.

An Italian secret police report of 1941 tells how: "an English lady, wife of an Italian officer living at Barnaba Oriana, 32, small villa [the Lombardi home address in Parioli] kept the light on during an air raid." Two years later with Allied forces approaching Rome, the Fascist secret police systematically began arresting anyone suspected of Allied sympathies. In most cases they were interned at the Bagno a Ripoli concentration camp near Florence.

Vera, "suspected of being an agent of the British secret services for the last ten years," was arrested on November 12, 1943, and held in Rome's women's prison. Three days later, an Italian Ministry of the Interior directive stated: "The lady mentioned [Vera Bate Lombardi] must be transferred north of the Po River—advise exactly where the lady should be kept." An answer came on November 15: "The lady should be kept at the Bagno a Ripoli." A later handwritten addendum to the document ordered that Vera's transfer must be "subject to agreement with relevant German authorities."

Seven days later, Vera was free. A joint Ministry of the Interior and Ministry of Defense directive, dated November 24, 1943, declared: "The person [Vera Lombardi] held in the Rome prison has been released on November 22, on the orders of the German Police Headquarters in Rome. It seems that Arkwright Vera is

Document from Chanel's police file revealing that Chanel applied for and received a visa to travel to Spain in 1943 via "the intermediary of German authorities." A 1948 Paris police report revealed Chanel gave no justification for the visa. It was granted by French authorities because of a direct order from the Paris SS chief, Karl Bömelburg.

free again . . ." (Arkwright was Vera's maiden name.) The document was signed by the provincial police commander.

Schellenberg had reached out and saved Vera.

BACK IN PARIS with Chanel, Dincklage arranged for her to be issued a passport and visa for Spain. The document was delivered on December 17, 1943. An official French notice accompanied the passport. It read in script: "Passport applied for and issued by the intermediary of German authorities . . . Passport 2652, delivered . . . for Spain." It was granted by French authorities because of a direct order from the Paris Chief of the Gestapo, Karl Bömelburg. (A year later a top secret British memo addressed to Churchill's secretary at 10 Downing Street, London, revealed: "there was conclusive evidence that [Vera Lombardi] was directly assisted on her journey [between Rome and Madrid] by the Sicherheitsdienst," Schellenberg's SD intelligence service.)

IN LATE DECEMBER 1943 or early in January 1944 Chanel and Dincklage (with Vera) left Paris by train for the Spanish border crossing at Hendaye. They broke their journey there in order to pass through the French-German-Spanish border control. And there Dincklage met with Schellenberg's liaison officer SS

SS captain Walter Kutschmann in civilian dress. Kutschmann, SS general Walter Schellenberg's liaison officer at the French border at Hendaye in 1944, was told to deliver a large sum of money to Chanel in Madrid that year. In 1946 he was number 182 on the list of wanted Nazi war criminals accused of killing thousands of Jews in Poland.

> My dear Francis,
>
> You may like to pass on to the Prime Minister the enclosed letter which we have been asked to forward by Mlle. Chanel, who claims to be a personal friend.

January 1944 letter from Henry Hankey, a senior diplomat at the British Embassy in Madrid. The letter reads: "My dear Francis, You may like to pass on to the Prime Minister the enclosed letter which we have been asked to forward by Mlle. Chanel, who claims to be a personal friend."

captain Walter Kutschmann, "who was told to deliver a large sum of money to Chanel in Madrid."

The Schellenberg MI6 report tells a slightly different version: "A week after Vera was freed she was flown to Madrid . . ."

Was Schellenberg's memory faulty or had he lost touch with Dincklage as his liaison officer?

At Madrid Chanel and Lombardi checked into the Hôtel Ritz. Chanel then went to meet with her friend Sir Samuel Hoare at the British Embassy. British diplomat Brian Wallace (code name Ramon), who had reported to London in 1941 about the Chanel-Vaufreland Abwehr mission, again assisted Chanel.

The Schellenberg MI6 interrogation discloses, ". . . with Schellenberg's permission Lombardi had also received a letter from Chanel delivered to her through [Reinhard] Spitzy urging [Vera] to see Churchill on her return to England." The contents of this letter have never been revealed, and the letter has never turned up in archives searched by the author. (Apparently Schellenberg believed Vera Lombardi intended to try to reach Britain from Madrid.)

Then the Schellenberg MI6 transcript reveals a startling event: "On her arrival at that city [Madrid] . . . instead of carrying out the part that had been assigned to her [Vera] denounced all and sundry as a German agent to the British authorities. The result of this, however, was not only was Chanel denounced as a German agent but also Spitzy. In view of this obvious failure, contact was immediately dropped with Chanel and Lombardi." (Dincklage must have known Reinhard Spitzy; the two men had worked for Abwehr chief Admiral Canaris.) The MI6 report adds, "Schellenberg does not know whether any communication was subsequently handed to Churchill through this woman."

Again Dincklage's role while in Madrid remains a mystery. Was his role as Schellenberg's contact officer divulged to the British? Was he forced to leave Madrid?

Soon after Vera's betrayal, Chanel asked senior British diplomat Henry Hankey at the British Embassy in Madrid to forward a letter to Churchill. Chanel's letter, sent just before she left Madrid for Paris, never mentions SS General Walter Schellenberg or the Modellhut mission. The letter is an appeal to her old friend to help Vera Lombardi, now suspected of being an SS agent because of her involvement with Chanel in the Modellhut mission.

Henry Hankey then forwarded Chanel's six-page handwritten letter to the prime minister's office at 10 Downing Street. The Churchill archives at Chartwell have preserved a copy of Chanel's letter, along with a note from one of Churchill's assistants establishing that Chanel's letter was received there; a few days later another Downing Street note establishes that Mrs. Churchill was shown Chanel's letter while the prime minister was away.

Here is the text of Chanel's letter to Churchill written by hand on notepaper from Hôtel Ritz, Place del Prado, Madrid:

My Dear Winston,

Excuse me to come & ask you in such moments as these . . . I had heard for some time that Vera Lombardi was not very happily treated in Italy on account of her being English and married with an Italian officer . . . You know me well enough to understand that I did everything in my power to pull her out of that situation which had indeed become tragic as the Fascists had simply locked her up in prison . . . I was obliged to address myself to someone rather important to get her freed and to be allowed to bring her down here with me . . . that I succeeded placed me in a very difficult situation as her passport which is Italian has been stamped with a German visa and I understand quite well that it looks a bit suspect . . . you can well imagine my dear after years of occupation in France it has been my lot to encounter all kinds of people! I would have pleasure to talk over all these things with you!

Enfin, Vera veut . . . en Italie où se trouve son mari. [In short, Vera wants to return to Italy to her husband.] Je crois qu'un mot de vous aplanirait toutes les difficultés et je rentrerais . . . tranquille en France car je ne peux pas l'abandonner là. J'espère que votre santé est meilleure. [I think a word from you would settle these difficulties and then I could return untroubled to France because I cannot abandon her (there). I hope your health has improved.] Je n'ose pas vous demander de me répondre mais naturellement un mot de vous serait un grand reconfort pour attendre la fin . . . [I do not dare to ask you to reply but naturally a word from you would be a great comfort as I wait the end . . .]

Croyez moi toujours très affectueusement . . .
[I remain always affectionately]
Coco Chanel

(Peut être Randolph peut me donner de vos nouvelles.)
[Perhaps Randolph could give me news of you.]

CHURCHILL WAS NOT in London to receive Chanel's letter. He was seriously ill in Tunisia with a temperature of 102 and had been bedridden with pneumonia since December 12, 1943. He had been in Tehran for a conference with Roosevelt and Stalin and had gone to Tunisia to see Eisenhower on a stopover. The prime minister was then moved to La Mamounia, a palace of a hotel in Marrakech, Morocco, on January 5. He would not return to London until January 19, 1944. Churchill's illness was a tightly kept secret, though Ambassador Hoare in Madrid may have known that Churchill was indisposed. In any event, the Modellhut mission was doomed. Chanel's reference to Churchill's health may have meant that she knew from Hoare that the prime minister had fallen ill.

By the time Chanel's letter arrived at 10 Downing Street,

Chanel and Dincklage were back in Paris. Later, Chanel would travel to Berlin to explain to Schellenberg why things had gone so poorly in Madrid.

In the aftermath of the Chanel-Dincklage failed mission at Madrid, Winston Churchill, the British spy agency MI6, and British diplomats would become tangled in the Vera Lombardi imbroglio. Later, Chanel would fear being blackmailed by the Modellhut actors.

IN MARCH 1944, a two-page hand-scribbled letter from Vera Lombardi arrived at the South Street, London, town house of Lady Ursula Filmer Sankey, Bendor's daughter. The letter contained a plea from Vera to her friend Ursula to intervene with her father and Churchill to get her out of Madrid and home to Rome. Vera's anxiety mounted over the weeks after Chanel's departure. She knew that the British suspected her of being an agent of the SS. And she feared the British would refuse to allow her to return to liberated Rome and Alberto Lombardi, her husband.

The appeal to Westminster's daughter arrived in London at a moment when Churchill was embroiled in a quarrel with the Americans over a Mediterranean strategy. The United States wanted to invade France to appease Stalin. Churchill wanted to attack through the Mediterranean Sea.

Over the months to come, the prime minister of Great Britain would devote precious time to saving Vera Lombardi.

SOME HISTORIANS AND BIOGRAPHERS have stated that Schellenberg's use of Chanel as an emissary to reach Churchill through Madrid was a harebrained idea. Sir Stuart Hampshire, a wartime officer of MI6, thought Schellenberg was badly informed about Churchill's determination to see the war through to Germany's capitulation.

Despite the Allies' January 1943 Casablanca agreement calling for Germany's unconditional surrender, senior officials in the United States and Britain believed that if Hitler could be done away with and hostilities with the United States and Britain suspended, the German military could check the Russian advance in eastern Europe and Germany. In this way a Communist takeover of Europe could be avoided.

By the spring of 1944 many members of Schellenberg's SS intelligence services and Abwehr military intelligence officers, among them Dincklage, had ceased to believe in an ultimate German victory. Members of the Abwehr intelligence service were soon to be merged under General Schellenberg into the SS Military Intelligence service—they were scanning the horizon for a possibility of negotiating an end to the war. And Schellenberg's growing desperation to open negotiations—his many maneuvers and stratagems—coincided with signals from the Allied and British politicians that an early end to hostilities with Germany was needed to stop Soviet advances into Germany and Stalin's invasion of all Europe.

The SS leader was not alone in seeking a new strategy for Germany. In 1943 German foreign minister Ribbentrop and Dincklage's boss, Abwehr chief Admiral Wilhelm Canaris, were communicating with senior Allied officers to shape a deal. As early as 1943, Dulles, the OSS chief in Bern, secretly sought an early accommodation with Germany through Swiss and Swedish intermediaries and sympathetic Germans and senior German officers. Dulles believed the United States and Britain needed to make arrangements with the Germans before the Russians overran Europe. He argued that the Casablanca declaration calling for unconditional surrender by Germany was "merely a piece of paper to be scrapped without further ado if Germany would sue for peace." Dulles contended: "Hitler had to go."

Thirty-eight-year-old Count Claus von Stauffenberg, chief of staff for the German Reserve Army, and fellow officers now acted. Their plan to assassinate Hitler, called Operation Valkyrie, also mandated that upon Hitler's death, there would be a quick peace deal with England to prevent the Soviets from overrunning Berlin and Bolshevizing it.

ON JULY 20, 1944, Stauffenberg attended a high-level conference presided over by Hitler. When Stauffenberg entered the führer's command post—Wolfsschanze (Wolf's Lair) near Rastenburg in East Prussia—he placed his briefcase, loaded with a fuse and explosives, near where Hitler sat. He then triggered the fuse to ignite the explosives stored inside the case and left the room.

Only one of the explosives went off, wounding Hitler. The plot had failed. Stauffenberg and his heroic fellow German officers paid with their lives. A few months later, Admiral Canaris was arrested by Schellenberg on Himmler's orders; there was evidence that Canaris had aided the plotters. The Abwehr was then merged with the SS. Canaris was murdered in April 1945 at Flossenburg concentration camp. At the same time Dincklage was transferred into the new SS military intelligence organization.

ELEVEN

COCO'S LUCK

The rich, the clever and well connected escaped punishment—they returned after the storm . . .

—FRENCH RESISTANT GASTON DEFFERRE

EARLY ON THE MORNING of Tuesday, June 6, 1944,
the French-language BBC broadcasts to France told of the
Allied D-Day landings at Normandy and proclaimed Paris would
soon be freed. Thousands of American, British, French, and other
Allied troops had landed on the beaches, parachuted onto roofs
and treetops, and glided in on planes only 73 miles (123 kilometers) from the center of Paris. France was startled. The news was
soon confirmed by radio and press reports. *Le Matin* headlined:
"France Is a Battlefield Again!"

It was a grim moment for Chanel and other Nazi collaborators. She and Jean Cocteau, Serge Lifar, and Paul Morand were
among hundreds whose names could be found on the blacklist
kept by the French Resistance. If the Germans were forced to
abandon Paris, Chanel and her friends faced trial and punishment
at the hands of men and women who had suffered humiliation
and worse under the Nazis. In the days that followed, Parisians
kept their eyes on the flagpoles atop nearly every public building
in Paris. Were the swastikas still there? If so, the Germans were
still around. For Parisians, an unadorned flagpole might mean
that the Germans had fled.

On the English coast at Portsmouth, Dwight D. Eisenhower,
Supreme Commander of the Overlord D-Day operations, seemed

to wear a perpetual grin on his face. Whereas, in Berlin, Hitler threw a tantrum. His once-favorite commanders, General Gerd von Rundstedt and General Erwin Rommel, the Desert Fox, had bluntly warned their master to "end this war while considerable parts of the German Army are still in being." Von Rundstedt was sacked; Rommel committed suicide, to save his family from Hitler's wrath.

At the Hôtel Lutetia, Dincklage, Momm, and their fellow Abwehr officers began packing their files or burning them. As they made preparations to leave Paris for Germany, Allied warplanes commenced bombing the Paris region. Slowly the Ritz emptied. Its German guests were going home to seek safety.

DINCKLAGE FLED sometime after the July 20 plot to assassinate Hitler had failed. Chanel, age sixty-one (though she could pass for fifty), soon moved into her rue Cambon apartment across from the Ritz in the breathless heat of August when bits of ash once again covered everything. As Allied bombers struck Paris suburbs, the Germans burned documents day and night just as the French had four years earlier when Paris was evacuated. Chanel wasn't totally alone; she had her butler, Léon, and her faithful maid, Germaine, at her side.

In Berlin, Schellenberg renewed efforts to meet with neutral arbitrators. He finally connected with Count Folke Bernadotte, a Swedish diplomat, and asked him to try to mediate a truce via British diplomats stationed in Stockholm. As a sign of sincerity, Schellenberg ordered his SS agents to free and turn over some American, French, and English prisoners being held at the SS camps of Ravensbruck and Neuengamme. It was his signal to the British that he and Himmler were no longer Nazi die-hards. It would later save Schellenberg's life.

As the Allied armies approached Paris, Chanel contacted Pierre Reverdy, her on-again, off-again lover of the past twenty years. In the very early days of the occupation Reverdy had made a trip to Paris to see Chanel before he joined a French resistance group to fight Germans. Chanel was not there. She was still with the Palasse family at Corbère. Now at Chanel's urging he set out to find and arrest Vaufreland. Chanel must have hoped that Vaufreland, the one Frenchman who could prove her connections to the Nazis, would disappear permanently.

With his partisan fighters, Reverdy located Vaufreland hiding at the Paris apartment of the Count Jean-René de Gaigneron. The baron was seized and hauled off with other *collabos* to a Resistance prison. Later he would be held at the Drancy camp on the outskirts of Paris—the very facility that had so recently housed Jewish families awaiting deportation to Nazi camps. All Vaufreland would say later about Reverdy's strange intervention was: "He had something against me."

Chanel's friend Serge Lifar had been rehearsing the Chota Roustavelli ballet at the Paris Opéra throughout June under opera masters Arthur Honegger and Charles Munch. Now, as Allied forces approached Paris, Lifar turned down an offer to be flown to neutral Switzerland in a private aircraft owned by Austrian conductor Herbert von Karajan. Instead, Lifar slipped into Chanel's apartment at the rue Cambon to hide. Chanel told a friend, "I couldn't walk around the apartment even half undressed because Serge might be hiding in a closet." Later, Lifar gave himself up to the purge committee of the Opéra, and was made to retire for one year—a slap-on-the-wrist punishment for his collaboration with the Nazis. Many of Coco's close friends had good reason to go into hiding. "Feelings of hatred and revenge permeated French society . . . there had been so much suffering, humiliation, and shame, so many victims of betrayal, torture, and deportation." Most Frenchmen had lived through four long years as prisoners, watched over and humiliated by a million or so Germans. People had sought to survive—some honorably; others, like Chanel, Vaufreland, Cocteau, and Lifar would soon be accused as *collabos*.

THE LAST TRAINLOAD of Jewish prisoners left France on their way to Auschwitz on August 17—days later desperate street fighting between German troops and Free French and Communist partisans broke out. The insurrection to free Paris of the hated Boche invader was under way as General Charles de Gaulle landed in Normandy. Meanwhile, General Philippe Leclerc's Free French troopers were advancing on the city.

Late in the evening of August 24, Leclerc's advanced column

arrived in Paris. The next day Leclerc tankers clad in GI khakis donated by the Americans, and French sailors, with their distinctive caps topped with a red pompom, invested key points of the city. All of France would be freed in the few months to come.

By August 25, Leclerc's army had taken Paris, German general Dietrich von Choltitz surrendered, and General Charles de Gaulle, head of the Provisional French Government, entered Paris to meet with Leclerc and other senior officers and aides.

The following day de Gaulle led his famous march down the Champs Élysées to Notre Dame for a solemn mass. Earlier, at the Hôtel de Ville he proclaimed, "Paris! Paris outragé! Paris brisé! Paris martyrisé! Mais Paris libéré"—words that made Parisians cry with joy. They were recorded in English history as: "Paris! Paris ravaged! Paris broken! Paris martyred! But Paris free!"

But for some, the words were ominous—meaning retribution was at hand.

To watch de Gaulle march down the Champs-Élysées to the Place de la Concorde, Chanel, Lifar, and a host of invited guests had gathered at the apartment of the Serts, which overlooked the

Humiliated German officers fallen into the hands of soldiers of the Second French Armored Division, Paris, August 1944.

German collaborators were hunted down in liberated France;
women who had fallen in with the German invader were humiliated.
Seen here are two women bearing Nazi swastikas on their shorn heads.

Place de la Concorde. If their biographers are to be believed, many
of them, including Chanel, her friend the Count de Beaumont,
and Lifar, were anxious about their highly visible roles as German
collabos. They hoped José-Marie Sert, the wartime Spanish ambassador to the Vatican (but living in Paris), might shield them from
the vengeance that would be meted out by de Gaulle's resistance
fighters.

Two weeks later, Chanel was arrested.

AFTER THE LIBERATION, French writer Robert Aron calculated that between thirty and forty thousand collaborators were
summarily executed.

To end this drumhead justice, de Gaulle's Provisional Government established special courts in mid-September 1944 to deal
with collaboration. Those found guilty faced execution, others
guilty of lesser forms of collaboration—the newly invented crime
of national unworthiness (*indignité nationale*)—were punished by
the loss of the right to vote, to stand for election and hold public
office, and to practice certain professions.

All over France the arrival of French and Allied troops released powerful forces. In Paris, amid wild celebration, German-language street signs around the Opéra and elsewhere were ripped down with bare hands. Many toasted freedom; others spewed revenge. For known collaborators, there was flight or death; if found, they risked being shot on sight. Handsome women, "horizontal collaborators," were dragged nude from their homes and had their heads shaved in public. Twelve thousand German troopers, officials, and hangers-on didn't make it out of Paris. Many would be imprisoned in French camps.

Among them was Dincklage's former wife, Catsy, suspected by the Free French intelligence officers of being a German intelligence agent. Just before the occupation she had been interned at Gurs, a French camp for German civilians. During the occupation she was released and then returned to Paris. After the war Catsy's half sister, Sybille Bedford, in a book about the period, claimed Catsy had suffered deprivation during the occupation because she was Jewish.

A secret postwar French intelligence report tells a different story, describing how Catsy worked with the Germans all during the occupation—protected by Dincklage and a host of Nazi friends. The file reveals that after the liberation, Catsy, terrified she might be caught by French resistance fighters, reported to the Paris police. She hoped to find protection but was immediately interned with other German nationals at the former SS holding camp for Jews at Drancy. Later she was held at a camp in Noisy-le-Sec, a Paris suburb. She was finally transported to a detention camp in Basse-Normandie, where she would remain a prisoner for eighteen months.

Catsy was released after repeated efforts by her lawyer. To free her, he presented the authorities with a recommendation for release written by the wife of a senior French officer. But secret French counterintelligence reports reveal that far from being a victim during the German occupation, Catsy was a collaborator, a black market dealer, and a spy for the Nazi regime. She had not lived in hiding as a Jew; instead, she "lived [the four years of the occupation] on the best of terms with the Germans . . . people she now pretends she abominated."

To gain her release, "Catsy collected letters from friends who were accomplices in her black market operations selling fine women's intimate apparel. She used these to try to prove [to liberation authorities] her loathing of the German occupation forces." The French secret report states: "Despite her testimony to French authorities, Catsy frequently received her ex-husband Hans Günther Dincklage at her rue des Sablons apartment." They were, after all, fellow Abwehr agents and friends. The report does not spare Dincklage: "Dincklage was an active and dangerous propaganda agent. He employed Mme Chasnel [*sic*] to obtain intelligence for his service." The report noted that as Allied forces approached Paris, "Catsy's friend SS Standartenführer Otto Abetz advised her to leave France." It concluded, "Maximiliane von Schoenebeck [Catsy] is an agent of the German intelligence service, and her presence in France is a danger to national security. We must assume she received orders to stay in France for the purpose of one day beginning to work again as a spy. She must be considered as undesirable in France."

Despite the fact that Catsy and Dincklage were officially expelled from France by ministerial decree dated July 5, 1947, Catsy managed to remain in France until her death at Nice in 1978 at age seventy-nine. The Schoenebeck family, in an interview at their home in Austria in the summer of 2010, stated that after the war Catsy was employed by Chanel, but they could offer no proof of this.

SINCE 1942 Chanel had been on an official FFI blacklist. Now, in the first week of September 1944, a handful of young FFI resistance fighters—*Fifis* as Chanel called them, the strong arm of the Free French purge committee—took Chanel to the office of the committee for questioning.

Chanel's biographers report that she scorned the armed youths with their sandals and rolled-up sleeves. However, the group that interrogated Chanel had no record of her secret work; they did not know the details of her collaboration with the Abwehr or her 1941 mission with Vaufreland in Madrid. Above all, they had no idea she had been the key figure in the Modellhut peace mission financed by Schellenberg in 1944.

By all accounts, Chanel was more insulted by the truculence and bad manners of the Fifis than by her arrest. After a few hours of interrogation by the *épuration* committee, she was back in her rue Cambon apartment. Her grand-niece, Gabrielle Palasse Labrunie, recalls that when Chanel returned home, she told her maid, Germaine: "Churchill had me freed."

Though there is no proof, Labrunie and some of Chanel's biographers believe that it was Prime Minister Churchill who intervened via Duff Cooper, the British ambassador to de Gaulle's provisional government, to have Chanel released. Biographer Paul Morand wrote that Churchill had instructed Duff Cooper to "protect Chanel."

Chanel's maid Germaine told Labrunie that soon after Chanel "left her rue Cambon apartment abruptly . . . she had received an urgent message from [the Duke of] Westminster" through some unknown person telling her: "Don't lose a minute . . . get out of France." Within hours, Chanel left Paris in her chauffeured Cadillac limousine headed for the safety of Lausanne, Switzerland.

Churchill's intervention to shield Chanel from prosecution has been the subject of speculation by biographers. One theory has it that Chanel knew Churchill had violated his own Trading with the Enemy Act (enacted in 1939, which made it a criminal offense to conduct business with the enemy during wartime) by secretly paying the Germans to protect the Duke of Windsor's property in Paris. The duke's apartment in the Sixteenth Arrondissement of Paris was never touched when the Windsors were exiled in the Bahamas, where the duke was governor. A Windsor biographer claimed "had Chanel been made to stand trial for collaboration with the enemy in wartime she might have exposed as Nazi collaborators the Windsors and a number of other highly placed in society. The royal family would not easily tolerate an exposé of a family member."

The royal family was so touchy about the duke's collaboration that Anthony Blunt, the royal historian, was sent to Europe in the final days of the war. Blunt, who was later exposed as a Russian spy, traveled secretly to the German town of Schloss Friedrichshof in 1945 to retrieve sensitive letters between the Duke of Windsor, Adolf Hitler, and other prominent figures. (The duke's correspondence with Hitler and the Nazis remains secret.)

Chanel certainly knew of the duke and his wife's pro-Nazi attitudes; she may have known about his correspondence with Hitler. MI6 agent Malcolm Muggeridge was in Paris at the liberation as a British liaison officer with the French *sécurité militaire*. He marveled at the way Chanel had escaped the purges: "By one of those majestically simple strokes which made Napoleon so successful a general, she just put an announcement in the window of her emporium that her perfume was available free for GIs, who thereupon queued up to get free bottles of Chanel No. 5, and would have been outraged if the French police had touched a hair on her head." Chanel managed to put off testifying before a court that decided the fate of Maurice Chevalier, Jean Cocteau, Sacha Guitry, and Serge Lifar."

CHANEL WOULD MAKE LAUSANNE one of her homes from 1944 onward. Dincklage was hidden by friends from the Allied occupation forces in Germany or Austria. Later, he joined Chanel at the four-star Beau Rivage hotel on Lake Leman, where Chanel resided before buying a house in the heights above the lake and forest of Sauvabelin, Lausanne.

With the end of World War II, Chanel made frequent trips to Paris. From there, she and Misia Sert traveled to Monaco and returned to Lausanne to buy drugs. As obtaining controlled substances was dangerous, the pair went to cooperative pharmacies outside France for their drugs, according to Misia Sert's biographers. They took for granted that their "powerful friends" would protect them.

Misia was "reckless and impatient. She made no attempt to hide what she was doing. Chatting at dinner parties or wandering through the flea market she would pause to jab a needle right through her skirt. Once in Monte Carlo she walked into a pharmacy and asked for morphine while a terrified Chanel pleaded with her to be more careful."

In Switzerland Chanel had privileged relations with a pharmacy in Lausanne, and she and Misia visited there to buy their drugs. "The two old friends had changed over the years: Chanel's gamine beauty had turned into simian chic, her shrewdness to vindictiveness. Misia, once full blown and radiant, had wasted away." On train trips to Lausanne "they sat deep in talk and laughter, distinguished and elegant. Habit—that weaver of old friendships—had made them indispensable to each other."

Misia Sert's biographers claimed that when Chanel was with

"her fellow collaborationist Paul Morand, Chanel still criticized Misia's relations with Jews and homosexuals; and she complained that Misia was a perfidious devourer of people, a parasite of the heart. But despite her hatred, she told Morand, whenever she needed someone she turned to Misia, for Misia was all women and all women were in Misia."

IN THE LAST FEW MONTHS of the war, Winston Churchill was desperately busy with the political aftermath of the death of Franklin D. Roosevelt, the Soviets grabbing Berlin, and the German surrender in May 1945. Yet he still found time to be involved in the affairs of Chanel and Vera Lombardi; the latter was, after all, a member of the British aristocracy and a personal friend of Churchill, the Duke of Windsor, and the Duke of Westminster, as well as close to members of the royal family.

From the winter of 1944 through the spring of 1945, Colonel S. S. Hill-Dillon at Allied Force Headquarters in Paris sent a number of messages to Churchill at 10 Downing Street. In one dispatch, he informed the prime minister that investigators wanted to know why Vera Lombardi had been "sent to Madrid on a specific mission by the German intelligence service." On December 28, 1944, P. N. Loxley, a senior officer of SIS-MI6 and the principal private secretary to Lord Alexander Cadogan, the permanent undersecretary of the Foreign Office, sent the following top secret dispatch to British Armed Forces Headquarters (AFHQ) in Rome. A copy was sent to Churchill's secretary at 10 Downing Street, Sir Leslie Rowan. (It contains a wrong date.):

When Madame Lombardi was in Paris in December 1941 [*sic*], her friend Madame Chanel deliberately exaggerated her social importance in order to give the Germans the impression that she [Madame Lombardi] might be useful to them, so that they would allow her to go to Madrid.

Independently, Lombardi appears to have had a fantastic notion about trying to arrange Peace Terms and thus end the war. While she was in Madrid, Madame Lombardi received letters from Rome by clandestine means. She is by no means anti-Fascist, but there is no indication that she was entrusted by the Germans with a specific mission.

While negotiating with Stalin in Moscow, Churchill found time, on October 14, 1944, to send this top secret personal telegram to General Wilson in Rome: "FROM MOSCOW TO FOREIGN OFFICE: I shall be glad to discuss with you on my homeward journey the case of Vera Lombardi née Arkwright who wishes to rejoin her husband in Italy. I shall be glad if you will have the security authorities at A.F.H.Q available."

TELEGRAM – OUT

[CYPHER]

FROM MOSCOW TO FOREIGN OFFICE

No. 2901   D. 14th October, 1944.
14th October, 1944.

IMPORTANT

TOP SECRET

HEARTY NO. 102

For Private Office.

Prime Minister to General Wilson.

Personal.

I shall be glad to discuss with you on my homeward journey the case of Vera Lombardi, née Arkwright who wishes to rejoin her husband in Italy. I shall be glad if you will have the security authorities at A.F.H.Q available.

CIRCULATION:-

Mr. Martin

I have told A.F.H.Q. that, in these circumstances, I cannot recommend her continued exclusion from Italy . . . I think [those] in Rome who are likely to meet Madame Lombardi socially should be warned that she is still under a cloud.

Previously Churchill's office at 10 Downing Street had been informed by a British official at the Foreign office:

from the outset [Vera Lombardi] was regarded with suspicion by our people in Madrid who found her story of her journey through Germany and German occupied territory unconvincing and contradictory. There was also conclusive evidence that she was directly assisted by the Sicherheitsdienst [Schellenberg's SS Intelligence service].

In Madrid, in the waning days of 1944, Vera's efforts to return to Rome seemed in vain. Then, just after the New Year of 1945, the British Foreign Office advised the Madrid Embassy in cipher: "Allied Forces Headquarters have withdrawn their objection and the lady is free to return to Italy. Prior notification of place and date of arrival will be necessary." Churchill had intervened.

Four days later, Downing Street sent a top secret note to Colo-

December 1944 top secret dispatch from British diplomat reporting how Chanel "exaggerated [Vera's] social importance in order to give the Germans the impression that she (Madame Lombardi) might be useful to them, so that they would allow her to go to Madrid . . ." (1941 date is an error.)

nel Hill-Dillon at Allied Force Headquarters in Paris: "I have shown the Prime Minister your letter of December 30 . . . about the case of Madame Lombardi; and Mr. Churchill asked me to thank you very much indeed for the enquiries made and all the trouble that had been taken in this matter." (The signature on the note is illegible.)

Vera was finally reunited with her husband, Alberto, in April or May 1945, as her thank-you letter to Churchill makes clear:

Rome, 9 May 1945

My Dear Winston,

Thank you with all my heart for what you found time to do for me and forgive me what I can't forgive myself. That you should have been obliged to give such a useless person a thought in a time when you certainly were saving the world. Randolph has been a great joy to us here and I shall sadly miss him. His English character and great big heart are the breath of life to me after being cooped up in these stifling countries five years.

Please God I'll get home soon and come up to breathe for a brief space.

Affectionately and gratefully,

(Sgd.) VERA

In the meantime, Alberto Lombardi had managed to bury his past connections with Mussolini. He went on to serve the Allies as he had the Fascist dictator. Vera Lombardi died from a severe illness in Rome a year after her return from Madrid.

A FEW MONTHS after Paris was liberated, French general Philippe Leclerc's armored division liberated the French city of Strasbourg and American troops broke out of the German trap at the Battle of the Bulge. Two months later, Soviet troops entered Auschwitz, the SS-run Polish death camp. Meanwhile, Dincklage had arranged through the Berlin Abwehr—now controlled by General Schellenberg—to have a German firm open negotiations with Swiss authorities with the aim of obtaining a permit for him to visit Switzerland. According to the Swiss Alien Police, a German firm—United Silk-Weaving Mill, Ltd., Berlin—sought permission for Dincklage to travel to Zurich for talks with the company's Swiss subsidiary and the German industrial commission in the Swiss capital of Bern. The company maintained that Dincklage was to negotiate the import of silk and the export of tools. In actuality, the transaction involved swapping Swiss-made artificial silk for German cast-steel tools. According to the United Silk-Weaving Mill, the deal was worth 1.2 million Swiss francs.

The Swiss authorities saw through the subterfuge. They denied Dincklage's entry permit in December 1944. The Swiss report is succinct: "The German citizen of the Reich, Hans Günther von Dincklage, resident of Berlin, is refused an entry permit into neutral Switzerland."

Later, Dincklage used a Swiss attorney to apply to become a naturalized citizen of Liechtenstein—which would automatically allow him to enter Switzerland. The Swiss Department of Justice and Police now advised Liechtenstein authorities that Dincklage was an unwelcome person. His application for citizenship was refused.

Bern had not forgotten how, in 1939, Dincklage had been on an Abwehr espionage mission in their country. The Liechtenstein authorities were told: "Information on Dincklage is negative, and he was banished from France in 1947." It would not be the last time Dincklage would try to get a legitimate permit to live in Liechtenstein or Switzerland.

IN PARIS, those in the know were wondering if Chanel's luck could hold out. In May 1946 at the Paris Cour de Justice, Judge Roger Serre opened a case against her. The case dossier on Chanel for this period has disappeared from national archives of the French Justice Department. All that remains is an index card with her name handwritten on it and the notation "art 75 I4787"—signifying that the file was related to a French article of the penal code dealing with espionage. According to the chief conservator of French twentieth-century archives, the card is a clear indication that "the special French court concerned with collaboration had opened a case under the French penal code concerning Chanel's dealing with the enemy in wartime."

By 1946 Judge Serre was eager to question Chanel. His French intelligence sources in Berlin turned up documents describing her as Abwehr agent F-7124, code name Westminster—the nom de guerre drawn from her lifelong friend and lover, Bendor, the Duke of Westminster. Serre's intelligence team also found that Vaufreland had written a number of reports for the Abwehr. However, they could find nothing written by Chanel. For this reason and because investigators never made the connection to Chanel's Modellhut mission for the SS, she was never formally arrested.

December 30, 1944, top secret letter from S. S. Hill-Dixon a senior officer at Allied Force Headquarters in Paris. Letter states ". . . Mme. Chanel has been undergoing interrogations by French authorities . . . it is clear that Mme. Chanel deliberately exaggerated Mme. Lombardi's social position in order to give the Germans the impression that if she were allowed to go to Madrid she might be useful to them. Mme. Lombardi herself seems to have had some curious notion of trying to arrange peace terms . . ."

Nevertheless, court orders were issued to bring her before Judge Serre.

Chanel knew how vulnerable she had become. She believed she was threatened—not only by Vaufreland—but by Theodor Momm and Walter Schellenberg. The main actors in the Modellhut mission clearly compromised her future in France. And Dincklage, too—what might he reveal under questioning? An astute observer later wrote, "Spatz . . . was her living hell." She was "like an angry sea captain walking the deck of a sinking ship." Pierre Reverdy knew of Chanel's treason and would later forgive her.

The interrogation of Baron Louis de Vaufreland began with his arrest by Reverdy and his résistance partisans. It would take five years for Vaufreland to be brought to trial at the Palais de Justice, the Paris court where Marie-Antoinette had been tried and sentenced to the guillotine during the horrors of France's revolutionary purges. On July 12 and 13, 1949, some 160 years later, Vaufreland stood accused of multiple crimes of aiding the enemy in wartime. He faced a single, solemnly robed judge and a four-member civilian jury.

AFTER BEING REPEATEDLY summoned by Judge Serre, Chanel finally appeared before Judge Fernand Paul Leclercq. Her interrogation by Leclercq was based on voluminous court records containing Vaufreland's testimony about her work for the Abwehr. An excerpt of the court stenographer's record of her testimony follows. It seems certain Chanel had been carefully coached by her lawyers:

> Chanel began by telling Judge Leclercq she had met Vaufreland in 1941 at the Hôtel Ritz and through the Count and Countess Gabriel de la Rochefoucauld.
>
> She added that Vaufreland gave the impression of being "a frivolous young man speaking a lot of nonsense. He was visibly of abnormal morals and everything in his manner of dressing and of perfuming himself revealed what he was. I didn't trust him. If he was in relations with certain Germans, they could only be of a sexual nature . . ." However, "he was an amiable boy and always ready to render service."

As Allied troops threatened to liberate Paris, Dincklage returned to Nazi Germany. In December 1944 he applied for permission to enter Switzerland—one of many efforts he made to join Chanel, who had fled to Lausanne. The Swiss refused his appeal.

Chanel admitted that at the time of their first meeting, Vaufreland knew all about her nephew, André Palasse, who was a prisoner of war in Germany at the time.

Leclercq didn't press Chanel as to how Vaufreland knew André was a prisoner in Germany or how he came to meet Chanel. In any case, according to Chanel's testimony, "Vaufreland claimed he could bring him [André] back. I accepted the offer Vaufreland spontaneously made . . .

"In fact my nephew was repatriated some months later, and I cannot personally say if this was due or not to an intervention by the Germans at the request of Vaufreland. He assured me that he had personally arranged [Palasse's] freedom, and I continue to believe it. . . . He seemed very desirous to please me . . . and I offered Vaufreland money but he refused, only asking me to loan him some furniture."

THE TEXT OF CHANEL'S TESTIMONY does not include Judge Leclercq's questions to Chanel as the judge went about the process of discovery. However, he pressed her to determine if she was in contact with German officials when meeting Vaufreland. To this Chanel volunteered, "Vaufreland had come to see me on several occasions under the pretext of giving me news of his efforts. Never did he come to my home, at least not into my

Index card from French archives with Chanel's name handwritten above the inscription "Art 75 I 4787," referring to a French Ministry of Justice file (never found) and related to Chanel's suspected collusion with the Germans in wartime.

personal dwelling, in the company of a German. It is possible he came into the store where I was never present and where indeed some Germans came to buy perfume. He never introduced me to any German, and the only German I knew during the Occupation was the Baron Dinchlage [*sic*], established in France before the war and married to an Israelite."

JUDGE LECLERCQ MUST HAVE studied the Vaufreland testimony to Judge Serre. Leclercq pressed Chanel to explain how it came about that she traveled to Madrid with Vaufreland.
    Chanel stated,

I met de Vaufreland in the train I had taken around the month of August 1941 to go to Spain. I obtained a passport through regular channels from the Police Préfecture . . . to obtain it and the visa I personally made the necessary arrangements with the German service . . . without any intervention on the part of Vaufreland. It was completely by accident that we met on the train. However, I was happy to find myself with him in Madrid because being born of a Spanish mother and speaking the language fluently, he rendered me service in a country where there had recently been a revolution and where police formalities were very strict . . . He never had an attitude I might suspect. After my nephew's return, I asked de Vaufreland to put some distance between his visits. In fact my nephew, whom I had asked to be friendly to de Vaufreland . . . didn't hide that after a year of captivity he couldn't bear that sort of person [homosexuals] . . . And as my nephew was living with me and to prevent any incidents between them— I believed it my duty to warn de Vaufreland.

Judge Leclercq put a series of questions to Chanel based on documents supplied by police and intelligence officers. When asked about her relations with Vaufreland's Abwehr masters Chanel replied: "I never knew any Germans by the names of Neubauer or Niebuhr . . . de Vaufreland did not present me to the Germans with whom he had relations."

Leclercq now questioned Chanel based on sworn testimony made by Vaufreland's Abwehr boss, German lieutenant Niebuhr, and Sonderführer Notterman (both men were now working for the U.S. Army counterintelligence service [CIC] in Germany).

When Chanel was told of Niebuhr's and Notterman's statements about their meetings, their relationships, and Chanel's trip to Spain, she replied: "I maintain I never asked anything from Vaufreland, neither for my nephew, nor for the trip I wanted to make to Spain."

Vaufreland had testified before Judge Serre that he helped Chanel get in touch with the Nazi authorities in charge of the Aryanization of property or businesses owned by Jews—in particular about the Wertheimer ownership of 90 percent of the Chanel perfume business. When questioned about this Chanel volunteered, "I never asked Vaufreland to be involved with the re-opening of my perfume business." Then, with reference to her use of Nazi laws to Aryanize Jewish businesses, Chanel dodged the question, saying, "The Chanel establishments were never sequestrated. There was a temporary administrator for around three weeks; and the business 'Aryanized' thanks to a scheme of the Wertheimer brothers with one of their friends . . . It is possible that Vaufreland overheard a conversation on this subject but I didn't ask anything of him."

Judge Leclercq went no further. He apparently did not know that Félix Amiot—a non-Jew with connections to Hermann

Göring—had taken over the Chanel perfume business in trust for the Wertheimers.

Chanel continued: "As for my Spanish trip, the official purpose of it was the purchase of primary material essential to the manufacture of perfume, and it was for this reason that I obtained my passport . . . It is true that I knew people in high circles in England, with whom I spoke by telephone thanks to the British Embassy in Madrid. I wanted above all to have news about the Duke of Westminster, who was very ill at the time . . . I personally knew Mr. Winston Churchill but I didn't phone him about this subject, not wanting to bother him at that time."

When confronted with Vaufreland's sworn statements that an Abwehr officer named Hermann Niebuhr had conferred with Chanel at her office and about an Abwehr-sponsored trip to Spain in 1941, she testified, "As for the alleged visit of Niebuhr to rue Cambon, I protest strongly against this assertion of Vaufreland, who never brought a German to see me. I can even say that I only saw him one time in the company of a German and that was on the last day of the Occupation, when he came by rue Cambon in the company of a German officer . . . "

Neither Judge Leclercq nor Judge Serre ever referred to Chanel's second trip to Madrid in 1944 for SS officer Walter Schellenberg. They may not have seen the documents in French intelligence files or, for political reasons, chose to ignore Chanel's collaboration with the SS. The court never questioned Chanel about her four-year wartime relationship with senior Abwehr officer Baron Hans Günther von Dincklage.

Judge Leclercq then advised Chanel that Niebuhr had given sworn testimony, confirmed by Vaufreland, that the Vaufreland-Chanel mission to Madrid in 1941 was financed by the Abwehr.

Chanel replied: "I protest against his declarations, which are clearly implausible. I have no memory of a German that Vaufreland would have introduced me to." Then, faced with Niebuhr's testimony, she said, "At the Ritz, one met many people in a mixed society . . . Vaufreland may have introduced me to this man whom I would very much like to see; and in any event I certainly didn't see him in uniform. He must have spoken French fluently which would have left me ignorant of his nationality."

Continuing, she ventured, "I certainly did not esteem Vaufreland and didn't hide it because I am in the habit of saying frankly what I think. As to the idea of sending me on a mission to England to approach the Prime Minister and the Duchess of York, Queen of England at the time, [the idea] doesn't stand up under examination; and I never received money from such an individual . . . [My financial] situation is sufficiently great for that to be ridiculous. In my opinion this individual [Lieutenant Niebuhr] tried by some fanciful declarations to explain his own relations with de Vaufreland."

Faced with the records that the Abwehr had registered her as one of their agents, Chanel argued, "I never was aware of my registration in a German service and I protest with indignation against such an absurdity . . . It is true I passed through the border post of Hendaye but I was never the object and neither was Vaufreland of special treatment on the part of the Germans. We spent two hours standing in a waiting room and after an hour, a German officer, seeing me very tired, had me given a chair. It is the only consideration of which I was the object." Then, Chanel added, "I remember now . . . Vaufreland told me that he too was leaving [Paris]. If he believed he had to signal our departure to this Niebuhr, he did it himself without my knowing about it, to undoubtedly avoid difficulties for us at the border."

Finally, Chanel told Judge Leclercq: "I could arrange for a declaration to come from Mr. Duff Cooper, former British Ambassador, who would be able to attest to the respect I enjoy in English society."

There is no record that Judge Leclercq made any attempt to discover why Chanel had maintained a long relation with Vaufreland, allowing him to stay at her Roquebrune villa on the Côte d'Azur in the spring of 1942, about the same time she and Dincklage were there.

LECLERCQ HAD PREVIOUSLY interrogated André Palasse. His testimony was to the point:

> Before the war, I was Director of the Chanel Silk Establishments. Made prisoner in 1940, I was repatriated in November 1941. Since it was impossible for me to resume the direction of the Chanel enterprise in Lyon, Mademoiselle Chanel . . . entrusted

A jury trial in session in Paris's Palais de Justice where Chanel
would give testimony about her trip to Madrid with
Abwehr spy Baron Louis de Vaufreland.

me with the post of Director of the company with headquarters
at 31, rue Cambon in Paris.

I didn't know Vaufreland before the war. I only made his
acquaintance several days after I was made Director . . . [when]
he declared that thanks to his relations with the Germans, I had
been liberated. Mademoiselle Chanel also told me that she had
asked Vaufreland to use all his influence to get me freed.

I met Vaufreland five or six times at Mademoiselle Chanel's
home. Then I lost sight of him from the beginning of 1942. I
cannot be sure that Vaufreland had me freed; I have no proof
of it. I repeat—I only knew what Vaufreland and Mademoiselle
Chanel told me.

ON JULY 13, 1949, Baron Louis de Vaufreland was found
guilty on a number of counts dealing with cooperation with the
enemy and sentenced to six years in prison. There is no record
of whether his sentence included time already served in prison.
Chanel returned to her safe haven in Switzerland, but Vaufreland's trial judge was still unsatisfied. The trial record adds, "The
answers Mademoiselle Chanel gave to the court were deceptive.
The court will decide if her case should be pursued."

There was no press coverage of Vaufreland's trial and no mention of Chanel. His sentence had come in the middle of other trials of Nazi collaborators. Judges and juries were overwhelmed with cases, and readers of the French press were inundated with reports of trials revealing Nazi war crimes.

Not the least of the trials covered in the international and French press was the trial of war criminal Otto Abetz—the Nazi general who as Berlin's representative in Paris during the occupation gave lavish parties at the German Embassy there. In July 1949 Abetz was sentenced to twenty years of hard labor. He was released in 1954 and died four years later in a car accident. His death, the newspapers speculated, may have been a revenge killing for sentencing Jews to the gas chamber.

CHANEL'S DENIAL of her cooperation with the Abwehr and her contradictions of Vaufreland, Lieutenant Niebuhr, and Sonderführer Notterman's testimonies were never questioned. Chanel was never confronted with a copy of the Abwehr warning to the Gestapo police post at the French-Spanish border town of Hendaye that Chanel and Vaufreland were to be assisted in crossing into Spain. Her nephew André's slips about Vaufreland's frequent visits to rue Cambon and his use of Chanel's office were passed over. There is no evidence Judge Serre or Judge Leclercq pressed Chanel to explain why if Louis de Vaufreland was so odious he was a frequent visitor at her rue Cambon offices and at the Ritz. And Judge Leclercq never questioned Chanel about her relations with Dincklage and her mission to Spain for the Abwehr in 1941. Finally, the court record is void of questions about Chanel's mission to Madrid for SS general Schellenberg. U.S. authorities didn't learn until after the war that Chanel's second mission to Spain for Himmler was financed by Schellenberg, or that his liaison officer in Hendaye, SS captain Walter Kutschmann, was a Nazi war criminal. They may never have been informed by U.S. intelligence sources of this crucial fact.

By 1949, few officials were interested in connecting the dots that led to Chanel's betrayal of France. The details of her collaboration with the Nazis were hidden for years in French, German, Italian, Soviet, and U.S. archives. Indeed, during the occupation of France, the German authorities pulled documents from French intelligence files and shipped them to Berlin. Later, they would be discovered in Nazi archives by Soviet intelligence officers in Berlin and shipped to Moscow. They remained there as a reference for Soviet intelligence until circa 1985. An agreement between Russia and France finally provided for thousands of files to be repatriated to the French military archives at the Château de Vincennes.

THE VAUFRELAND INVESTIGATION in France and Germany took some five years and involved police and intelligence organizations in Berlin and Paris. Details in French intelligence files were known only to a few—and British and French intelligence services did not share information. Vaufreland's testimony and the statements of the German Abwehr officers who had dealt with Chanel in Paris (both Niebuhr and Notterman were working for Allied intelligence services after 1945) were found in hundreds of typescript pages recently declassified by French and German authorities.

French men and women who lived through the occupation had closed their eyes to the atrocities of the Nazis. When asked about their lives during that era, many replied, "The days of the German occupation of France were hard times. During the war years, strange things happened . . . better to put all that behind us."

AFTER TESTIFYING at the Vaufreland trial, Chanel quietly slipped back across the French border to a house she had bought and redecorated near Lausanne. Her four years of collaboration never really became a public issue.

Dincklage spent time hiding in postwar Germany as Allied interrogators sought out former Abwehr and SS officers. Later, he sought refuge at his aunt's estate, Rosencrantz Manor near Schinkel in northern Germany.

In October 1945 he was on his way to Rosencrantz with an American GI named Hans Schillinger, a friend of Chanel's former photographer Horst. Suddenly the two men were stopped by a British patrol as they crossed the Nord-Ostsee canal in the British zone of Germany. Dincklage was in trouble. He was found to be carrying more than $8,000, 1,340 Norwegian kroner, 100 Slovak koruna, and 33 gold pieces at a time when it was a crime to transport large sums of undeclared foreign currency across Allied zones.

He and Schillinger were arrested and the money impounded as British authorities launched an investigation.

During questioning by British military police, Schillinger admitted "he received the money from Mademoiselle Chanel of Société des Parfums Chanel while he was on leave in Paris. Chanel had asked him to deliver the money to Dincklage."

The British finally confiscated the money and the men were released. Much later when a British officer questioned Chanel in Paris they received the following reply to a question put to her: "Mademoiselle Chanel has stated she does not want the money back as it might involve her in trouble with the French government for being in possession of undeclared foreign currency. [S]he therefore desires that it be donated to any charity the authorities wish to name." There is no record of how the British finally disposed of the confiscated money.

In December 1945, Dincklage reached Rosencrantz Manor, where his mother, Lorry, had been living during and since the war. Shortly thereafter, Dincklage joined Chanel in Switzerland.

The Rosencrantz estate near Kiel, Germany, where Dincklage lived for a short time while he tried to get permission to join Chanel in Switzerland.

TWELVE

COMEBACK COCO

I have never known failure.

—COCO CHANEL

A N AGING C H A N E L was not ready for a pleasant retirement in Switzerland—with or without Dincklage at her side. Years earlier she had told photographer Horst, "I am tired! Naturally, it is a lie. I am well and full of ideas for many things in the future."

Chanel's life was far from over. Her collaboration with the Nazis, her visceral anti-Semitism, and her attempt to use Nazi Aryanization laws to harm the Wertheimers were largely now ignored. In the years following her testimony at the trial of Louis de Vaufreland, Chanel led a low-key life in voluntary exile at Lausanne. Dincklage was there. However, there were rumors the couple was estranged. Gabrielle Palasse visited Auntie Coco often. Her father, André, was recuperating at a villa overlooking Lake Leman—a gift from Chanel. Over time his condition improved and he and his new wife moved to a house in Brittany.

From 1945, Chanel began buying the silence of those who had inside knowledge of her relationships with the Abwehr and Schellenberg's SS. And she continued inventing stories about her childhood, her love affairs, and her wartime activities. When Chanel saw a draft of Louise de Vilmorin's *Mémoires de Coco,* she told her biographer Paul Morand, himself a former Vichy official, that she didn't like what Vilmorin wrote. Instead, from Switzerland, she commissioned another French author, Michel Déon, later elected to the Académie Française on the strength of his fiction writing, to ghostwrite her memoirs. After a year, he produced a three-hundred-page manuscript based on "lengthy dialogues" with Chanel. A month later, this book too "was not to her taste." Chanel never spoke to Déon but sent word via a friend, Hervé Mille, the editor of *Paris Match*. Mille told Déon that Chanel wanted him to know that "in these three hundred pages there is not a single sentence that is not hers, but now that she sees the book as it is, she thinks it is not what America is expecting."

According to Morand, Déon concluded: "Chanel had a childhood fear of abandoning the world of her dreams and confronting the realities of existence."

EXILED IN SWITZERLAND, Chanel's spirits were low. As the years slipped by she mourned the loss of one friend after another. In the early fall of 1950 she visited Paris and the ailing Misia Sert. Worn and feeble, still abusing drugs at seventy-eight, Misia recalled that long ago she had been one of the favorite models for Renoir and other French Impressionists. The visit turned into a last goodbye. Misia died with Chanel at her side. Then Bendor passed away shortly after attending Queen Elizabeth's coronation and Étienne Balsan was killed in a car accident as Boy Capel had been years before.

Chanel still worried about the power others had over her: Vaufreland, her Abwehr partner; Theodor Momm; Walter Schellenberg; and, of course, Dincklage. They were living witnesses to her collaboration with the Nazis.

In June 1951 Chanel heard through Momm that Schellenberg had been released from prison because he was incurably ill with liver disease. His six-year prison sentence, issued by a Nuremberg Military Tribunal for war crimes, had been cut short. While awaiting trial, the incarcerated Schellenberg had written his memoirs. Now he worked at them with a German journalist, rewriting the work into a book about life as SS Reichsführer Heinrich Himmler's right-hand man. The book was eventually titled *The Labyrinth*.

Theodor Momm must have told Chanel that Schellenberg was now seeking a publisher for the book, and she realized the dan-

Walter Schellenberg, once Himmler's right-hand man, seen here after his surrender to Allied agents, 1945. Later, he would be tried and convicted of war crimes. When he was freed, due to ill health, Chanel paid his expenses in exile.

ger. She arranged through her COGA Trust (the acronym is a combination of the first letters of Coco and Gabrielle) to finance a comfortable retreat for Schellenberg and his wife, Irene, at a house in the Swiss lake district. But the Swiss authorities didn't want a convicted war criminal living in Switzerland, and he was evicted. Schellenberg had managed to obtain a false Swiss passport in the name of Louis Kowalki; he then went into hiding with Irene at a villa at Pallanza, Italy, on the shores of Lake Maggiore.

From Germany, Momm again alerted Chanel that Schellenberg was being treated for his liver disease in Pallanza and was in desperate need of money to pay his physician, Dr. Francis Lang, and the Italian clinic where he received medical care.

Professor Reinhard Doerries, Schellenberg's principal biographer, tells what happened next:

> Dr. Lang and his wife visited Schellenberg in Pallanza . . . while talking about financial matters, Doctor Lang must have intimated [to Schellenberg] he was in considerable financial straits since he had covered from his own pocket Schellenberg's medical and other expenses in the amount of Swiss Fr 20,000. Dr. Lang tells how "Schellenberg then contacted Chanel and explained his dire financial problems . . . the lady of haute couture soon arrived [at Pallanza] in a black Mercedes, curtains drawn. She gave Schel-

lenberg about Swiss Fr 30,000 [the doctor ventured the sum might have been in French Francs]."

To explain Chanel's gesture, Dr. Lang said, "During the war Schellenberg had been helpful to her and to others in the fashion world."

Walter Schellenberg died in Turin at age forty-two on March 31; he was buried there on April 2, 1952. After his death, his wife wrote to Momm: "Madame Chanel offered us financial assistance in our difficult situation and it was thanks to her that we were able to spend a few more months together." After Schellenberg's death, Irene returned with her children to Düsseldorf, where she sought a publisher for her husband's autobiography. Chanel knew of this and may then have received a promise from Irene Schellenberg that Chanel would not be named if her husband's memoirs were published.

DINCKLAGE, despite being banned from Switzerland for his work as a German spy, lived for several years with Chanel in Lausanne and Davos. According to friends, Spatz still looked the handsome German officer. There is a photograph of Chanel and Spatz taken circa 1949 in Switzerland; Dincklage in a handsome long coat and homburg hat looks the distinguished retired officer. The couple seems relaxed. Those who knew him at the time remembered him as an aging playboy: a man of striking bearing and impeccable good manners.

Chanel's biographer Pierre Galante wrote that the Dincklage-Chanel idyll continued. "They spent time together at a Swiss ski resort taking short trips to Italy . . . Mademoiselle's Swiss friends, her three lawyers, dentist, doctor, rheumatism specialist, and an eye specialist often saw them together—and there were rumors of a possible marriage." Then one day Chanel's Spatz vanished.

Dincklage had left Chanel to become a permanent resident of Spain's Balearic Islands—a sunny resort on the Mediterranean with an agreeable climate not unlike that of Sanary-sur-Mer, the former spy's 1930 hunting grounds. He lived on a handsome pension paid regularly through Chanel's COGA Trust. No one seems to know if Chanel and Dincklage met again.

Pierre Galante interviewed Chanel's friends at the time. Asked

Chanel and Dincklage,
Switzerland, 1949.

to describe her mood following Dincklage's departure, they painted her as "a charming, simple, lively woman. She entertained friends frequently, either in the hotels where she was staying or in restaurants in 'old' Lausanne. Her menu varied very little. She almost always ordered vegetable soup, filet mignon, unbuttered rice, and fruit compote." They also reported that Chanel danced and shopped with friends, especially at more affordable stores. "She dined out, here and there, quite often with her physician whom she was fond of and later invited him and his wife to stay at La Pausa."

Chanel hardly spoke of fashion. A friend said, "It was as though it did not interest her anymore. Or almost . . . One day [a friend] wore a blouse that Coco did not like; Coco could not resist taking a pair of scissors and making a few changes on the spot."

Photographer Horst offered a different picture in 1951: "Chanel was somewhat lost at that time in her life; she seemed bored. Her hair was different, and she had started to pluck her eyebrows. She didn't look like the Chanel I had known."

WHAT WAS THIS extraordinary woman—still brimming with creative ideas and energy—to do next? At seventy, Chanel had one singular and enduring asset: her talent. She continued to garner admiration and affection from Pierre Wertheimer—despite their quarrels over the past forty-some years. Sometime earlier, Pierre Wertheimer had discovered that Chanel was making perfume in Switzerland. It was a clear breach of the 1924 agreement she had signed to sell all rights to her line of perfume and cosmetics to Société des Parfums Chanel, a company of which the Wertheimers owned 90 percent.

In the spring of 1947 Wertheimer and his lawyer called at René de Chambrun's Paris offices on the avenue des Champs-Élysées. Pierre Wertheimer wanted to make a deal. He offered Chanel $50,000 and a small additional percentage of annual sales of Chanel No. 5. Chambrun then upped the ante, demanding a higher payout on annual sales. Their negotiations would last for most of a day—bickering over what eventually became large sums of money. During the long, drawn-out discussions Chambrun left the room, ostensibly to obtain approval from his client in Lausanne via a private telephone line in a suite a few doors away. In fact, he went outside to talk to Chanel in person. She had waited all day to hear the Wertheimers' proposals.

Early the next day an agreement was reached: Chanel would get $350,000 in cash and 2 percent of all sales—more than a million dollars a year (equivalent to about $9 million today). The dividends were to be deposited at Chanel's account at the Union de Banques Suisse. Later, Chanel told a friend, "Now, I'm rich."

Indeed, back in 1947 Pierre Wertheimer had made a shrewd calculation. Had he sued Chanel in French court, it would have exposed Chanel's Nazi connections, her relations with Dr. Kurt Blanke, and her attempt to Aryanize the Wertheimer holdings. In court the secret arrangements between the Wertheimers and Félix Amiot might have come out, along with the payment of a large sum of money to Amiot in 1939 and Amiot's deal to build warplanes for Hermann Göring's Luftwaffe. Even Gregory Thomas's secret mission might have become public. The negative press would have damaged the Chanel name; the lucrative trademark the Wertheimer family cherished might be tarnished forever. Wertheimer was protecting the franchise that would bring the family unimagined riches. Years later—by 2008—a bottle of Chanel No. 5 was being sold "every thirty seconds."

IN 1970, after a relation that lasted thirty years, Chanel fired
René de Chambrun. (Later they would be reconciled.) At the time
she ventured, "I cannot stand lawyers, police officers and soldiers."
Then, despite her disdain for attorneys, Chanel hired Robert
Badinter, a brilliant international lawyer who years later would
become famous for having worked to banish the death sentence
by guillotine in France.

Biographer Pierre Galante relates how Badinter became Chanel's attorney: "I'm Jewish," he said. "Perhaps you do not know
that, Mademoiselle."

"Yes," Chanel replied, "and it doesn't bother me at all. I have
nothing against Jews."

Chambrun and his wife, Josée, never said a word about Chanel in public. The couple had escaped punishment after the war
because of their immensely powerful connections—just as Chanel
had managed to have Winston Churchill save her. For many years,
Chambrun had defended Chanel with all his skill. Despite Chambrun's having personal knowledge of Chanel's wartime collaboration, he protected her and lied in a BBC retrospective about her
relations with Dincklage, and about her 1944 mission to Berlin.

A transcript of the BBC interview, last broadcast in 2009,
records Chambrun saying, when asked about Dincklage, "I know
that at one point, because she talked to me about him, there was
a German tennis player, noble, Dincklage, and I know that she
helped him financially. And that's all I know about all the gossip
that has gone around Coco."

When asked about Chanel's mission to Spain in 1944, he
replied, "I don't see her interest *in* the mission. She was, uh—
I think if it had been proposed to her, she would have refused it.
That's *my* Chanel, that's what I think she would do. It's none of
my business. Her business that I *know* was that she did help this
former tennis player, actually helped him, but all the talk about
engineering a separate peace, to me, is ballyhoo."

Chambrun had been Chanel's faithful knight for more than
thirty years.

IN THE FALL of 1953 Chanel wrote to Carmel Snow of *Harper's Bazaar*: "I thought it would be fun to work again . . . you

know I might one day create a new style adapted to today's living . . . I feel that this time has come." Pierre Wertheimer agreed; this would be an excellent way to enhance the Chanel franchise.

The Paris fashion world swirled with rumors. "Mademoiselle Chanel is going to come back! Chanel is returning to couture!" She told the press, "I still have perhaps two or three things to say." As Christmas 1953 approached, the media reported that "Chanel will make a comeback in February." Some of the Parisian couturiers congratulated her, while others trembled. She now pulled together a few of her old staff and hired some new people. Her hands were often painful from arthritis; she was, after all, over seventy. Cecil Beaton, the photographer and costume designer, noted that Chanel's fingers "seemed strong enough to shoe a horse." She crawled about on hands and knees, pinning hems herself, her straw boater always on to conceal her bald spots, the ever-present Camel cigarette between her lips.

A few weeks before the show, she told *Vogue*: "I will start with a collection . . . About one hundred [pieces] . . . It won't be a revolution . . . It will be a collection made by a woman with love." Chanel's first postwar show opened on February 5, 1954—once again the fifth because she was convinced five was her lucky number. It wasn't this time. The Paris cognoscenti nodded politely through Chanel's careful choreography staged in her opulent renovated salon. A reporter from the major French daily *L'Aurore* wrote, "Everyone had come hoping to find again the atmosphere of the collections that had bowled over Paris in the years gone by. But there is nothing of that left, only mannequins who parade before an audience that cannot bring itself to applaud." The reporter added: "A rather melancholic retrospective." Lucien François of *Combat* (at one time Camus' newspaper) wrote a devastating piece about Chanel's first collection after the war: "Her dresses were good for cleaning offices." Chanel's models were "likened to a herd of geese."

After the show, Pierre Wertheimer visited Chanel at her rue Cambon showroom. He found her on her knees, pinning hems on dresses. He stayed there, watching her work, and then walked her back to the Ritz. "You know, I want to go on," she told him. "I want to go on and win."

"You're right," he responded. "You're right to go on."

But despite the ho-hum French press reaction and a slap from the Brits, who thought her show was a flop, the American media was impressed. *Life* reported, "[Chanel] has influenced all of today's collections. At seventy-one, she brings us more than a style—she has caused a veritable tempest. She has decided to return and to conquer her old position—the first." *Harper's Bazaar* and *Vogue* agreed. Marlene Dietrich came to the rue Cambon and ordered several suits—among them the tailored suits, *tailleurs Chanel,* that would become famous by 1956.

Chanel's creations may have been successful but Chanel's fashion business was in deep financial trouble. Her comeback had cost some 35 million francs (equivalent to almost $800,000 in 2010). The company was broke. Chanel's guardian angel, Pierre Wertheimer, stepped in again. In the spring of 1954, Chanel and the Wertheimer organization signed a final business deal: she sold the Wertheimers her fashion company, her commercial real estate, and all her holdings bearing the Chanel name. The Wertheimers would pay all of her expenses: her rooms at the Ritz, her domestic help, telephone bills, postage, and other costs of living. All she had to do was assist with the development of new perfumes and run her couture house. It was a priceless deal for Chanel. In the years to come, it would turn out to be a money machine for the Wertheimers.

In the fall of 1956 Chanel presented another collection to warm reviews. The *New York Times* reported from Paris: "[Chanel's] return to the couture scene last February led the fashion world to expect a startling revolution on her part, [but] it did not materialize. She designed in the same spirit as she displayed before the war, but in the last eight months the eye of fashion has become accustomed to the Chanel look. Its ease, casualness and understatement meet a need in the life of many women today."

Chanel was back in business—and blessed again. That year she introduced her famous *tailleurs Chanel.* And that same year, the English edition of Schellenberg's memoirs, *The Labyrinth,* appeared with an introduction by British historian Alan Bullock, who later wrote an influential and critically acclaimed biography of Hitler. There was not a word about Chanel.

Once again, Coco could breathe a sigh of relief.

As befitting a fashion queen, Chanel was invited to Dallas,

Texas, by the dynamic and innovative Stanley Marcus, renowned for displaying outlandishly expensive items in his Dallas store. In his Christmas catalogues he offered his-and-hers matching bathtubs, his-and-hers airplanes, and miniature submarines. In 1957 Chanel arrived in Dallas to receive a Neiman Marcus award for Distinguished Service in the Field of Fashion—ironically the executive accompanying Chanel to Dallas was H. Gregory Thomas, now president of the Chanel perfume company.

Chanel thought American customs vulgar, but again, and ironically, she wanted to visit a Texas ranch. A visit to Marcus's brother's Black Mark farm was arranged along with a ranch-style dinner and a show of bronco riding and roping.

Alas, it turned out that Chanel didn't like the taste of western food, so she dumped her plate of barbecued meat and beans under the table and right onto the elegant satin slippers of another guest, Elizabeth Arden, seated next to her—Coco had struck again.

Returning to Paris via New York, Chanel was interviewed by a reporter from *The New Yorker* at the Park Avenue Waldorf-Astoria hotel. The reporter found her "sensationally good looking, with dark brown eyes, a brilliant smile, and the vitality of a twenty-year-old, and when giving a firm handshake said, *'I'm très, très fatiguée.'* It was the assurance of a woman who knows she can afford to say it."

And there were other honors. Years later the Broadway producer Frederick Brisson proposed to do a musical called *Coco,* with Katharine Hepburn in the title role. It all somehow came together when Hepburn spent a few days with Chanel in Paris. The actress recalled that on her visit to Paris, she accidentally interrupted Chanel's afternoon nap. "I left Paris knowing I could play Chanel," said Hepburn.

INCREDIBLE AS IT MAY SEEM, sometime after 1962, Chanel, aged seventy-nine, took a new beau into her life. François Mironnet was a single man when Chanel hired him as a butler. He apparently bore a resemblance to Bendor, Duke of Westminster. According to Lilou Marquand Grumbach, Coco's intimate assistant and friend, it was "almost love at first sight." Mironnet soon became her companion and confidant. He would offer her his arm when she needed help on the stairs, and he'd remind her to take

The famous rue Cambon staircase re-created for the
Broadway musical *Coco* starring Katharine Hepburn,
1970. The Chanel suits (*tailleurs*) as worn by the
actresses are authentic Chanel designs.

her medications. To reward his loyalty, Chanel taught Mironnet
to design jewelry. He was often beside her at her private table in
the Ritz dining room. Forgetting the thirty years that distanced
the two, Chanel fell in love with François, recalled Grumbach,
who saw the couple together every day. According to her, Chanel
once asked him to marry her.

Janet Wallach, one of Chanel's biographers, had another take:
she believed Chanel feared solitude. "In the last moment of her
life she surrounded herself with females . . . switched her lovers,
the fashion world believed, from men to women. Her young and
beautiful models, some of them lesbians, all of them modeled in
her image, became the object of her affection." Chanel was simply
lonely, and while she may have flirted with her beautiful models,

Chanel, in spectacles, watches a fashion show from her spiral staircase
on rue Cambon.

she was desperate for companionship. She needed a man at her side, and François Mironnet was her last male friend.

Claude Delay, French writer, psychoanalyst, and an intimate friend of Chanel's, had yet another idea: Chanel's many love affairs, her infatuations, her attentions to François Mironnet were foretold by Chanel's own words: "No matter the age, a woman who is unloved is lost—unloved she might as well die." As she aged, Chanel's expressions mellowed. But she still managed to overpower.

Chanel posed for *Vogue* in one of her hallmark suits, with furs and a toque. Despite the careful work of her personal *maquilleuse,* Chanel at age eighty-one was like a leaf on a withering tree—and even more dependent on her evening injection of morphine.

Ten months before her death, Cecil Beaton photographed Chanel, and there was that look, that "enduring allure."

A CROWNING MOMENT for Chanel came eight months before her death. Claude Pompidou, wife of French president Georges Pompidou, had been Chanel's client and admirer for

Sketch of Chanel.

many years. In June 1970, she invited the designer to dinner at the presidential home at the Élysée Palace. After the reception, if biographer Pierre Galante is to be believed, Chanel remarked, "In my day one did not invite one's dressmaker for dinner."

GABRIELLE "COCO" CHANEL passed away in her rooms at the Ritz on the night of January 10, 1971. She was attended by Jeanne, her chambermaid. Her last words were, "Well, that's how one dies."

A bit before seven o'clock on the cold morning of Thursday, January 13, a closed casket bearing Chanel's body was brought into the magnificent Church of the Madeleine, a few minutes' walk from rue Cambon and the Hôtel Ritz. It was still dark outside. Paris was nearly silent. About nine o'clock the guests entered the church: Lilou Marquand Grumbach on the arm of Salvador Dalí, six of Chanel's mannequins dressed in Chanel suits, her old friends Serge Lifar and Lady Abdy, and a host of Chanel's compet-

Claude Pompidou, wife of the President of
the French Republic, was a regular client of
Coco Chanel. Seen here at the
Maison de Chanel in 1962.

itors: among them Yves Saint Laurent and Marc Bohan of Dior.
Luchino Visconti sent two wreaths of red roses.

After the mass the coffin was put into a Renault hearse and
driven to Lausanne, where Chanel had ordered a marble vault
bearing the heads of five lions and a simple cross with her name.

Chanel's fortune at her death—held in trust by COGA and
administered by grand-niece Gabrielle Palasse Labrunie and Swiss
attorneys—was estimated to exceed some $10 million, worth
about $54 million in 2010. Almost everyone wanted a piece of it.

On the third Wednesday of March 1973, Chanel's former
attendant—the man supposed to have been her last love, François
Mironnet—appeared before the judges at the principal civil tribunal of Paris. Mironnet was claiming a part of Chanel's fortune.
He offered as proof of his claim a letter Chanel left. According
to the letter, Chanel had bequeathed Mironnet $1 million, her

Lausanne property, and her jewels. His claim was contested by Chanel's Swiss lawyer and a representative of Union de Banques Suisses on the orders of Gabrielle Labrunie. Still, Mironnet's claim was supported by a number of Paris celebrities: among them, Jean Cau, former secretary to Jean-Paul Sartre and an award-winning writer for *L'Express, Le Figaro,* and *Paris Match*; Jacques Chazot, a friend of Chanel's and a well-known dancer; and Chanel's "lady-in waiting and secretary, Lilou Marquand Grumbach." Lilou claimed that Chanel had read the letter giving Mironnet the fortune to her in May 1968. When the document was exhibited in court, it was declared "false" by Swiss and "authentic" by French experts.

How did it all end? The matter was settled out of court, according to Gabrielle Labrunie. She did not elaborate.

Three years later, on the night of March 24, 1976, Dincklage died not far from the führer's Eagle's Nest where, in earlier days, Hitler had received the Duke and Duchess of Windsor. Among the last persons to meet Dincklage was a woman he lived with in a village near Berchtesgaden, Schönau am Königssee, Hurberta von Dehn, who came from a Bavarian aristocratic family, and a Dr. Herbert Pfistere. When asked what he remembered about Dincklage's last years, Dr. Pfistere said that Dincklage told him he had been imprisoned for a short time after the war and that he had been an SS officer.

Dincklage was cremated in nearby Salzburg, and his ashes were delivered to Hannover—hometown to the Dincklage family for more than a hundred years. There, in a lakeside memorial cemetery, his ashes were interred alongside the Hannover dead of two world wars and victims of Allied bombings. It was a fitting end for a German warrior, a man who had served his country for more than forty years and in two wars.

Eleven months later, Louis de Vaufreland died at age sixty-five at a villa outside Paris. The Abwehr's paid agent in wartime Paris and Chanel's nemesis after the war had a checkered career after being released from prison. He was involved in a number of fraudulent schemes in France and in Ireland, including trying to sell counterfeit $100 bank notes and pretending to be a police officer. He served time at Fresnes and Santé prisons in 1956.

In 1951 French intelligence sources reported Vaufreland was seen at Donald Maclean's villa, La Sauvageonne, near Saint-

Maxime on the Côte d'Azur. It was the same moment that Maclean and Guy Burgess, members of the Cambridge Five spy ring, fled Britain for the Soviet Union.

Gregory Thomas, the retired president of Chanel, Inc., died at eighty-five in Florida. Thomas, a decorated World War II OSS officer and an officer of the French Légion d'honneur, had once gone undercover as Don Armando Guevaray Sotto Mayor to aid the Wertheimer family in occupied France. On retirement, Thomas had been with the Wertheimer family in various senior positions for more than thirty years. As a wine enthusiast, he was a founder and *grand maître* of the Commanderie de Bordeaux in the United States—an elite group of lovers of the Bordeaux wines.

Epilogue

And forever shalt thou dwell
In the spirit of this spell.

—Ralph Waldo Emerson, *Wide World*

In the twilight years of her life, Chanel was celebrated for her creative genius. André Malraux, French historian and one of Charles de Gaulle's favorite ministers, ventured, "From this century, in France, three names will remain: de Gaulle, Picasso, and Chanel."

For all sorts of reasons the name Chanel remains a worldwide icon. One could count her enormous appeal as a designer by the royalty and distinguished women she dressed and perfumed after her comeback: Madame Georges Pompidou, wife of the president of France; Jacqueline Kennedy, who was wearing a pink Cha-

For the 1961 film *Last Year at Marienbad*,
Chanel designed dramatic feather and lace costumes
for leading lady Delphine Seyrig.

Louis Malle's 1958 film *The Lovers* features actress
Jeanne Moreau in Chanel's "little black dress."

nel suit on the day her husband was assassinated in Dallas; and
actresses Jeanne Moreau, Romy Schneider, Elizabeth Taylor, and
Marilyn Monroe, who claimed Chanel No. 5 was the only thing
she wore in bed.

Jean Cocteau's take on Chanel is less heroic. "She looks at you
tenderly, nods her head, and you're condemned to death!"

In the 1962 movie *Boccaccio '70* by director Luchino Visconti,
Romy Schneider, in a classic Chanel suit, surrounds herself
with expensive trinkets, including Chanel No. 5 perfume.

Two views: one heroic, one demonic.

Pierre Reverdy, romantic poet and nineteenth-century man, believed women were weak—and in love would fall under the spell of a man, do his bidding. He loved Chanel as well and as deeply as any man and wanted to believe Chanel had fallen under Dincklage's power—"Spatz was her damnation."

Reverdy may have had the measure of Chanel's solitude and distress. He never knew the depth of her collaboration. As a good Catholic he put aside his disgust for what Chanel had done during the war and absolved Chanel for her weakness and her condemnable acts with the Germans. This Catholic poet believed Chanel needed to be free from guilt.

Before he died at seventy in 1960 at the Abbaye Saint-Pierre, a Benedictine monastery at Solesmes, Reverdy blessed Chanel in poetry. This determined and dedicated resistance fighter who had fought the German invader and the Vichy regime and had broken with his friends for their collaboration with the Nazis, willed Chanel a final epitaph:

> *Dear Coco, here is*
> *The best of my hand*
> *And the best of me*
> *I offer it thus to you*
> *With my heart*
> *With my hand*
> *Before heading toward*
> *The dark road's end*
> *If condemned*
> *If pardoned*
> *Know you are loved.*

NOTES

ABBREVIATIONS

ADV   Archives du Département du Var
APP   Archives de la Préfecture de Police
ASM   Archives de la Ville de Sanary-sur-Mer
BCRA   Bureau Central de Renseignements et d'Action (Central Bureau
          of Intelligence and Operations)
BMT   Bibliothèque municipale de Toulon
BNA   British National Archives, Kew
BNF   Bibliothèque nationale de France
BRO   Berlin Registry Office
CARAN   Centre d'accueil et de recherche des Archives nationales
CHADAT   Centre historique des archives, département de l'armée de terre,
          files of the 2ème Bureau, Army Intelligence
EFP   Eidgenössische Fremdenpolizei, branch of federal police in
          charge of foreigners, Bundesarchiv, Switzerland
HRC   Harry Ransom Center, University of Texas at Austin
HRO   Hanover Registry Office
KEW   British National Archives
LASH   Landesarchiv, Schleswig-Holstein
MDN   Ministero della Difesa Nazionale, Rome
MVN   Mairie de la Ville de Nice
NARA   U.S. National Archives
PVM   Paris-Var-Méditerranée
SB   Schweizerische Bundesanwaltschaft
SSF   Services spéciaux français
USWD   U.S. War Department
VD   Vesna Drapac, "A King is killed in Marseille . . ."
V1   *Vendémiaire* article: "Gestapo über alles"
V2   *Vendémiaire* article: "La Fébrile Activité . . ."
ZO   *Zones d'ombres 1933–1944*, pp. 50–52

PROLOGUE

xv   "Despite her age": Paul Morand, *The Allure of Chanel*, p. 181.
xv   Gabrielle Chanel had barely been laid to rest: Hebe Dorsey, "Looking
     Back," *International Herald Tribune*, September 26, 1972.
xv   "a dangerous agent": Ibid.
xvi " . . . to hell with politics": A comment by Knopf senior editor and V.P.,
     Victoria Wilson, December 2010.
xvi Paxton's book proved: Robert O. Paxton, *Vichy France, Old Guard and
     New Order, 1940–1944*.

xvi "was not in the Gestapo": Milt Frudenheim, "Chanel's Past Haunts Exhibit," *The Salt Lake Tribune,* September 29, 1972.

xvi "loved eating": Dorsey, *International Herald Tribune,* September 26, 1972.

xvi "He is not German": Ibid.

xvii Years later: When I briefed Chanel biographer Edmonde Charles-Roux on my findings and showed her French counterintelligence documents in the spring of 2009, she admitted that in 1974, when she was finishing the Chanel biography (*L'Irrégulière*), she had been manipulated into believing Dincklage was a playboy by Chanel's lawyer, René de Chambrun.

xvii Boches: "Boches" was a pejorative term for Germans used by the French in World Wars I and II.

xviii Chanel was released: Gabrielle Palasse Labrunie, telephone interview with author, Yermenonville, France, November 8, 2009.

xviii During the postwar process: Ousby, *Occupation,* p. 310.

xix French police had identified: CARAN Z/6/672 greffe 5559. German Abwehr personnel document: *Personalalbogen, 159, Paris, den 9. Juni 1941.* Also Shirer, *The Rise and Fall of the Third Reich,* p. 1044.

xix Serre, forty-eight years old: *Annuaire de la Magistrature,* n.p.

xix Slowly, Serre, a painstaking investigator: CARAN Z/6/672 greffe 5559. APP BA 1990. SSF. CARAN: An index card, inscribed "Gabrielle Chanel" with the mention art. 75 I 4787 signifying: "an investigation of Chanel is opened under the French penal code, article 75: dealing with the enemy."

xix But French police and court documents: CARAN Z/6/672 greffe 5559.

xix Serre would never learn: SSF document.

xx Nor did he know that Dincklage: Ibid; BNA, KV2/159, Ledebur file.

CHAPTER ONE: METAMORPHOSIS — GABRIELLE BECOMES COCO

3 "If you're born without wings": As quoted in Sylviane Degunst, *Coco Chanel: Citations,* pp. 8, 44.

3 The added "s": There are numerous examples of the *s* and other letters being deleted in French family names or words, such as Surène for Suresne and Quénel for Quesnel. Chasnel was and still is a not-uncommon French family name.

4 "From my earliest childhood": Edmonde Charles-Roux, *Chanel* (London: Jonathan Cape, 1976), p. 40.

4 "Why Moses?" Marcel Haedrich, *Coco Chanel,* p. 120.

4 "I only fear Jews": Ibid.

9 "What followed": Paul Morand, *The Allure of Chanel,* pp. 54–55.

CHAPTER TWO: THE SCENT OF A WOMAN

10 "Neglect taught Misia independence": Arthur Gold and Robert Fizdale, *Misia,* p. 26.

10 For the next few years: Ibid., p. 38.

11 "enthroned at his [Diaghilev's] side": Ibid., p. 4.

11 "[I] was drawn": Ibid., pp. 197–198.

13 "I remained forever": Morand, *The Allure of Chanel*, p. 65.

13 300,000 gold francs: $769,000 in today's money. Henry Gidel, *Coco Chanel*, p. 131.

14 "The woman who hasn't": Ibid.

15 Chanel was wearing: Axel Madsen, *Chanel: A Woman of Her Own*, p. 82.

15 7,000 francs: Ibid.

15 In simple terms the cost: A 2010 Union Bank of Switzerland analysis of inflation.

15 Two German cavalry officers: Landesarchiv (LASH), Büro für Kriegstammrollien, SW 29 (Berlin, Germany) Military Government of Germany, Fragebogen, undated document. Schleswig-Holsteinisches (Schleswig, Germany) "Dincklage" file.

15 Each had fought: U.S. War Department, *Histories of the German Army 1914–1918*, p. 729.

15 "A people continually torn": Shirer, *Berlin Diary*, p. xiii.

16 Theodor Momm's wealthy family: The official name of the firm was Th. Momm & Co. Baumwoll-spinnerei und Weberei (Michael Foedrowitz's e-mail to author, August 2008).

16 With the coming to power of Hitler: Militärregierung, U.S. Army Military Government files, DET, 1.370 circa 1946. Momm's NSPD number given as: 4 428.309.

16 joined the military intelligence service: SSF doc. 814; Dincklage Army Major—biographic entry, Bundesarchiv Berlin.

16 Dincklage's father: Landesarchiv Antrag "Request." War Department Histories, 23565, Government Printing Office, Washington, D.C., 1920. Memoire in Swiss archives.

16 Dincklage's English-born mother: CHADAT 7NN2973.

17 The Dincklages shared: Christian Ingrao explores the Völkisch myth in *Croire et détruire—les intellectuels dans la machine de guerre SS.*

17 Years later: SS general Heinrich Himmler quoted in Robert G. L. Waite, *Vanguard of Nazism*, p. 29. Dincklage's connection with the Free Corps is found in Marcel Haedrich, *Coco Chanel*, p. 137; Manfred Flügge, *Amer Azur: Artistes et écrivains à Sanary*, p. 61: "One heard from Sybille Bedford that [Dincklage] participated in the assassination of Rosa Luxemburg in 1919." Manfred Flügge, interview in Paris by author, September 13, 2009.

17 According to French counterintelligence: SSF, Dec. 814.

17 But Spatz was certainly: MI6, Ledebur report, BNA.

18 Isabelle Fiemeyer described: Chanel experienced a moment of religious fervor in Venice while she prayed and mourned Boy Capel. There, she began a lifetime habit of collecting religious cards with prayers to Catholic saints: Saint Thérèse de l'Enfant-Jesus, Saint Agatha, the Madonna of the Oliviers, and a prayer card dedicated to "The Blessed Pierre Marie Louis Chanel (1803–1841)" of her family. She kept the cards in a small wallet along with a note written in her hand: "I am a Roman Catholic; in case of a serious accident or transportation to hospital, I request a Catholic priest come to me. If I die I request the blessing of the Catholic Church, signed Chanel, 31, rue Cambon, Paris" (author's translation).

When Chanel died in 1971, the wallet was found in her handbag along with photographs of her nephew, André Palasse and his two grand-daughters. Isabelle Fiemeyer, *Coco Chanel: un parfum de mystère*, pp. 65–66.

18 Chanel biographer Pierre Galante: Galante, *Mademoiselle Chanel*, p. 50.

19 The city had "forgotten the black years": Ibid., p. 51.

20 "liberated from prejudices": Ibid., p. 64.

21 "Chanel launches": Ibid., p. 54.

21 "Women were no longer to exist": Madsen, *Chanel: A Woman of Her Own*, p. 116.

21 In one of her maxims: Vaughan translation of Chanel's citations, proverbs, and maxims found at Citations Chanel: http://www.citation-du-jour.fr/

21 "Chanel's genius": Gold and Fizdale, *Misia*, p. 230.

21 "An orphan denied a home": Morand, *L'Allure de Chanel*, p. 32; my translation.

22 The swank flat: Galante, *Mademoiselle Chanel*, p. 60.

22 "but the greatest concentration": Pierre Assouline, *Simenon: A Biography*, p. 73.

22 Later, Chanel and her entourage: Galante, *Mademoiselle Chanel*, p. 2.

22 "Love affairs between writers and artists": Ibid., p. 62.

23 Chanel's newfound friends: Wallach, *Chanel: Her Style and Her Life*, p. 42.

23 "You do not know dear": Fiemeyer, *Coco Chanel: Un parfum de mystère*, p. 87; my translation.

23 "What would become of dreams": Edmonde Charles-Roux, *Chanel*, p. 220.

24 She was generous and tactful: Ibid., p. 224. Today, the manuscripts are kept at Yermenonville, France, at the home of Gabrielle Palasse Labrunie.

25 Prince Félix chose Dmitri: On the night of December 16, 1916, two men, with the help of British secret agents, managed to poison Rasputin. They then clubbed him almost to death. But the "holy monk" would not die. They finished the deed with gunfire and threw his nearly dead body in the icy river Neva, where he died of hypothermia. Dmitri Pavlovich was later suspected of having shot the monk.

26 Rumors now spread: Gidel, *Coco Chanel*, p. 171.

29 "It was like a winning lottery ticket": Madsen, *Chanel: A Woman of Her Own*, p. 135.

30 "I want you to meet": Galante, *Mademoiselle Chanel*, p. 146.

30 "But if you want": Ibid.

33 She would come to believe: Haedrich, *Coco Chanel: Her Life, Her Secrets*, p. 156.

34 an individual whose: APP BA 1990.

CHAPTER THREE: COCO'S GOLDEN DUKE

36 Mademoiselle is more: French *Vogue*, March 2009, p. 295.

36 One biographer claimed: Paul Morand, *The Allure of Chanel*, p. 157.

37 "a man of great generosity": Ibid., p. 186; my translation.

38 Chanel and the prince met: Claude Delay, *Chanel solitaire*, p. 125. Janet Wallach, *Chanel: Her Style and Her Life*, p. 2. Delay, a respected French psychoanalyst and prize-winning author, is the only Chanel biographer to tell this anecdote of Chanel and the prince. It may be one of Chanel's many inventions, but her brief affair with the prince was also confirmed to this author by Edmonde Charles-Roux in 2010.

38 Legend holds that the butler: Charles-Roux, *Chanel*, pp. 249–50.

38 "The Duke frightened me": Chanel to her friend, the Russian refugee and designer Lady Iya Abdy, in Field, *Bendor, the Golden Duke of Westminster*, p. 183.

39 Chanel was "a little like Cinderella": Galante, *Mademoiselle Chanel*, pp. 96–99.

39 To them, she was "the former demimondaine": APP BA 1990.

39 In one of her more sarcastic moods: Delay, *Chanel solitaire*, p. 126.

39 "He had a yacht": Field, *Bendor, the Golden Duke of Westminster*, p. 184.

39 "I loved him": Morand, *The Allure of Chanel*, p. 158.

41 One of Bendor's chums: Ridley George, *Bend'Or, Duke of Westminster*, p. 74.

41 Churchill thought Bendor: Ibid., pp. 196–197. Churchill and Bendor fought side by side in the Boer War. They were together on the Western Front in 1918 with the Prince of Wales.

41 A French lady described Bendor: Charles-Roux, *L'Irrégulière*, pp. 417–18; my translation.

41 When his homosexual brother-in-law: Homosexual activity was a criminal offense in Britain in 1931. The Seventh Earl of Beauchamp held the Order of the Garter and carried the Sword of State at King George V's coronation in 1909. He was a pillar of the Church of England and the House of Lords, and was the father of Lady Lettice's seven children. He was ruined and fled to France. Lady Lettice, Beauchamp's wife of twenty-nine years, divorced him. The king's reaction to Beauchamp's evildoings was, "I thought that men like that shot themselves" and "I thought that people only did that abroad." When the devastated Lady Lettice suffered a "nervous collapse," she went to live with her brother, claiming to Bendor that she had never heard of homosexuality and could not understand what her brother was talking about. Field, *Bendor, the Golden Duke of Westminster*, pp. 244–47.

41 Chanel could match: Morand, *The Allure of Chanel*, pp. 136–38; my translation.

42 In another picture: Wallach, *Chanel: Her Style and Her Life*, p. 72.

42 In a *Vogue* photo: Ibid., p. 75.

42 In one rare photo: Chanel was addicted to Camel cigarettes according to Gabrielle Palasse Labrunie. Interview by author at Yermenonville, France, June 9, 2009.

43 Another snapshot shows: Photo in Charles-Roux, *Le Temps Chanel*, p. 244.

43 There is also a delightful November 1929 snapshot: Justine Picardie, *Coco Chanel*, p. 166.

43 "Rumor is busy": Field, *Bendor, the Golden Duke of Westminster*, pp. 184–85.

44   "My real life began with Westminster": Haedrich, *Coco Chanel*, p. 124.
46   "A very charming picture": Sir Winston Churchill Archive Trust, CHAR 2157.
46   "The famous Chanel turned up": Churchill may be referring to the fact that Vera had been with Mrs. Churchill on the Western Front as a nurse in World War I. Field, *Bendor, the Golden Duke of Westminster*, p. 201.
46   "Chanel is here in place of Violet": Ibid.
46   "[Chanel] created elegant clothes" Wallach, *Chanel: Her Style and Her Life*, p. 166.
47   "She really had two real loves": Galante, *Mademoiselle Chanel*, p. 95.
47   His scheme was to convince Chanel: Field, *Bendor, the Golden Duke of Westminster*, p. 201.
47   A picture taken at her La Pausa retreat: Photo in Wallach, *Chanel: Her Style and Her Life*, p. 82.
48   Bendor purchased it: Galante, *Mademoiselle Chanel*, p. 116. Note: author Charles-Roux states Chanel used her own money: Charles-Roux, *Chanel*, p. 255.
48   When completed by Chanel: Galante, *Mademoiselle Chanel*, p. 120.
48   "I never wanted to weigh": Ibid., p. 141.
48   Chanel's friends thought: Ibid., p. 111.
48   She steadfastly refused: Field, *Bendor, the Golden Duke of Westminster*, p. 185.
49   "All I want": Ibid., p. 207.
49   "those Jews": Roger Peyrefitte, *Les Juifs*, pp. 71–72.
51   "The Duke makes frequent trips": APP BA 1990, Chanel file; my translation.
51   The Sûreté suspected him: Ibid.
51   "I never tried to get him": Morand, *L'Allure de Chanel*, p. 192; my translation.
52   Misia was crushed: Edmonde Charles-Roux, *L'Irrégulière*, p. 458.
52   One legend has it: Marcel Haedrich, *Coco Chanel: Her Life, Her Secrets*, p. 130.
53   Coco scorned nights out: Henry Gidel, *Coco Chanel*, pp. 237–38.
53   The maxims included: Ibid., p. 238.
53   He left a touching few lines: Ibid., p. 240; my translation.
54   "Imagine": Gold and Fizdale, *Misia*, p. 240.
54   "One must not let oneself be forgotten": Haedrich, *Coco Chanel*, p. 205.
54   While the duke wandered around: Field, *Bendor, the Golden Duke of Westminster*, p. 225.
54   Loelia remembered Chanel: Galante, *Mademoiselle Chanel*, pp. 113–14.
55   Dincklage and his German half-Jewish wife: Reliable sources and biographer Edmonde Charles-Roux (*L'Irrégulière*, p. 545) write that Dincklage and wife were traveling and living on the Côte d'Azur from 1928. French police and counterintelligence sources claim he entered France in 1929.
55   Dincklage had earned this plum posting: CHADAT 7NN 2620.
56   "We were by the sea": Marje Schuetze-Coburn, Bill Dotson, Michaela Ullmann, *Against the Eternal Yesterday—Essays Commemorating the Legacy of Lion Feuchtwanger*, p. 26.
56   The Dincklages were not the first: CHADAT 7NN 2620.

57   It was good cover: The Abwehr often used agents from Jewish families. Being Jewish was good cover, and the Abwehr could threaten reprisals against the agent's families in Germany. Jews cooperated with the intelligence service either by patriotism for their German homeland or, after 1933, as a means of protecting themselves and their families from Nazi persecution.

57   And Maximiliane had solid credentials: German Abwehr officers Ledebur and Feihl stated that Maximiliane owned shares in I. G. Farben. The author Sybille Bedford, Catsy's half sister, speaks of Catsy's mother as being wealthy in her own right.

57   A 1929 German Registry document: German archives of Berlin, 1929: "Dincklage," p. 139.

57   Indeed, French military intelligence: CHADAT 7NN 2973.

57   A 1934 secret Sûreté document: November 17, 1934. Ibid.

58   "There were Huxley picnics": Sybille Bedford papers, HRC, Box 46–1, July 1932.

58   Coton described Sanary: Jacques Grandjonc and Theresia Grundtner, *Zones d'ombres 1933–1944: Exil et internement d'Allemands et d'Autrichiens dans le sud-est de la France,* pp. 50–52.

58   Coton later wrote: Ibid.

59   Later, Coton's spying: CHADAT 7NN2973.

60   In 1931, the shift in political sentiment: Warsaw: Archiwa Akt Nowych; du Plessix Gray, *Them,* p. 136.

CHAPTER FOUR: A HOLLYWOOD DIVERTISSEMENT

61   God makes stars: Samuel Goldwyn.

61   about $14 million: This figure was arrived at using the Consumer Price Index.

61   "The Italian Wizard": Meredith Etherington-Smith, *Patou,* pp. 121–30.

62   Chanel had taken women: Bet Moore, "Two for the Runway," *Los Angeles Times,* May 4, 2005.

62   Later, Chanel would say: In a telephone conversation with the author on September 6, 2009, Gabrielle Palasse Labrunie confirmed Chanel's judgment of Hollywood as "vulgar." Also Edmonde Charles-Roux, *L'Irrégulière,* pp. 474–75; my translation.

62   "There are great Jews": Delay, *Chanel solitaire,* p. 149.

62   "What looked young last year": *Vogue,* cited in Etherington-Smith, *Patou,* p. 115.

62   His stars were to be dressed: "Mlle Chanel to Aid Films," *New York Times,* January 20, 1931.

63   She and husband, José-Maria Sert: Arthur Gold and Robert Fizdale, *Misia,* pp. 249–57.

63   "Tatar charm": Ibid.

63   "Coco and Misia were seen": Ibid., p. 231.

63   "a snobbish little pederast": Francis Steegmuller, *Cocteau: A Biography,* p. 389.

63   Although both were fervent Catholics: Together, the Serts begged the French Catholic episcopacy for an annulment of their marriage. Roussy

would die later in 1938 of tuberculosis, and the Serts would reunite. Gold and Fizdale, *Misia*, pp. 281, 303–12, 332, 335.

64 At a suite in the Hotel Pierre: "Chanel Visits America," *New York Times*, March 8, 1931.

64 Dressed in a simple rose-red jersey: Ibid.

64 Astute as ever: Ibid.

64 "rather bewildered at the score": Ibid.

64 "If blonde": *Los Angeles Examiner*, March 17, 1931.

65 "gawked at Paris mannequins and laughed": Galante, *Mademoiselle Chanel*, pp. 159–61.

65 "Two Queens Meet": Ibid.

65 "actors [were] strong": Ibid.

67 "I never was a dressmaker": Paul Morand, *L'Allure de Chanel*, p. 59; my translation.

67 Chanel had hoped: *Sunday Express* (London), February 21, 1932, as cited in Galante, *Mademoiselle Chanel*, p. 162.

68 "The Hollywood atmosphere": Charles-Roux, *Chanel*, pp. 269–70.

70 "Chanel made a lady": Madsen, *Chanel: A Woman of Her Own*, p. 194.

CHAPTER FIVE: EXIT PAUL, ENTER SPATZ

71 "a bath of nobility": Pierre Galante, *Mademoiselle Chanel*, p. 164.

71 In a rare photograph: When Boy Capel realized that Chanel, being slightly cross-eyed, needed glasses, he arranged for her to see a specialist. Still, Chanel refused to wear spectacles. Janet Wallach, *Chanel: Her Style and Her Life*, p. 104.

71 "bright, a dark golden color": Madsen, *Chanel: A Woman of Her Own*, p. 197.

72 "I am timid": Marcel Haedrich, *Coco Chanel: Her Life, Her Secrets*, pp. 236–37.

72 Age had not weakened: Janet Flanner, "31 rue Cambon," *The New Yorker*, March 14, 1931, p. 25.

72 "Mademoiselle Chanel": Ibid.

72 "I signed something": Galante, *Mademoiselle Chanel*, p. 149.

74 Despite the world economic crisis: Wallach, *Chanel: Her Style and Her Life*, pp. 87–92.

74 "All those bluebloods": Madsen, *Chanel: A Woman of Her Own*, p. 109.

74 "It's disgusting": Galante, *Mademoiselle Chanel*, p. 166.

74 Germany's next most powerful man: Robert S. Wistrich, *Who's Who in Nazi Germany*, p. 78.

75 Canaris cooperated: Ibid., p. 29.

75 Later, Himmler's SS: Abwehr, from German *abwehren*, "to ward or fend off," was the intelligence and counterintelligence (spy and spy-catching) agency of the military Reichswehr, later the Wehrmacht under Hitler. David M. Crowe, *Oskar Schindler*, p. 15.

75 Operating under diplomatic immunity: CHADAT 7NN2973.

75 By 1932 the Dincklages: Ibid.

75 Writing about Dincklage's power of attraction: Manfred Flügge, *Amer*

Azur: Artistes et écrivains à Sanary, pp. 61–62, and from Flügge's interview with Sybille Bedford in Chelsea, England, January 2000. Edmonde Charles-Roux, *L'Irrégulière* (p. 556) tells how Dincklage provided "physical satisfaction" to Chanel and his many mistresses.

75   The two naval officers: In their book, *Zones d'ombres,* Jacques Grandjonc and Theresia Grundtner reveal how a French naval officer, Charles Coton, befriended the Dincklages in 1930 at Sanary and that Dincklage was known to be a German agent. For Charles Coton, see Jacques Grandjonc and Theresia Grundtner, *Zones d'ombres, 1933–1944: Exil et internement d'Allemands dans le Sud-Est de la France,* pp. 50–52. For Gaillard, see CHADAT 7NN 2973.

76   Within weeks of arriving in Paris: Vans were hired from Gustav Knauer, Wichmannstrasse 62. The couple moved to 64, rue Pergolèse.

76   She was issued: Dincklage letter to Herr Goersch circa 1958; letters 1961; PAdAA Document 681/5, October 3, 1933.

76   French police and military intelligence: CARAN F/7/15327 "Feihl Statement," PAdAA, Deutsche Botschaft file.

76   Dincklage had also planted: Ibid.

76   By 1934 the Berlin Nazi machine: CHADAT 7NN 2737.

77   In Paris: Ibid.

77   The French military counterintelligence service: Ibid.

77   The Inter Press dispatch: Ibid.

78   Finally, the report confirmed: Ibid.

79   According to one biographer: Charles-Roux, *Chanel,* p. 290.

79   In the February 24, 1933, edition: *Le Témoin,* February 24, 1933, n.p.

79   No man before Iribe: Charles-Roux, *Chanel,* pp. 290–91.

79   Iribe had become: Ibid.

80   She was "devastated": Gabrielle Palasse Labrunie, telephone interview with author, September 7, 2009.

81   "I need it to hold on": Isabelle Fiemeyer, *Coco Chanel: Un parfum de mystère,* p. 109. Sedol, a strong French sedative, was manufactured by Theraplix. It contained morphine chlorhydrate.

81   "My baby has a heart": Wallman/Wartell/Crosby, *My Woman,* recorded by Ted Lewis and his band, Columbia Records 2635-D. Chanel sang it while driving with Gabrielle Palasse Labrunie. Telephone interview with Labrunie, September 6, 2009.

81   "Your Queen succeeds": Randolph Churchill, "Mlle Chanel's Tribute," *Daily Mail,* June 20, 1934.

81   "We are strong": William L. Shirer, *Berlin Diary,* p. 21.

81   He was tracked: CHADAT 7NN 2719.

82   "The Germans are by no means": BNA, letter on British Embassy Berlin letter paper, dated January 3, 1935.

82   The editors revealed: Wistrich, *Who's Who in Nazi Germany,* p. 38.

83   Allard's postwar book: *Quand Hitler espionne la France,* pp. 38–50.

83   The newly single Dincklage: Ledebur report, FSS. Ledebur named the two girls "the Joyce sisters."

83   The letter makes a feeble attempt: German Foreign Ministry Archives, 1934.

83   "To the Honorable Ambassador": Ibid.

84 Prior to Dincklage's: CHADAT 7NN 2973. While photos of Dincklage and Lucie Braun were mentioned as attached, only the latter photo remains in the file.
85 "I fear I shall not": Telegram dated December 2, 1935, Chartwell Trust.
85 His former agent in Toulon: CHADAT 7NN 2973.
86 By November 1938: Ibid.
86 A French agent in Bayonne: Ibid. Aga Baltic was a Swedish manufacturer of a Superhetterodyne radio receiver made in 1938. "Le Grand Livre de la TSF" (old radios), http://www.doctsf.com/grandlivre/index .php.
87 The report continues: Ibid.
87 "Even if no direct proof exists": Ibid. Signed Le Capitan Adjoint, Paillole. Paul Paillole was "one of the best-known figures of wartime French counter espionage, a senior intelligence officer for the Free French and a leading member of the French Resistance." Douglas Porch, *The French Secret Services: From the Dreyfus Affair to the Gulf War,* p. 44. The occupation of France by the Germans froze expulsion measures against Germans. It took until 1947 for the French to legally expel Hans Günther von Dincklage and wife Maximiliane.
87 And what of Catsy?: CHADAT 7NN 2973.
88 "He is seen in Toulon": Ibid. The report then lists seven license plate numbers, including German, Italian, and British ones. Dincklage's own automobile was registered in Monaco. The report does not give the type of automobile that Dincklage was driving.
88 Finally, French authorities: Dessoffy's full name was Countess Dessoffy de Czerneck et Tarko, née Bonneau du Chesne de Beauregard. CHADAT 7NN 2650.
88 The Deuxième Bureau now: CHADAT 7NN 2973.
88 French counterintelligence services: Ibid.
88 The report is a summary: Ibid.
89 In December of that year: Ibid.
89 Months before the Nazi: SSF file, "Dincklage." With the German occupation of France, Maximiliane von Dincklage was one of many German nationals released from the Gurs camp. She would live in occupied Paris during the war. Her family incorrectly believed that as a Jew she might have been obliged to wear a yellow Star of David sewn on her clothing. Schoenebeck family interview by research assistant Sally Gordon-Marks, Hinterstoder, Austria, July 3, 2009.
89 When questioned about Dincklage: Marcel Haedrich, *Coco Chanel: Her Life, Her Secrets,* p. 148.
89 Her grand-niece, Gabrielle Palasse Labrunie, who knew Dincklage well: Gabrielle Palasse Labrunie, interview with author, May 18, 2009.
89 Among them: Pierre Lazareff, *Deadline: The Behind the Scenes Story of the Last Decade in France,* trans. by David Partridge, n.d., p. 110.
89 Pierre Lazareff: Known as "Pierre in suspenders," Lazareff was a giant of the French press ca. 1931: editor of *Paris-Soir*; later, founder of *France-Soir* (2 million copies sold in 1970); and a television personality.
89 Abetz assured his listeners: Lazareff, *Deadline: The Behind the Scenes Story of the Last Decade in France,* pp. 100, 111, 117.

CHAPTER SIX: AND THEN THE WAR CAME

90 "Medieval children playing": Pablo Picasso, *New York Review of Books*, Nov. 25–Dec. 8, 2010, p. 27.

90 *Paris Herald* newsman: Shirer, *Berlin Diary*, pp. 6–8.

92 By June, the Ritz boutiques: Roulet, *Ritz: A Story That Outshines the Legend*, p. 99.

92 Chanel's salesgirls: Edmonde Charles-Roux, *L'Irrégulière*, p. 524.

92 "The first time I saw": Gabrielle Palasse Labrunie, telephone interview with author, April 28, 2009.

93 It was a French version: Charles-Roux, *Chanel*, p. 298.

93 The keystone to peace: Gabrielle Palasse Labrunie, interview with author, Yermenonville, France, April, 27, 2009; Leslie Field, *Bendor, the Golden Duke of Westminster*, p. 262.

95 "because two gentlemen": Wallach, *Chanel: Her Style and Her Life*, p. 19.

96 she "enraged" her: Ibid., p. 112.

96 "Chanel is finished": Galante, *Mademoiselle Chanel*, p. 169.

96 swathing the performers: Charles-Roux, *Chanel*, p. 304.

98 Cocteau remembered: Madsen, *Chanel: A Woman of Her Own*, p. 220.

99 British *Vogue*: Ibid., p. 221.

99 The Chanel collection: Charles-Roux, *Chanel*, p. 302.

100 Clare Boothe Luce: Clare Boothe Luce, *Europe in the Spring*, pp. 61, 63, 126.

101 It was payback: Charles-Roux: *Chanel*, p. 305.

101 "How could I suppose": Haedrich, *Coco Chanel: Her Life, Her Secrets*, p. 142.

101 His anti-Semitism: Edmonde Charles-Roux, interviewed by the author, Paris, April 21, 2009.

101 Chanel's ex-lover: Field, *Bendor, the Golden Duke of Westminster*, p. 265.

102 They believed she was a British agent: ADGMD, personal records, Lombardi, Alberto, No. B728.

102 Italian archives tell: *Archivio centrale dello Stato* (ACS), handwritten letter to the Justice Minister from Lombardi concerning his wife, Vera Bate: timbro della SPD 12.8.41, data in alto 23.8.41, n. 111684 A4-24.8.41.

102 "Mrs. Lombardi": ACS, Ministry of Interior, Envelope 216, Vera Lombardi report.

102 One week later: Ibid.

103 From the time he was mobilized: Gabrielle Palasse Labrunie, interview with author, Yermenonville, France, April, 27, 2009.

103 "Oh, Iribe!": Galante, *Mademoiselle Chanel*, p. 141.

104 "There is nothing worse than solitude": Ibid.

104 "I've closed the business": Charles-Roux, *L'Irrégulière*, pp. 536–37; my translation.

104 "war was a time to hide": Ibid., p. 535.

104 They were furious: Ibid., pp. 533–34.

104 What would Paris wartime: Ibid., p. 534.

104 "Life is about combat: Paul Morand, *L'Allure de Chanel*, p. 206; my translation.

105 "In spite of repeated denials": The article, "Gems of Far East Blend With Gowns," by Kathleen Cannell, did not appear in the *New York Times* until May 6, 1940.

106 He knowingly assured: Gidel, *Coco Chanel,* pp. 292–93.

106 The reports amused: Ibid., p. 302.

107 During one such alert, Coward: Claude Roulet, *Ritz: A Story That Outshines the Legend,* pp. 106–7.

107 Most French families: "Half-Year Mark," *Time,* March 11, 1940.

107 It was worse: "GERMANY: To Paris," *Time,* May 20, 1940, p. 32.

108 A million and a half men: Ousby, *Occupation,* p. 6. Vividly put: had the French war dead of 1914–1918 risen up and marched at an ordinary pace through the Arc de Triomphe, it would have taken eleven days and eleven nights for them to pass through.

108 "What they do with this information": Ousby, *Occupation,* p. 22.

108 A few men: Ibid., p. 14.

108 The French generals: Michael Bloch, *The Secret File of the Duke of Windsor: The Private Papers 1937–1972,* p. 149.

109 Winston Churchill visited: Roulet, *Ritz: A Story That Outshines the Legend,* pp. 103–4.

109 "Hitler and his cohorts": A.P.H. in *Punch,* London, February 14, 1940, as cited in Luce, *Europe in the Spring,* Preface.

109 "Last week long-dreaded World War II": "Half-Year Mark," *Time,* March 11, 1940.

110 They abandoned their mistress: Roulet, *Ritz: A Story That Outshines the Legend,* p. 109.

110 While Europe held its breath: Swiss National Archives N7811B.A.6.

110 Driving a Fiat Topolino: Ibid. License plate no. L 878995.

111 But French counterintelligence: CHADAT 7NN 2650.

111 Dessoffy, the daughter: du Plessix Gray, *Them,* p. 170.

111 had become Dincklage's witness: CHADAT 7NN 2650.

111 Edmonde Charles-Roux recalled: Edmonde Charles-Roux, interview by author, Paris, April 21, 2009.

111 Indeed, with all mail from Germany: ADV 158W848.

111 Moving from one Swiss canton: Schweizerisches Bundesarchiv: Lugano police report dated December 1, 1939, and signed "Botta." In 1939, it was illegal to be in Switzerland without prior permission from Swiss federal or cantonal authorities. Strict laws forced foreigners to register either at a hotel or with the local police. The registration formulas were then collected every evening by a police officer and passed to the Swiss central registry in Bern for routine checking. Any undesirable alien could be immediately penalized and expelled.

111 It turned out: Ibid.

112 Within a few days: Schweizerisches Bundesarchiv, Police de Sûreté, November 24, 1939.

112 A Swiss police officer now called on Dincklage: Ibid.

112 Dincklage used his good looks: FSS documents.

112 Later, the Swiss discovered: From a summary of documents translated by Michael Foedrowitz, 2009, found in Swiss National Archives.

113 They would soon show up: NARA WAAG, Secret Jan. 26 1946, U.S.

Forces Summary. Schweizerisches Bundesarchiv, November 24, 1939, report.

113 In banner headlines: "GERMANY: To Paris," *Time*, May 20, 1940, p. 32.

114 Broadcasting from the German Rundfunk: William L. Shirer, *Berlin Diary*, pp. 332–33.

114 Hitler's orders to his army: Ibid., p. 335.

114 According to Shirer: Ibid., p. 385.

114 Panic seized Paris: *Harper's Bazaar*, October 1939.

115 Clare Boothe Luce was listening: Boothe Luce, *Europe in the Spring*, p. 230.

CHAPTER SEVEN: PARIS OCCUPIED — CHANEL A REFUGEE

116 "For a woman": Charles-Roux: *Chanel*, p. 265. This phrase is translated "cannot betray one's senses."

116 "The airplane has proved": Will Brownell and Richard N. Billings, *So Close to Greatness: A Biography of William C. Bullitt*, p. 255.

116 "The streets are utterly deserted": William L. Shirer, *Berlin Diary*, pp. 412–13.

117 Chanel's trip from Paris: Four million refugees were on the roads of France in June 1940. Vaughan, *FDR's 12 Apostles*, p. 28.

117 "No American after tonight": "Foreign News," *Time*, June 17, 1940, p. 32.

118 "The best the French could hope for": "Foreign News," *Time*, July 1, 1940, p. 25.

118 After Chanel and Larcher crossed the river Garonne: Gabrielle Palasse Labrunie, interview with author, Yermenonville, France, April 27, 2009.

119 Just after noon on June 17: Ousby, *Occupation*, p. 63; Montagnon, *La France dans la guerre de 39–45*, p. 179.

119 Chanel was aghast: Labrunie used Chanel's word for "betrayal": *"trahison."* Labrunie interview, April 27, 2009.

120 "the shipwreck of France": Ousby, *Occupation*, p. 63.

120 "This guy is breaking": Montagnon, *La France dans la guerre de 39–45*, p. 187.

121 For many French men and women: In six weeks in May and June 1940, the French army had suffered 120,000 wounded and 120,000 killed or dead of their wounds. The Germans had suffered 45,000 dead; the Belgians 7,500; the Dutch 2,900; the British 6,800. Montagnon, *La France dans la guerre de 39–45*, p. 207.

121 "The Germans weren't all gangsters": Marcel Haedrich, *Coco Chanel: Her Life, Her Secrets*, p. 144.

121 "scorn, anger, hate": Shirer, *Berlin Diary*, p. 422.

122 Soon, the Nazis forced Pétain: Ibid., pp. 79–81.

122 "Statute on Jews": Thomas Wieder, "Découverte du projet de 'statut des juifs,'" *Le Monde*, October 5, 2010, p. 10.

122 If Vichy was now: Labrunie interview, May 19, 2009.

123 News from André: Katharina and the girls learned that André could have escaped the Maginot Line before capture. His four-man unit had been sharing one bicycle. When it was André's turn to have the bicycle, he could have easily fled. Instead, he let his comrade use the bike to flee hours before the line surrendered. On arriving home, the man wrote to Mme Palasse, telling of André's deed and his probable capture by the Germans.

124 A friend of Chanel's: André-Louis Dubois, *À travers trois Républiques*, pp. 56–60.

124 At Vichy: Haedrich, *Coco Chanel: Her Life, Her Secrets*, p. 143.

125 The Paris Chanel returned to: Allan Mitchell, *Nazi Paris: The History of an Occupation, 1940–1944*, pp. 13–14.

126 "Thanks to the artificial exchange rate": Frederic Spotts, *The Shameful Peace: How French Artists and Intellectuals Survived the Nazi Occupation*, p. 33.

126 Formally correct: For descriptions of the German invaders in Paris, 1940, see photos and text, David Pryce-Jones, *Paris in the Third Reich*, pp. 3–29.

128 On a crisp fall morning: Francine du Plessix Gray, *Them*, p. 218.

130 Dincklage was back: CHADAT 7NN 2973. The British National Archives, Kew, and the National Archives in France contain BCRA (General de Gaulle's intelligence service) documents about Dincklage as an Abwehr agent in France.

130 At age fifty-seven, Chanel: Labrunie interview, May 18, 2009.

131 "On orders from Berlin": CARAN AJ/40/871, "Seizure of the Ritz." See Claude Roulet, *Ritz: A Story That Outshines the Legend*, p. 107. Dincklage's intervention allowing Chanel to stay at the Ritz is confirmed in a *Time* magazine article of June 1998. Edmond Charles-Roux, in *L'Irrégulière*, and author Alex Madsen offer separate versions of how Chanel returned to the Ritz in August 1940. Writer Pierre Galante avoids the subject.

131 In fact, only certain non-Germans: Ibid. "Instruction About Hôtel Ritz" issued by *Der Militärbefehlshaber in Frankreich* command order, Paris, February 2, 1941.

131 Everyone entering or leaving: See CARAN AJ/40/871, "Instruction about Hôtel Ritz" issued by *Der Militärbefehlshaber in Frankreich* command order, Paris, February 2, 1941. For distinguished Nazi guests, see Roulet, *Ritz: A Story That Outshines the Legend*, pp. 108–9.

131 For those allowed entry: Roulet, *Ritz: A Story That Outshines the Legend*, p. 111.

132 "In times like these": Henri Amouroux, *La Vie des Français sous l'Occupation*, p. 141.

132 Chanel believed: Haedrich, *Coco Chanel*, p. 136.

132 Chanel "was seen everywhere": Galante, *Mademoiselle Chanel*, p. 181.

132 "I never saw the Germans": Haedrich, *Coco Chanel: Her Life, Her Secrets*, p. 136.

132 Dincklage dined often: CARAN F/7/15327. Folder 209 "FEIHL."

133 The Serts and their friends: APP DB 540.

133 Chanel preferred hosting: Gabrielle Palasse Labrunie to author in Yermenonville, France, June 9, 2009.

134 Nazi collaborator Fern Bedaux: SSF document. Fern Bedaux used the French term *"une intoxiquée."*

134 "the exterminating angel": Morand, *The Allure of Chanel,* p. 10.

135 He and his "pro-German" wife: Madsen, *A Woman of Her Own,* p. 242.

135 But for a truly amusing evening: Barbara Lambauer, "Francophile contre vents et marée? Otto Abetz et les Français, 1930–1958," *Bulletin du Centre de Recherche Français de Jérusalem* 18 (2007): 159. The Rothschild furniture referred to belonged to Baron Élie Robert—who was a prisoner of the Nazis in Germany during the war.

135 "Coco Chanel . . . indulged": Ousby, *Occupation,* p. 112.

135 "That's the way you overthrow ": Ibid., p. 84.

135 Josée raved: In her memoirs about her father, Josée talks often of Chanel. See Yves Pourcher, *Pierre Laval vu par sa fille,* pp. 213, 215, 313.

136 "in a blacked-out Paris": Pourcher, *Pierre Laval vu par sa fille,* pp. 213–14; my translation.

137 The American Hospital at Neuilly: Keating in an unpublished paper, 1981, found in Hal Vaughan, *Doctor to the Resistance,* pp. 44, 46–48.

137 Even the French staple: Donald and Petie Kladstrup, *Wine and War: The French, the Nazis, and the Battle for France's Greatest Treasure,* pp. 112–16.

CHAPTER EIGHT: DINCKLAGE MEETS HITLER; CHANEL BECOMES AN ABWEHR AGENT

138 "À la guerre comme à la guerre" (Dincklage's quip): Du Plessix Gray, *Them,* p. 218.

138 In early 1941: CHADAT 7NN 2717.

138 In Berlin, Dincklage: CHADAT 7NN 2973.

139 However, a document: CARAN 117M128.

140 "D [Dincklage] is [now] on very bad terms": The French-owned Yugoslavian Bor mines were confiscated by the Nazis in 1940. In a baffling further revelation, French counterintelligence states, "The Gestapo, after having failed to liquidate von D . . . has now decided to get along with him." For Dincklage in Berlin and the Gestapo's attempt to kill him, see CHADAT 7NN 2973: For Vaufreland in Berlin and Tunisia, see BNA document, item 317, H57/139.

140 Meanwhile, Vaufreland had earned: CARAN Z/6/672 greffe 5559, Vaufreland, Abwehr personnel file, Personalbogen, June 9, 1941.

141 They would help Chanel: Ibid. Vaufreland tells how he knew before he met Chanel of her desire to get André Palasse home from Germany.

141 When they returned to Paris: Ibid.

141 A London Free French report: French, British, and American diplomatic reports and intelligence assessments substantiate the London report. BNA: British dispatches, January 20, 1941, Z 407/132/17 and Z 5423. American Consul, Casablanca, letter, May 30, 1941. CARAN 171 mi/125 and 127: "Most Secret, June 25, 1944 Report, Members of German services."

142 Sometime in the spring of 1941: CARAN Z/6/672 greffe 5559.

142 the Abwehr enrolled: APP BA 1990.

143   "Leaving Paris at 20:10 hours": For telegram, CARAN Z/6/672 greffe 5559.
143   Wallace: Edmonde Charles-Roux states that Brian Wallace used "Ramon" as his code name when Chanel was in Madrid in 1943 on her second mission for the Nazis. See Charles-Roux, *L'Irrégulière*, p. 595.
143   "MI, Copy. Enclosure": BNA document 1139.
146   Chanel and Vaufreland: CHADAT 7NN 2717.
146   Vaufreland arranged for Chanel: Vaufreland testimony before Cours de Justice, CARAN Z/6/672 greffe 5559.
146   "Now it was [Chanel's] turn": Edmonde Charles-Roux, *Chanel*, p. 320.

CHAPTER NINE: CHECKMATED BY THE WERTHEIMERS

147   "War or peace she lived": Haedrick, *Coco Chanel: Her Life, Her Secrets,* p. 146.
147   In a 1941 essay: For Sartre, see ibid., p. 157.
149   The telegram read: Jeremy Josephs, *Swastika Over Paris*, p. 70.
149   John Updike noted: John Updike, "Qui qu'a vu Coco?" *New Yorker,* September 21, 1998, pp. 135–36.
149   Chanel had no doubt: Gold and Fitzdale, *Misia*, p. 287.
150   As promised: Vaufreland stated in testimony after the war that a [Prince] Ratibor gave him letters of recommendation to Dr. Blanke, "from whom I wanted to obtain the return of Mlle Chanel's perfume business . . . les Parfums Chanel, of which Mssrs. Wertheimer were the majority shareholders . . . and catalogued a 'Jewish business' assigned to a temporary commissioner." CARAN Z/6/672 greffe 5559; the text of Vaufreland's letter to French prosecuting Judge Roger Serre, December 2, 1946, pp. 34–36. Other documents reveal that the wife of Vaufreland's friend Prince Ernest Ratibor-Corvey was a friend of Dincklage. Dincklage used Princess Ratibor-Corvey as a letter drop in Switzerland in 1939.
150   With the occupation of France: MBF document.
150   Until 1944 he played a key role: Martin Jungius and Wolfgang Seibel at the University of Konstanz wrote how Dr. Blanke

displayed intelligence, determination, and devotion to his convictions . . . committing his energy and resourcefulness to the development of effective machinery for the economic persecution of the Jews . . . Blanke's wartime activities reveal much about [Nazi] bureaucratic perpetrators during the Holocaust . . . In occupied France, Blanke showed no inhibitions against depriving many thousands of Jewish property-owners of the material basis for their existence, rendering them even more defenseless against the attacks of the SS, the Gestapo, and the Nazis' French collaborators . . . Blanke personally carried out supervisory visits to the businesses of Jewish owners, himself ordered the punishment of violations of the anti-Jewish ordinances, and knew full well the impact the measures he ordered had on specific individuals. Blanke's particular commitment was to exclude Jews from the French economy. In France his victims were not the middle-class Jewish neighbors whom he had known in his hometown, but typically the Jewish tradesmen and shop-owners of the Parisian suburbs (many of them East European in origin), as well as the more prominent Jews whose names are emphasized in "The De-Jewification [*sic*] of the French Economy." These were the stereotyped targets of German anti-Semitism, and Blanke . . . accepted the Nazis' anti-Semitic cliches. Blanke was one of the indispensable bureaucrats of the Holocaust . . .

Jungius and Seibel, "The Citizen as Perpetrator: Kurt Blanke and Aryanization in France, 1940–1944," *Holocaust and Genocide Studies* 22, no. 3 (Winter 2008): 441–74.

150 Kristallnacht: On the Night of Broken Glass, November 9–10, 1938, 91 Jews were murdered and 25,000 to 30,000 were arrested and placed in concentration camps; 267 synagogues were destroyed and thousands of homes and businesses were ransacked throughout Germany and Austria.

151 SECM: Société d'Emboutissage et de Constructions Mécaniques. Transfer of 50 million French francs to Amiot's aviation company in August 1939, CHADAT 7NN 2659. A French counterintelligence report states, "Amiot had given the plans for the Amiot 370 bomber."

151 via a bank transfer: The funds were transferred to Amiot via the Banque Manheimer-Mendelson in August 1939. Ibid.

151 "We said goodbye": Bruno Abescat and Yves Stavridès, *L'Express,* July 11, 2005, p. 1.

152 They flocked to cinemas: Between 1940 and 1945, Americans and refugees in New York had nostalgia for Paris and France, a sentiment prominent in major U.S. cities. The defeat of France at the time was the subject of books, magazine pieces, and Hollywood feature films. Typical was the 1942 movie *Casablanca,* with Humphrey Bogart, Ingrid Bergman, and Paul Henreid.

152 "a big-boned, jagged-faced": For a description of Thomas, see NARA, OSS Personnel File, "Thomas, Herbert Gregory," Entry 168A, Box 2. Aline Countess of Romanones, an OSS agent in Madrid, worked for Thomas, code named Argus, at the OSS Madrid station. Her description confirms Thomas's size. Aline Countess of Romanones, *The Spy Wore Red,* p. 83.

153 A vice president: National Archives, NARA, OSS Personnel File, "Thomas, Herbert Gregory," Personal History Statement, SA-One.

154 Second, he had to secure: *Jasmin de Grasse,* the natural essence needed to produce the Chanel No. 5 perfume, is grown only in Grasse in southern France and had to be shipped to the United States in large quantities. Some experts believe Thomas shipped a concentrate, *absolu de jasmin;* 40 to 50 kilograms of the concentrate would be enough for a few years of production. Though illegal, it could be carried by suitcase to Lisbon by train and then by boat to New York.

John Updike wrote in *The New Yorker* that "seven hundred pounds of jasmine had to be smuggled [by Thomas] from Grasse, France, to Hoboken." Updike, "Qui qu'a vu Coco?" *New Yorker,* September 21, 1998, pp. 135–36. The New York Toilet Goods Association told the

State Department in 1941: "A pound of precious natural aromatic product [like jasmine] may sell for as high as four or five thousand dollars in 1941." For the formula being in a Chanel company safe, see Véronique Maurus, "No. 5., l'éternel parfum de femme," *Le Monde,* April 20, 1997, p. 9. Use of anti-Semitic laws, see Updike, "Qui qu'a vu Coco?" *New Yorker.* NARA: American Perfume Association letter to Department of State, March 25, 1941. For "seven hundred pounds of jasmine," see Updike, "Qui qu'a vu Coco?" *New Yorker.* The Chanel No. 5 classic bottle, designed in 1924 by Jean Helleau, has been on display at the Museum of Modern Art in New York City since 1958. No. 5 would become the favorite scent of Marilyn Monroe, Catherine Deneuve, and Vanessa Paradis. In 2010, a 0.25 (7.5ml) bottle sold for over $100 in major U.S. cities and overseas. In 1942: For the date of Thomas's travel: "Studies Cosmetic Needs," *New York Times,* August 18, 1940. Thomas's pseudonym was found thanks to Peter Sichel in a note entitled *Commanderie de Bordeaux History.* Address and C.V. of Thomas from: NARA, OSS Personnel Name File, Thomas, Entry 168 A, Box 2. After the United States entered World War II in December 1941, Thomas took a leave of absence for the Wertheimer firm and worked for General William "Wild Bill" Donovan's Office of Strategic Services (OSS). As Chief of Station at Madrid and Lisbon, he headed all U.S. intelligence-gathering activities on the strategic Iberian Peninsula. He was also responsible for running OSS agents into France. With war's end, the Wertheimers rewarded Thomas by appointing him president of Chanel, Inc., in 1945, a job he kept until he retired in 1972. Allen Dulles, a senior officer of the OSS (and later, head of the CIA), interviewed Thomas for a job with the OSS. In April 1942, Dulles wrote: "Thomas has rather extraordinary qualifications and is quite an impressive fellow. If he checks out satisfactorily, I think we should make use of him."

155 "The feats accomplished": Details of the Thomas mission for the Wertheimers in France in 1940, drawn from Bruno Abescat and Yves Stavridès, "Derrière l'empire Chanel," *L'Express,* August 11, 2005, p. 2; Phyllis Berman and Zina Sewaya, "The Billionaires Behind Chanel," *Forbes,* April 3, 1989, p. 104; and Updike, "Qui qu'a vu Coco?" *New Yorker.* Thomas's appointments as president and later chairman of Chanel, Inc., from: "Executive Changes," *New York Times,* April 14, 1971. See www.zoominfo.com/people/Sichel_Peter_14493897.aspx.

155 Sichel believes: Peter Sichel, e-mail messages to author, October 2007 and May 2008. The Louis d'Or was first introduced by Louis XIII in 1640. The name derives from the depiction of the portrait of King Louis on one side of the coin. The French royal coat of arms is on the reverse.

155 In a 1989 interview: For gangsters' help, see Berman and Sewaya, "The Billionaires Behind Chanel," *Forbes.*

155 From other sources: The *Excalibur* was used as a troop ship by the U.S. Army. She was sunk off the North African coast in November 1942 during a sea battle surrounding the invasion of North Africa by U.S. and U.K. forces.

CHAPTER TEN: A MISSION FOR HIMMLER

156 "She wanted to live": Charles-Roux, *L'Irrégulière*, p. 356.
156 On Monday morning: *Le Matin*, Monday, November 9, 1942, front page.
156 Another newspaper assured: *Le Petit Parisien*, November 10, 1942, front page.
156 "President Franklin D. Roosevelt's baby": Churchill's words, borrowed from a phrase spoken by Talleyrand in 1812 after the Battle of Borodino, were spoken at the Lord Mayor's Day luncheon in London on November 10, 1942.
157 "horizontal collaborator": Carmen Callil, *Bad Faith: A Forgotten History of Family, Fatherland and Vichy*, p. 305. BBC broadcasts, see Frederic Spotts, *The Shameful Peace: How French Artists and Intellectuals Survived the Nazi Occupation*, p. 255.
157 The Free French knew: For Josée Laval de Chambrun's possessing Jewish paintings stolen by Nazis from the Schloss family and Rosenberg collections, see Callil, *Bad Faith: A Forgotten History of Family, Fatherland and Vichy*, pp. 335, 352.
157 The *Life* magazine article: "Black List," *Life*, August 24, 1942, p. 86.
157 Now he was condemned: See CARAN F/7/14939, "Black List," 27/12/43, "Black List," *Life*, August 24, 1942, p. 86. Chambrun told the *New York Times* in October 1941 that all allegations were "ridiculous." René de Chambrun, *Mission and Betrayal*, p. 140.
157 "Darlan and Juin": Yves Pourcher, *Pierre Laval vu par sa fille*, p. 270; unpublished manuscript.
158 "It's tough, collaboration is": For more information on Chambrun's collaboration, see CARAN F/7/15327, folder 208 3. For Chambrun representing National City Bank and General Motors (GM) in Paris and its businesses in occupied France, and for GM's investments in Nazi Germany, see Pierre Abramovici, *Enquête avec Carine Lournaud. Un rocher bien occupé. Monaco pendant la guerre 1939–1945*, pp. 78–79. Chambrun was Marshal Pétain's godson. He acted as a link between Pétain and Laval and between Vichy and the United States. When Paris was liberated, the Chambruns hid near Paris. René de Chambrun's arrest was ordered by French authorities. Later, he appeared before Parquet du Cour de Justice of the Département de la Seine and was cleared of all charges on August 11, 1948. Source M. Vallée-M. Vielledent, Parquet de la Cour de Justice du Departement de la Seine, 11 Aout 1948, Affaire: Pineton de Chambrun René, Ordonnance de Classement. He was also reappointed to the bar in France, his "patriotism unquestioned." See also "Rapport de René de Chambrun au Juge Marchat lors de son inculpation, au lendemain de la Libération," mimeographed document, n.d. See David Thompson's *A Biographical Dictionary of War Crimes Proceedings, Collaboration Trials and Similar Proceeding Involving France in World War II*, written and compiled for the Grace Dangberg Foundation, Inc., http://reocities.com.

158   The winter of 1943: www.meteo-paris.com.

158   By year's end: Vaughan, *Doctor to the Resistance,* p. 78.

158   Paris, once the center: Mitchell, *Nazi Paris: The History of an Occupation, 1940–1944,* pp. 94–98.

159   Dincklage and Chanel had to wonder: Quote about Chanel's remark on Côte d'Azur, found in Antony Beevor and Artemis Cooper, *Paris After the Liberation, 1944–1949,* p. 134. Death List: CARAN F/7/14939, "Black List," 27/12/43. See also APP BA 1990.

159   Dincklage knew he was: See: French BCRA counterintelligence report, CHADAT 7NN 2973.

159   Momm wanted Dincklage: BNA, KV2/159. In Ledebur's file, he identifies Momm's brother precisely as head of the Abwehr economic espionage service in Istanbul: "IWi K.O. Istanbul, Turkey." (The letters "IWi K.O." signify economic espionage in a foreign state.) The author corresponded with Theodor Momm's daughters, Monika and Kathrin (last names withheld by the author), in Germany. Monika was at first willing to meet the author's German assistant in mid-January 2010. Monika stated that her sister, Kathrin, had papers and photos related to Chanel's mission in 1943. However, Kathrin decided at the last moment and for as long as Momm's wife (name withheld) was alive that she would not agree to reveal any "private documents/letters." From Michael Foedrowitz (author's research assistant in Berlin), e-mails to author, January 26 and February 8, 2010.

159   Chanel would have moved: Gabrielle Palasse Labrunie confirms that her aunt wanted to keep Dincklage in Paris. Gabrielle Palasse Labrunie, telephone interview with author, February 12, 2010.

160   Dincklage would accompany: BNA, KV2/159, Joseph von Ledebur-Wicheln file.

160   In the early winter: Ibid.

160   While in Berlin: For Dincklage's mother—Valery Cutter von Dincklage, known as "Lorry"—being at Rosenkranz, Schinkel, near Kiel in 1943, see Swiss file, L878995 Hf. By 1945, more than half of Kiel would be destroyed by Allied bombings.

161   Dincklage returned to Paris: Joseph von Ledebur-Wicheln File, National Archives, Kew.

161   "It was established": Gidel, *Coco Chanel,* p. 315; my translation.

161   James Lonsdale-Bryans: A handwritten note by the MI5 stated: "He went to Italy with the knowledge of the Foreign Office in order to develop his contacts. He greatly exceeded his instructions." MI5 decided against having him arrested, due to the possible support he was receiving from members of Parliament (potentially including Neville Chamberlain) and the embarrassment this would have caused. Lonsdale-Bryans was on friendly terms with powerful members of the British aristocracy: Lord Halifax, the Duke of Buccleuch, and Lord Brocket, who also were Nazi sympathizers.

161   In Nazi Germany: Robert S. Wistrich, *Who's Who in Nazi Germany,* p. 114.

161   As early as fall 1942: Reinhard R. Doerries, *Hitler's Intelligence Chief, Walter Schellenberg,* p. 107.

162 "a way out": Ibid., p. 172.

162 "university-educated intellectual": William L. Shirer, *The Rise and Fall of the Third Reich*, p. 653.

162 "the sixth most powerful man: Anthony Cave Brown, *Bodyguard of Lies*, p. 457.

162 "By all counts": NARA, Schellenberg file, p. 224.

162 With Himmler's approval: Doerries, *Hitler's Last Chief of Foreign Intelligence: Allied Interrogations of Walter Schellenberg*, p. 39.

163 "Pheiffer told me": MI6 and Service Spécial document, SSF and BNA, KV2/159.

164 "Dincklage had been": Ibid.

165 In 1938: Ibid. For Dincklage's spy work in Switzerland, see Swiss file L878995 Hf.

165 "I couldn't use Dincklage": Quotes from SSF and BNA, KV2/159 Ledebur file.

165 "Dincklage had trouble": Ledebur file at KEW, ibid. I was unable to determine which archives Ledebur consulted.

165 For Ledebur, the case: Ibid.

166 Ledebur may never have learned: SSF document.

166 A secret postwar report: NARA December 27, 1946, report, U.S. Political Advisor in Germany, CI-FIR/130. I failed to find information giving the exact amount of money Chanel received from the SS or how the SS funds were dispersed. Chanel and Dincklage must have needed large sums of money to finance their mission in Madrid. After the war Kutschmann was wanted in Germany for having participated in the mass murder in 1942 of Polish Jews and the murder of thirty-six Polish intellectuals in 1941. Sometime in 1945 he escaped to Argentina disguised as a Carmelite monk. He disappeared into Argentina by the time a warrant was issued for his arrest by West German authorities in 1967.

166 About the same time: Doerries, *Hitler's Intelligence Chief, Walter Schellenberg* p. 85.

166 While in Turkey: In 1943, Ambassador Papen and Abwehr agent Erich Vermehren were asked to meet with Archbishop (later Cardinal) Francis Spellman in Istanbul. The Gestapo learned of Vermehren's "peace initiative" and had him recalled to Germany. Vermehren defected to the British in Istanbul. He and his wife were sent to England. It is possible that Rittmeister Momm wanted Dincklage to take over Vermehren's job in Turkey with the Abwehr. For Schellenberg's discussions with Ambassador Papen, see ibid., p. 136.

167 He and his colleagues: Uki Goñi, *The Real Odessa*, pp. 9–10.

167 Schellenberg was so concerned: Doerries, *Hitler's Intelligence Chief, Walter Schellenberg*, p. 77.

167 By the late summer . . . Major Theodor Momm: From German National Archives: NSDAP v. 1.5.37 Nr. 4428309. Momm's Abwehr unit was identified as Abwehrstelle, Wehrbezirke–Generalkommando–Headquarters Military Districts. See also APP GA LI2.

167 Arriving in Berlin: The date of Momm's visit to Berlin is erroneous in the British transcript of Schellenberg's interrogation. It is incorrectly

recorded as April 1944. It may have been a slip by Schellenberg or a fault in transcribing the interrogation file. A host of archival documents at Kew and Churchill's Chartwell papers place Momm's visit in the late fall or early winter of 1943. NARA, Schellenberg file, p. 65.

167   Dincklage immediately made preparations: It is not clear that Momm returned to Paris at this time. He may have communicated Schellenberg's summons to bring Chanel to Berlin via telephone or a secure SS cable system.

168   they could travel: Chanel's travel arrangements, arrival, and stay in Berlin were reconstructed by Michael Foedrowitz.

169   "I was finished": Schellenberg quote in Doerries, *Hitler's Intelligence Chief, Walter Schellenberg,* p. 240.

169   The April date: See APP BA1990, Report on Chanel's passport. 1944 Chartwell documents for the date of Chanel's letter from Madrid.

170   "interned with [her] husband": Lombardi was not imprisoned.

170   "[Pietro] Badoglio": Badoglio was an Italian general and politician. On July 24, 1943, when Italy had suffered several setbacks in World War II, Mussolini summoned the Fascist Grand Council, which voted no confidence in Mussolini. The following day Il Duce was removed from government by King Victor Emmanuel III and arrested. Badoglio was named prime minister of Italy and, while mass confusion in Italy reigned, he eventually signed an armistice with the Allies. According to Italian documents, at the time of the Schellenberg-Chanel meeting, Colonel Alberto Lombardi, Vera Bate Lombardi's husband, headed an Italian unit in the Mediterranean Theater of Operations and was engaged in fighting Allied units. Mussolini was later rescued by German troops and set up an Italian government above the Po River in North Italy under the Nazis.

171   "Dincklage was to act": Chanel, Momm, and Dincklage's visit is covered in NARA, "Final Report," Schellenberg file, 65; OSS file, XE001752, Box 195, 65. For Dincklage being a member of the Abwehr and SD, and for Schieber, see Doerries, *Hitler's Last Chief of Foreign Intelligence: Allied Interrogations of Walter Schellenberg,* pp. 164–65; see ibid., p. 240, for details of how the report was prepared, and the fact that material was omitted by the British when shared with OSS. The report is incomplete as it appears in NARA; I have been unable to locate the material concealed by the British. In Schellenberg's biography, *The Labyrinth,* he fails to mention Chanel, her visit, his plan to use her to contact Churchill, or her generous care of Schellenberg after his release from an Allied prison for war crimes. Doerries, *Hitler's Last Chief of Foreign Intelligence: Allied Interrogations of Walter Schellenberg,* p. 164.

171   Charles-Roux in her biography: *Chanel* (London: Jonathan Cape, 1976), pp. 332–37. Despite a request, I was never able to obtain a copy of the letter.

171   During the early war years: ACS, Minister of the Interior, Political Police, April 21, 1941, report.

171   Her letter, "My Dear": The Sir Winston Churchill Archive Trust, CHAR 2/255, Bate, letter, June 1935.

172   Vera, "suspected": Italian National Archives, King's Provincial Police Headquarters, November 12, 1943.

172 "The person [Vera Lombardi]": Italian National Archives, King's Provincial Police Headquarters, November 24, 1943.

173 "Passport applied for": APP BA 1990. Chanel's birth date is given incorrectly as ten years later—in 1893. I never discovered who issued Vera Lombardi's passport used to travel to Paris and Madrid from Rome.

173 a direct order from the Paris Chief: Ibid.

173 "there was conclusive": CHAR 20/198, Letter, Pierson Dixon to Rowan, September 30, 1944.

174 Walter Kutschmann: Goñi, *The Real Odessa*, p. 241.

174 "A week after Vera": NARA, December 10, 1946, report. NARA, Schellenberg file, 65.

174 At Madrid: Documents including Chanel's handwritten letter to Churchill uncovered at the British National Archives at Kew. Churchill's private papers at Chartwell, and Count Joseph Ledebur's testimony after the war, confirm what happened when Chanel arrived in Madrid in the winter of 1943–1944.

174 "with Schellenberg's permission": NARA, Schellenberg file, 65.

174 "On her arrival at that city": Ibid.

176 "Peut être Randolph": Randolph Churchill was a close friend to Chanel. Note from Hankey and Chanel letter from Sir Winston Churchill Archive Trust, Chartwell, CHAR 20/198 A.

176 Churchill was not in London: Information about Churchill's illness, see Field Marshal Lord Alanbrooke, *War Diaries,* pp. 497–515.

177 Later, Chanel would travel: Les Archives du Monde, February 8–9, 2004, 81. Paragraph drawn from Charles-Roux, *L'Irrégulière,* p. 601.

177 The letter contained a plea: CHAR 20/198A. The envelope addressed to Lady Sankey is from Hôtel Ritz stationery—raising the possibility that Vera was staying at the hotel, presumably at Chanel's expense. From the moment Vera was released from the Roman prison, she was penniless.

CHAPTER ELEVEN: COCO'S LUCK

180 "France Is a Battlefield Again": *Le Matin,* June 7, 1944, front page.

180 It was a grim moment: CARAN, F/7/14939. Chanel's name appears on a list in an F.F.I. report dated "27.12.43."

180 On the English coast: Stephen E. Ambrose, *The Supreme Commander: The War Years of General Dwight D. Eisenhower,* p. 419.

181 Whereas, in Berlin: William L. Shirer, *The Rise and Fall of the Third Reich,* p. 1041.

181 Von Rundstedt was sacked: Ibid. For Rommel's suicide and funeral, pp. 1078–80.

181 As Allied bombers struck: *Paris-Soir,* June 7, 1944, front page. Soot from burning documents: Centre historique des archives nationales, *La France et la Belgique sous l'Occupation allemande 1940–1944,* p. 46. Living at rue Cambon: Telephone interview with Gabrielle Palasse Labrunie, February 12, 2010.

181 In Berlin: Until Germany surrendered a year later, Schellenberg never ceased trying to find a way out for himself and Himmler. They knew

246 NOTES TO PAGES 182–188

what fate was reserved for them at the hands of the Allies. See Doerries, *Hitler's Intelligence Chief, Walter Schellenberg,* pp. 302, 327. Hal Vaughan, *Doctor to the Resistance,* p. 158.

182   With his partisan fighters: Cyril Eder, *Les Comtesses de la Gestapo,* p. 208.

182   "He had something": CARAN Z/6/672 greffe 5559.

182   Chanel's friend: Lifar rehearsals, evacuation, and at Chanel's apartment, see David Pryce-Jones, *Paris in the Third Reich,* p. 188.

182   "I couldn't walk": Galante, *Mademoiselle Chanel,* p. 185.

182   "Feelings of hatred": Frederic Spotts, *The Shameful Peace: How French Artists and Intellectuals Survived the Nazi Occupation,* p. 254.

183   "Paris ravaged!": Éric Roussel, *Charles de Gaulle,* p. 450; my translation.

183   To watch de Gaulle's march: see Arthur Gold and Robert Fizdale, *Misia,* p. 292.

184   Two weeks later: Charles-Roux, *Chanel,* p. 345.

184   After the liberation: Pryce-Jones, *Paris in the Third Reich,* p. 206.

185   Among them: SSF.

185   During the occupation: Ibid.

184   After the war: Report of von Schoenebeck family, interviews by Sally Gordon-Mark, Griesser Haus, Hinterstoder, Austria, July 1–3, 2009.

185   A secret postwar French intelligence report: SSF.

185   She had not lived in hiding: Ibid.

185   To gain her release: Ibid. Among others who furnished a favorable reference was Catherine Jouhakoff, who furnished women's lingerie to Catsy.

186   "Dincklage was an active": Gabrielle Chanel's name as originally written, mistakenly, on her birth certificate of 1883.

186   "Catsy's friend": Abetz's telephone warning to Catsy von Schoenebeck was given to Catsy's maid, Mme Bartuel, at her apartment at 77, rue de Longchamp, Paris.

186   The Schoenebeck family: Interview with Schoenebeck family, Sally Gordon-Mark, Hinterstoder, Austria, July 3, 2009.

186   Since 1942: CARAN F/7/14939.

186   Now, in the first week: Chanel was suspected by French intelligence services of supplying "intelligence for the enemy." APP BA 1990. Letter from CARAN junior archivist to Sally Gordon-Mark, Paris, July 2, 2008.

186   Chanel's biographers report: Galante, *Mademoiselle Chanel,* p. 186; Marcel Haedrich, *Coco Chanel: Her Life, Her Secrets,* p. 148; Axel Madsen, *Chanel: A Woman of Her Own,* p. 262.

187   "Churchill had me freed": Gabrielle Palasse Labrunie, telephone interview with author, November 8, 2009.

187   "protect Chanel": Paul Morand, *The Allure of Chanel,* p. 178. Edmonde Charles-Roux confirmed Duff Cooper's intervention. Edmonde Charles-Roux, telephone interview with author, Paris, January 12, 2010.

187   Chanel's maid Germaine: Gabrielle Palasse Labrunie, telephone interview with author, February 12, 2010. Labrunie reconfirmed that Chanel's maid, Germaine, had told her of Ambassador Cooper's message from Westminster.

187   "had Chanel been made to stand trial": Charles Higham, *The Duchess of Windsor: The Secret Life,* pp. 359–62.

188   "By one of those": Madsen, *Chanel: A Woman of Her Own,* p. 263.

188 Chanel made frequent trips: Gold and Fizdale, *Misia,* pp. 300–1.

189 "When Madame Lombardi": Sir Winston Churchill Archive Trust, CHAR 20/198A, letter from P.N. Loxley, December 28, 1944.

189 "December 1941": This date is an error. Lombardi didn't get to Paris until late October 1943.

190 "from the outset": CHAR 20/198 letter, Pierson Dixon to Rowan, September 30, 1944.

190 "Allied Forces Headquarters": Telegram, Foreign Office to Madrid, D. 3:10. p.m. January 4, 1945. CHAR 20/198.

191 "I have shown the Prime Minister": See January 8, 1945, Top Secret to Colonel Hill-Dillon. CHAR 20/198.

191 "My Dear Winston": CHAR 20/198.

191 General Schellenberg: SS General Schellenberg took over the Abwehr after the arrest of Admiral Canaris for treason in 1945.

192 According to the Swiss Aliens Police: Swiss Federal Archives, letter of the United-Silk Weaving Mill Ltd., Kreefeld, Berlin, November 21, 1944, to Swiss Legation, Bern. Translation by Michael Foedrowitz.

192 The Swiss authorities saw: Résumé of Dincklage matters, Swiss National Archives, JAEGGI, November 1950, and Bern, January 15, 1950.

193 "the special French court": Letter from CARAN senior archivist to Sally Gordon-Mark, Paris, July 2, 2008.

194 Nevertheless, court mandates: CARAN Z/6/672 greffe 5559.

194 "Spatz . . . was her living hell": "Derrière l'empire Chanel," Charles-Roux, *L'Irrégulière,* pp. 646–48; my translation.

194 Pierre Reverdy knew of Chanel's: Charles-Roux, *L'Irrégulière,* p. 649; my translation.

194 The interrogation: For various reasons, Vaufreland was freed and re-arrested during this five-year period. The jury was selected because they had no record of collaboration with the enemy. The procedures of trial for collaborators with the Nazi regime during the occupation were decided by General Charles de Gaulle's provisional government in September 1944.

194 Her interrogation by Leclercq: Memorandum prepared by Jules-Marc Baudel, Esq., who analyzed French legal documents to assist the author.

194 "Chanel began by telling": Testimony of Gabrielle Chanel, June 4, 1948, Cour de Justice, Paris, before Judge Fernand Paul Leclercq. CARAN Z/6/672 greffe 5559.

199 There is no record: Cyril Eder, *Les Comtesses de la Gestapo,* p. 204

199 "Before the war": CARAN Z/6/672 greffe 5559, Testimony of André Palasse, forty-two years old, nephew of Chanel, before Judge Roger Serre on November 20, 1947.

200 six years in prison: Ibid.

200 "The answers Mademoiselle Chanel gave": Ibid.

202 "The days of the German occupation": Based on numerous statements made to the author in 1953 and later.

202 Hans Schillinger, a friend: Axel Madsen, *Chanel: A Woman of Her Own,* p. 264.

202 Suddenly the two men: Interview with Volkmar von Arnim by Michael Foederwitz, Schinkel, Germany, August 11, 2008. Also BNA Foreign Office file.

202   He was found to be carrying: BNA Foreign Office file. Beglaubigte Abschrift (authenticated transcript), Certificate, signed Capt. A. H. Haynes, December 3, 1945.

203   He and Schillinger were arrested: BNA, March 16, 1948, War Office letter. To a Mrs. Pollack.

203   During questioning: BNA. Letter from Major General to German Internal Affairs Department, Foreign Office, London, November 13, 1947.

203   "Mademoiselle Chanel has stated": Great Britain, Zonal Executive Offices, B.A.O.R. 1, Letter from Major General to Foreign Office, London, Feb. 25, 1948.

CHAPTER TWELVE: COMEBACK COCO

204   "I have never known failure": Morand, *The Allure of Chanel*, p. 174.

204   An aging Chanel: Valentine Lawford, *Horst*, p. 192.

204   However, there were rumors: Gabrielle Palasse Labrunie, telephone interview with author, September 9, 2010.

204   When Chanel saw a draft: Paul Morand, *The Allure of Chanel*, p. 178.

205   "was not to her taste": Morand, *The Allure of Chanel*, p. 179.

205   "in these three hundred": Ibid.

205   "Chanel had a childhood fear": Ibid.

205   In June 1951: ECR, Chanel, pp. 357–58. Wistrich, *Who's Who in Nazi Germany*, p. 222.

206   "Dr. Lang and his wife": Doerries, *Hitler's Intelligence Chief*, p. 284, drawn from Dr. Lang's memoirs.

207   "Madame Chanel offered us": Charles-Roux, *Chanel*, p. 380.

207   "They spent time together": Pierre Galante, *Mademoiselle Chanel*, pp. 189–90.

207   Asked to describe her mood: Ibid.

208   Chanel hardly spoke of fashion: Ibid.

208   "Chanel was somewhat lost: Lawford, *Horst*, pp. 322–24.

209   In the spring of 1947: Bruno Abescat and Yves Stavridès, "Derrière l'empire Chanel," *L'Express*.

209   "Now, I'm rich": Galante, *Mademoiselle Chanel*, p. 193.

209   "every thirty seconds": "Chanel No. 5 Perfume History," Dulcinea Norton-Smith, http://www.suite101.com/content/icons-chanel-no-5-perfume-a44263, February 11, 2008.

210   "I cannot stand lawyers": Claude Delay, *Chanel solitaire*, p. 242.

210   A transcript of the BBC interview: René de Chambrun lived to be ninety-two, and died in 2002. The BBC documentary *Reputations* was last broadcast on BBC 4 on January 29, 2009. Date of first broadcast unknown.

210   In the fall of 1953: Galante, *Mademoiselle Chanel*, pp. 204–9.

211   A reporter from the major French daily: Ibid., p. 209.

211   "Her dresses were good": As quoted by Charles-Roux in *Le Figaro Madame*: conversation Edmonde Charles-Roux et Audrey Tautou, May 11, 2009.

211 "likened to a herd of geese": Edmonde Charles-Roux, interview with author, Paris, April 21, 2009.

211 "You know, I want to": Charles-Roux, *Chanel*, p. 367.

212 "[Chanel] has influenced": Galante, *Mademoiselle Chanel*, pp. 210–11.

212 Marlene Dietrich came: Ibid., p. 212.

212 The company was broke: Ibid., p. 207.

212 In the spring of 1954: Ibid., p. 217. Also Gidel, *Coco Chanel*, p. 350.

212 "[Chanel's] return": "Ease and Casualness Abound in Chanel's Autumn Showing," *New York Times*, October 6, 1954.

212 As befitting a fashion queen: Marcus, *Minding the Store*.

213 The reporter found her: Lillian Ross, "The Strong Ones," *The New Yorker*, September 28, 1957.

213 "I left Paris": Madsen, *Chanel: A Woman of Her Own*, p. 315.

213 "almost love at first sight": Lilou Marquand, *Chanel m'a dit*, p. 125.

214 To reward his loyalty: Marcel Haedrich, *Coco Chanel: Her Life, Her Secrets*, pp. 256–57.

214 Forgetting the thirty years: Marquand, *Chanel m'a dit*, p. 127.

214 "In the last moment of her life": Janet Wallach, *Chanel: Her Style and Her Life*, p. 160.

215 "No matter the age": Delay, *Chanel solitaire*, pp. 252–53.

215 "enduring allure": Wallach, *Chanel: Her Style and Her Life*, p. 165. Photographs: ibid.; Edmonde Charles-Roux photo collection, *Le Temps Chanel*, p. 330; Lawford, *Horst*, p. 154.

216 "In my day": Galante, *Mademoiselle Chanel*, p. 263.

216 "Well, that's how one dies": Ibid. Also Isabelle Fiemeyer, *Coco Chanel: Un parfum de mystère*, p. 161.

217 On the third Wednesday: Bruno Dethomas, *Le Monde*, March 23, 1973, found in *Le Monde, Les Grands Procès: 1944–2010*, pp. 211–13.

218 His claim was contested: Ibid.

218 Still, Mironnet's claim was supported: Ibid.

218 Lilou claimed that Chanel: Ibid.

218 When the document was exhibited: Ibid.

218 How did it all end: Telephone conversation with Gabrielle Palasse Labrunie, March 26, 2010.

218 Dincklage was cremated: German memo from Florian M. Beierl to the author, November 2009, and in a memo to me from Michael Foedrowitz, my research assistant in Berlin, April 3, 2010.

EPILOGUE

220 "From this century": Charles-Louis Foulon, *André Malraux et le rayonnement culturel de la France*, p. 99; Michel Guerrin, "André Malraux, la culture en solitaire," *Le Monde*, June 25, 2010.

221 "She looks at you tenderly": Galante, *Mademoiselle Chanel*, p. 260.

222 "Spatz was her damnation": Edmonde Charles-Roux, *L'Irrégulière*, p. 648; my translation.

222 "Dear Coco": Reverdy poem reprinted in ibid., p. 649; my translation.

BIBLIOGRAPHY

ARCHIVES

Archives de la ville de Sanary-sur-Mer, France:
Series 12: Police générale étrangers, réfugiés

Archives départementales du Var, France:
158 W 848

Archives de la Préfecture de Police, Paris, France:
Series BA: 1745, 1846, 1990, 2140, 2141, 2176, 2369, 2430
Series DB: 540
Series GA: D2, R8, L12, P8, S6, T2

July 29, 2009, letter from Commissaire divisionnaire françoise Gicquel, Cabinet du Préfet, Service des archives et du musée

Bibliothèque nationale de France:
"Paris-Var-Méditerranée," 1935–36, 1938, JO-55926

Bundesarchiv, Berlin: SS files, federal archives

Central Archives of the State Archives, Archivio centrale dello Stato, documents of Mussolini's secretary:
Ordinary correspondence, envelop 1726, file no. 523074

Centre Historique des Archives du Département de l'Armée de terre CHADAT, Vincennes, France:
Series 7NN 2ème Bureau : 2145, 2162, 2164, 2268, 2402, 2502, 2515, 2641, 2650, 2655, 2659, 2708, 2717, 2719, 2735, 2736, 2737, 2752, 2973

Centre de Recherches des Archives Nationales CARAN, Paris, France:
Series AJ/40 German/economic files: 871
Series F/7/ Police: 14713, 14714, 14939, 14940, 14946, 15142, 15299, 15305, 15327, 15332
Series 3AG2 prefix 171/MI/ BCRA Files:
112, 119, 125, 127, 128, 326
Series 3W/354 Archives de Berlin: Bordereau 2597, Bordereau 2745, no. 4
Series Z/6/762 greffe 5559 Justice File

The Chartwell Trust, West Kent, UK:
1/272/83
2/255/25–27

20/173/44
20/181/19
20/198A/62, 63, 65–69, 71–82, 86–92

Hanover Registry Office:
Standesamt Nr 0193 Eintrag 7181

Harry Ransom Center, University of Texas at Austin:
Sybille Bedford Papers, Box 46.1

Landesarchiv, Berlin State Archives:
Bestand B Rep 012
Abt. 460 Nr. 1789, reference D 120—Denazification file
Abt. 611 Sta Nr. 53778 Citizenship file
Abt. 761 Nr. 18049 Reparation file

Ministero della Difesa, Rome, Italy:
Prot. n. M_D/GMIL V 16 5/0367479.

Archivio di Stato—Ministry of the Interior, Political police, personal records,
Rome, Italy: B728, "Lombardi Alberto."

National Archives and Records Administration, College Park, Maryland
"Walter Schellenberg," File no. XE001752, Box 195
RG No. 319, Stack Area 270, Row 84, Compartment 8, Shelf 3
"OSS-Schellenberg," Entry 125A, Box 2, Folder 21
RG No. 226, Stack Area 190, Row 7, Compartment 19, Shelf 3
"OSS-Schellenberg," Entry 171, Box 10, Folder 61
RG No. 226, Stack Area 190, Row 9, Compartment 10, Shelf 6
"CIA Name File—Alois Brunner," RG N 263, Stack Area 2000,
Row 6, Compartment 4, Box 9

National Archives, Kew, England:
Registry nos. Z 407/132/17 and Z 5423/1698/17
Letter signed Eric Phipps, British Embassy, Berlin, January 3, 1935
File no. CG503503184
File: Premier 3/181/10

Politisches Archiv des Auswärtigen Amts, Deutsche Botschaft Paris, Political
Archives of German Foreign Office, German Embassy, Paris:
Akte 681c press attaché, 2 volumes. 1933–36
Akte 681/5 c Paris IV press attaché, File 1
General activites
Akte 1726

Services spéciaux, France, including:
Renseignements généraux
Sûreté nationale
Sûreté générale

Swiss Federal and Cantonal Archives, Bern, Switzerland:
File Nos.: C.16.1373 1939–1940; 878995 1950

United States Department of State, Washington, D.C.:
RG 59, Central Decimal File 1940–44, 800–20252/29 Lombardi, Vera

Archival searches for author were carried out in the following locations by the following individuals:

United States (Carolyn C. Miller)

National Archives and Records Administration, College Park, Maryland
United States Holocaust Memorial Museum, Washington, D.C.

Germany and Switzerland (Michael Foedrowitz)

Aufstellung der benutzten Archive und Institutionen
Militärgeschichtliches Forschungsamt MGFA, Potsdam
Politisches Archiv des Auswärtigen Amtes PAdAA, Berlin
Stadtarchiv Hannover
Landesarchiv Berlin
Bundesarchiv Berlin
Bundesarchiv-Militärarchiv Freiburg BAMA
Stadtarchiv Kaufbeuren
Wehrmachtsauskunftsstelle WASt, Berlin
Archivgemeinschaft Gettorf
Landesarchiv Schleswig Holstein LASH, Schleswig
Schweizerisches Bundesarchiv BAR, Bern
Freie Universität Berlin, Institut für Meteorologie
Archives cantonales vaudoises
Einwohnermeldeamt Gemeinde Berchtesgaden
Einwohnermeldeamt Gemeinde Schönau

Texas (Milanne Hahn)

The Sybille Bedford Papers, Harry Ransom Center of the University of Texas, Austin, Texas

France (Sally Gordon-Mark)

Archives du Département du Var, Draguignon
Archives de la Préfecture de Police, Paris
Archives de la Ville de Paris
Archives de la Ville de Sanary-sur-Mer
BDIC, Nanterre
Bibliothèque Municipale de la Ville de Toulon
Bibliothèque Nationale de France, Sites Mitterrand et Richelieu, Paris
Cabinet du Ministre de l'Intérieur, Mission des Archives Nationales, Paris
Centre d'Accueil et de Recherche des Archives Nationales, Paris
Centre des Archives Contemporaines Fontainebleau
Centre Historique des Archives du Département de l'Armée de Terre Vincennes

Établissement de Communication et de Production Audiovisuelle de la Défense, Ivry-sur-Seine
La Mairie de la Ville de Nice
Service spécial, Paris

Rome (Francesca Di Pasquale)

Archivio centrale dello Stato
Archivio della Direzione generale per il personale militare del Ministero della difesa
Archivio di Stato di Genova
Archivio di Stato di Roma
Biblioteca dell'Archivio centrale dello Stato
Biblioteca di storia moderna e contemporanea
Biblioteca Universitaria Alessandrina

Britain (Philip Parkinson)

British Library, London
British Library Newspaper Library, London
Churchill College, Cambridge
Hurlingham Polo Association, Little Coxwell, Faringdon
National Archives, Kew, London
Westminster Reference Library, London

Warsaw (Joanna Beta)

Archiwum Akt Nowych
Archiwum Państwowe m. st. Warszawy
Instytut Pamięci Narodowej

CORRESPONDENCE AND INTERVIEWS
(WITH AUTHOR UNLESS OTHERWISE STATED)

Abramovici, Pierre. Paris. March 2009.
Almeida, Fabrice d'. Historian and director of l'Institut d'Histoire du Temps Présent. April, 2009.
Arnim, Alexandra, and Baron Volkmar von. August 11 and 16, 2008.
Baudel, Jules-Marc. Avocat Honoraire, Ancien Membre du Conseil de l'Ordre. On legal matters connected with the indictment of Chanel and the trial of Louis de Vaufreland. Paris. March 3, 2010.
Charles-Roux, Edmonde. April 21, 2009. Paris, France. Telephone interviews throughout 2010.
Engelhardt, Baron Wilfried von. Hinterstoder, Austria. July 3, 2009. Interview by Sally Gordon-Mark.
Flügge, Manfred. Paris. December 2009.
Foedrowitz, Michael. Berlin and Paris. August 2008. Personal communication with author and telephone consultations, 2008–2010.
Griffith, Aline, Countess of Romanones. January 2008.
Higham, Charles. Telephone interview with Philip Parkinson, research assistant. London. April 2008.

Klarsfeld, Serge. L'Association des fils et filles des déportés juifs de France, correspondance, 2008.

Labrunie, Gabrielle Palasse. Interviews in person and by telephone, April 2009–April 2010. Yermenonville, France.

The Momm Family. Interview with Michael Foedrowitz. February–March 2010.

Muller, Florence. Fashion historian. March 2009.

Munchhausen, Ernst-Friedemann Freiherr von. August 8, 2008.

Ozanam, Yves. Interview with Michael Foedrowitz. March 4, 2010, at the Palais de Justice in Paris.

Roese, Manfred. Archive society, Gettorf, Germany. August 7, 2008. Interview with Michael Foedrowitz.

Schmidt, Eric. June 6, 2009.

Schoenebeck, Baron Andre von. Hinterstoder, Austria. July 3, 2009. Interview by Sally Gordon-Mark.

Sichel, Peter. Telephone conversations and e-mails with author. New York, 2007–2010.

Testa, Eleanor. Archivist of the Mémorial de la Shoah. June 11, 2008, Paris.

Tiedt, Marietta. Hinterstoder, Austria. July 3, 2009. Interview by Sally Gordon-Mark.

BROADCAST

Chanel: A Private Life. BBC Two documentary, first broadcast January 1995.

ARTICLES

Abescat, Bruno, and Yves Stavridès. "Derrière l'empire Chanel." *L'Express,* July 4–12, 2005.

Angus, Christophe. "Chanel: un parfum d'espionage." *L'Express,* March 16, 1995.

Arnaud, Claude. "Mademoiselle L'oeil noir frondeur, un petit tailleur mythique, un jersey enchanteur, un N° 5 universel, une allure libérée mais disciplinée, des rencontres inouïes, Cocteau, Diaghilev ou Renoir . . . Portrait impressioniste de Gabrielle Chanel." *Vogue,* March 2009.

"Ascot's Brilliant Pageant—Brilliant in Spite of Rain Threat." *The Daily Mail,* June 20, 1934.

"Battle of Births." *Time,* February 5, 1940.

Berman, Phyllis, and Zina Sewaya. "The Billionaires Behind Chanel." *Forbes,* April 3, 1989, 165.

Bernstein, Richard. "An Archive Puts Faces on Nazis' Young Victims." *New York Times,* December 18, 1984, A2.

Berton, Gilles. "Au ban de la nationale." *Le Monde,* November 7, 2008.

"Black List." *Life,* August 24, 1942, 86.

"Blum's Debut." *Time,* June 15, 1936.

Blumenthal, Ralph. "U.S. Suit Says French Trains Took Victims to the Nazis." *New York Times,* June 13, 2001.

Bower, Brock. "Chez Chanel." *Smithsonian,* July 2001, 60.

Brady, James. "The Truth About Chanel from Her Last Amour." *Crain's New York Business,* April 25, 2005, 3.

"Brunner Tried in Absentia for Sending Orphans to Deaths." *Toronto Star,* March 3, 2001.

Cannell, Kathleen. "Gems of Far East Blend with Gowns." *New York Times,* May 6, 1940.

Ceaux, Pascal. "Soixante ans de douleur dans une valise." *Le Monde,* September 2006, 3.

Chauffour, Celia. "Le Musée d'Auschwitz doit préserver la mémoire collective." *Le Monde,* September 2006, 3.

"Chanel Arrives, Perfumed and Wearing Pearls!" *Illustrated Daily News,* March 17, 1931, 12.

"Chanel étudie une réorganisation mondiale" and "Chanel renouvelle ses dirigeants et revoit ses structures." *Les Échos,* January 16, 2008.

"Chanel l'album de sa vie, de sa fortune et de sa gloire." *Paris Match,* January 23, 1971.

"Chanel, the Couturier, Dead in Paris." Obituary, *New York Times,* January 11, 1971.

"Chanel Visits America." *New York Times,* March 8, 1931.

Churchill, Randolph. "Mlle Chanel's Tribute." *Daily Mail,* June 20, 1934.

"Coco, encore et toujours." *Vogue,* March 2009, 150.

"Concentration Camp Near Paris Is Closed." *New York Times,* September 10, 1945.

Cousteau, Patrick. "Coco Chanel vue par les RG." *Minute,* April 29, 2009.

Cox, Edwin. "Private Lives." *Los Angeles Times,* March 27, 1940, A14.

Coyle, Gene. "Spy vs. Spy." *The Intelligencer: Journal of U.S. Intelligence Studies* 17, no. 2 (Fall 2009): 61.

Davies, Lizzy. "Coco Chanel Back in Vogue as France Celebrates an Icon." *Guardian,* August 25, 2008.

Delavoie, Sophie. "De Fulco pour Coco." *Vogue,* March 2009, 245.

Dethomas, Bruno. "Coco Chanel et son maître d'hôtel." *Le Monde,* March 23, 1973.

Dixon, Jane. "Women Behind the News." *Los Angeles Times,* February 1, 1931, A4.

Dorsey, Hebe. "Looking Back on the Life of Chanel." *International Herald Tribune,* September 26, 1972.

Drapac, Vesna. "A King Is Killed in Marseille: France and Yugoslavia in 1934." In "French History and Civilization," a paper presented at 2005 Georges Rude Society conference. http://www.h-france.net/rude/2005conference/Drapac2.pdf.

"Erich Vermehren." *The Independent,* May 3, 2005.

Flanner, Janet. "31 rue Cambon." *New Yorker,* March 14, 1931, 25.

"France Admits Guilt but Says 'Jews Have Been Given Enough.'" *Times of London,* February 17, 2009.

"Free Trade." *Time,* October 12, 1936.

"French Jews Sent to a Nazi Oblivion." *New York Times,* April 1, 1943.

Frudenheim, Milt. "Chanel's Past Haunts Exhibit." *Salt Lake Tribune,* September 29, 1972, 20.

"Germany Cornered." *Time,* April 22, 1940.

"Gestapo über alles." *Vendémiaire,* September 4, 1935.

Gildea, Robert. "How to Understand the Dreyfus Affair." *New York Review of Books,* June 10, 2010, 43–44.

Grassin, Sophie. "Chanel aurait été folle de vous! Edmonde Charles-Roux à Audrey Tatou." *Mme Figaro,* April 18, 2009, 84.

———. " 'Coco Avant Chanel': Portrait de Femme." *Mme Figaro,* April 18, 2009, 80.

———. "Edmonde Charles-Roux à Audrey Tautou. 'Chanel aurait été folle de vous!' " *Mme Figaro,* April 18, 2009, 84.

Grimes, William. "Recovering Lost Relatives from Holocaust Oblivion." *New York Times,* September 20, 2006.

Guerrin, Michel. "André Malraux, la culture en solitaire." *Le Monde,* June 25, 2010.

"Half-Year Mark." *Time,* March 11, 1940.

"H. Gregory Thomas, Chanel Executive, 82." Obituary, *New York Times,* October 10, 1990.

Hilberg, Raul. " 'C'est un travail sans fin' . . ." Interview with Thomas Wieder. *Le Monde,* October 20, 2006.

"Hitler Endorsed by 9 to 1 in Poll on His Dictatorship, but Opposition Is Doubled." *New York Times,* August 19, 1934.

"If Blonde, Use Blue Perfume, says Chanel." *Los Angeles Examiner,* March 17, 1931, 5.

Jungius, Martin, and Wolfgang Seibel. "The Citizen as Perpetrator: Kurt Blanke and Aryanization in France, 1940–1944." *Holocaust and Genocide Studies* 22, no. 3 (Winter 2008): 441–74.

Katz, Yaakov. "Int'l Hunt on for Top Nazi Fugitive." *Jerusalem Post,* December 28, 2005.

"King of Perfume." *Time,* September 14, 1953.

Krick, Jessa. "Gabrielle 'Coco' Chanel 1883–1971 and the House of Chanel." The Costume Institute, The Metropolitan Museum of Art, October 2004, www.metmuseum.org.

"La fébrile activité de 'la Gestapo' en France." *Vendémiaire,* September 11, 1935.

Lambauer, Barbara. "Francophile contre vents et marée? Otto Abetz et les Français, 1930–1958." *Bulletin du Centre de Recherche Français de Jérusalem* 18 (2007): 153–60.

Le Bars, Stéphanie. "Institutions juives, Cimenter une communauté dispersée." *Le Monde,* June 23, 2008.

Long, Tanya. "Paris Purge Jails Many by Mistake." *New York Times,* September 8, 1944.

"Mademoiselle Chanel Here, Hollywood-Bound." *New York Times,* March 5, 1931.

Mandelbaum, Jacques. "Nuit et brouillard, affaire trouble." *Le Monde,* August 22, 2006.

Marguin-Hamon, Elsa. "Une campagne anti-sémite en 1290." *Historia,* October 2006.

Maurus, Véronique. "No. 5, l'éternel parfum de femme." *Le Monde,* April 20, 1997.

Merrick, Mollie. "Hollywood in Person." *Los Angeles Times,* December 19, 1932, A5.

Miller, Margaux. "Audrey Tatou, ou le fabuleux destin de Coco." *Mme Figaro,* December 13, 2008, 92.

"Mlle Chanel, New Czarina of Film Fashions, Arrives." *Hollywood Daily Citizen*, March 17, 1931, 4.

"Mlle Chanel, Paris Stylist, Meets Stars." *Los Angeles Evening Herald*, March 17, 1921, A-15.

"Mlle Chanel to Wed Her Business Partner; Once Refused the Duke of Westminster." *New York Times*, November 19, 1933.

"Mme Chanel." *New York Times*, March 15, 1931.

Moore, Beth. "Two for the Runway." *Los Angeles Times*, May 4, 2005, E-1.

De Moubray, Jocelyn. "Obituary: Jacques Wertheimer." *The Independent*, February 10, 1996.

"No, Without Bayonets." *Time*, July 20, 1936.

Nye, Myra. "Society of Cinemaland." *Los Angeles Times*, March 22, 1931, 24.

Obituary of Vera Lombardi Arkwright, *Il Messaggero*, May 24, 1947.

"On and Off the Avenue, Feminine Fashions." *New Yorker*, March 19, 1932, and August 27, 1932.

"Parfums Chanel Sued by Designer." *New York Times*, June 3, 1946.

Paris Letter column. *New Yorker*, December 3, 1933.

"Perfume Industry Hit by Lack of Oils." *New York Times*, February 12, 1941.

Philip, P. J. "France Crippled by Wild Cat Strikes; Blum Is in Power." *New York Times*, June 5, 1936.

———. "Paris Ends Strikes," *New York Times*, September 18, 1936.

———. "300,000 on Strike in France as Blum Prepares to Rule." *New York Times*, June 4, 1936.

"Present & Future Plans." *Time*, April 8, 1940.

"Return of Welles." *Time*, April 8, 1940.

Riding, Alan. "The Fight Over a Suitcase and the Memories It Carries." *New York Times*, September 16, 2006.

Roberts, Glenys. "Movie-makers Fight over Coco's Life Story—from Chanel No. 5 to Nazi Spy." *Prada's Meadow*, June 9, 2007, www.forum.purseblog .com.

Ross, Lillian. "The Strong Ones." *New Yorker*, September 28, 1957.

Salsman, Richard M. "The Cause and Consequences of the Great Depression, Part 1: What Made the Roaring '20s Roar." *The Intellectual Activist* 18, no. 6 (June 2004): 16.

Savigneau, Josyane. "Le Vel' d'Hiv avant le désastre." *Le Monde*, October 31, 2008.

Schultz, Jeff. "Paris Memories Horrible, Indelible." *Atlanta Journal-Constitution*, August 7, 2005, B1.

Sischy, Ingrid. "The Designer Coco Chanel." *Time*, June 8, 1998.

Skidelsky, Robert. "The Remedist." *New York Times*, December 12, 2008.

"Strong Nerves." *Time*, June 19, 1936.

"Studies Cosmetic Needs." *New York Times*, August 18, 1940.

"Style Creator Tells How to Become 'Chic.'" *Los Angeles Times*, March 18, 1931, A1.

Thurman, Judith. "Scenes from a Marriage: The House of Chanel at the Met." *New Yorker*, May 23, 2005.

"Tradition Upheld by Noted Star" and "Style Creator Praises Modes?" *Los Angeles Times*, December 2, 1931, 7.

Trescott, Jacqueline. "Detention Camp Archive Donated by Red Cross to Holocaust Museum." *Washington Post*, July 3, 1998, D-2.

Updike, John. "Qui qu'a vu Coco?" *New Yorker,* September 21, 1998.
Whitaker, Alma. "Sugar and Spice." *Los Angeles Times,* March 29, 1931, 21.
Wieder, Thomas. "Découverte du projet de 'statut des juifs.'" *Le Monde,* October 5, 2010, 10.
Wildman, Sarah. "Paris' Dirty Secret." *Jerusalem Report,* November 1, 2004, 26.

BOOKS

Abramovici, Pierre. *Un rocher bien occupé. Monaco pendant la guerre 1939–1945.* Paris: Editions du Seuil, 2001.
Alanbrooke, Field Marshal Lord. *War Diaries.* London: Weidenfeld & Nicolson, 2001.
Allard, Paul. *Quand Hitler espionne la France.* Paris: Les Éditions de France, 1939.
Ambrose, Stephen E. *The Supreme Commander: The War Years of General Dwight D. Eisenhower.* Garden City, N.Y.: Doubleday & Company, 1969.
Amouroux, Henri. *La Vie des Français sous l'Occupation.* Paris: Librairie Arthème Fayard, 1990.
Annuaire de la Magistrature. France: Sofiac, 1996.
Arthaud, Christian. *La Côte d'Azur des écrivains.* Aix-en-Provence: Édisud, 1999.
Assouline, Pierre. *Simenon: A Biography.* Translated by Jon Rothschild. New York: Alfred A. Knopf, 1997.
Atelier vidéo-histoire du Lycée Jean-Baptiste-Say. *Paris, carrefour des résistances.* Paris: Paris-Musées, 1994.
Barth, Jack. *International Spy Museum Handbook of Practical Spying.* Preface by Peter Earnest. Washington, D.C.: National Geographic Society, 2004.
Bedford, Sybille. *Jigsaw.* London: Penguin Books, 1990.
———. *Quicksands: A Memoir.* London: Penguin Books, 2006.
Beevor, Antony, and Cooper Artemis. *Paris After the Liberation 1944–1949.* London: Penguin Books, 2007.
Berg, A. Scott. *Goldwyn: A Biography.* New York: Riverhead Trade, 1998.
Bloch, Michael. *The Secret File of the Duke of Windsor: The Private Papers, 1937–1972.* New York: Harper & Row, by arrangement with Bantam Press in Great Britain, 1988.
Bothorel, Jean. *Louise, ou, la vie de Louise de Vilmorin.* Paris: Éditions Grasset & Fasquelle, 1993.
Breward, Christopher. *Fashion.* New York: Oxford University Press, 2003.
Brissaud, André, Fabrice Laroche, Jean Mabire, and François d'Orcival. *Histoire secrète de la Gestapo,* 4 vols. Geneva: Éditions Farnot, 1974.
Brown, Frederick. *For the Soul of France: Culture Wars in the Age of Dreyfus.* New York: Alfred A. Knopf, 2010.
Brownell, Will, and Richard N. Billings. *So Close to Greatness: A Biography of William C. Bullitt.* New York: Macmillan Publishing Co., 1987.
Browning, Christopher. *The Origins of the Final Solution.* Lincoln: University of Nebraska Press, 2004.
Buisson, Patrick. *1940–1945 Années érotiques: Vichy ou les infortunés de la vertu.* Paris: Éditions Albin Michel, 2008.
Bullock, Alan. *Hitler: A Study in Tyranny.* London: Penguin Books, 1962.

Burrin, Philippe. *France Under the Germans: Collaboration and Compromise.* New York: The New Press, 1998.

Cadogan, Sir Alexander. *The Diaries of Sir Alexander Cadogan, O.M. 1938–45.* New York: G. P. Putnam's Sons, 1972.

Callil, Carmen. *Bad Faith: A Forgotten History of Family, Fatherland and Vichy France.* New York: Alfred A. Knopf, 2006.

Catherwood, Christopher. *Winston Churchill: The Flawed Genius of World War II.* New York: Berkeley Publishing Group, 2009.

Cave Brown, Anthony. *Bodyguard of Lies.* New York: Harper & Row, First Edition, 1975.

Charles-Roux, Edmonde. *Chanel.* London: Jonathan Cape, 1976.

———. *Le Temps Chanel.* Paris: La Martinière/Grasset, 1979.

———. *L'Irrégulière ou mon itinéraire Chanel.* Paris: Grasset, 1974.

Chauvy, Gérard. *Histoire secrète de l'Occupation.* Paris: Editions Payot, 1991.

Christophe, Francine. *Guy s'en va. Deux chroniques parallèles.* Paris: l'Harmattan, n.d.

———. *Une Petite Fille privilégiée.* Paris: l'Harmattan, n.d.

Cline, Sally. *Zelda Fitzgerald: Her Voice in Paradise.* New York: Arcade Publishing, 2003.

Cointet, Jean-Paul. *Expier Vichy: L'Épuration en France, 1943–1958.* Paris: Perrin, 2008.

Coles, S. F. A. *Franco of Spain.* London: Neville Spearman Limited, 1955.

Collins, Larry, and Dominique Lapierre. *Is Paris Burning?* New York: Warner Books, 1991.

Cowles, Virginia. "The Beginning of the End Flight from Paris: June 1940." In *Reporting World War II, Vol. 1: American Journalism 1938–1944,* Library of America. New York: Penguin Books, 1995, 53–62.

Crowe, David M. *Oskar Schindler.* New York: Basic Books, 2004.

de Chambrun, René. *Mission and Betrayal.* Stanford, Calif.: Hoover Institution Press, 1993.

Degunst, Sylviane. *Coco Chanel: Citations.* Paris: Éditions du Huitième Jour, 2008.

Delay, Claude. *Chanel solitaire.* Paris: Éditions Gallimard, 1983.

Doerries, Reinhard R. *Hitler's Intelligence Chief, Walter Schellenberg.* New York: Enigma Books, 2009.

———. *Hitler's Last Chief of Foreign Intelligence: Allied Interrogations of Walter Schellenberg.* Portland, Ore.: Frank Cass Publishers, 2003.

Dreyfus, Jean-Marc, and Sarah Gensburger. *Des camps dans Paris.* Paris: Librairie Arthème Fayard, 2003.

Dubois, André-Louis. *À travers trois Républiques.* Paris: Plon, 1972.

du Plessix Gray, Francine. *Them.* London: Penguin Books, 2006.

Dutton, Ralph, and Lord Holden. *The Land of France.* New York: Scribner's, 1939.

Eder, Cyril. *Les Comtesses de la Gestapo.* Paris: Grasset, 2006.

Edwards, Michael. *Perfume Legends: French Feminine Fragrances.* Carlsbad, Calif.: Crescent House Publishing, June 1998

Escoffier, A. *L'Aide-mémoire culinaire.* Preface by Michel Escoffier. Paris: Flammarion, 1919 Re-édition.

Etherington-Smith, Meredith. *Patou.* London: Hutchinson & Co., 1983.

————. Traduit de l'anglais par Marie-Françoise Vinthière. *Patou.* Paris: Les Éditions Denoël, 1984.

Everett, Peter. *Matisse's War.* New York: Vintage Books, 1997.

Farago, Ladislas. *The Game of the Foxes.* London: Pan Books Ltd., 1973.

Field, Leslie. *Bendor, the Golden Duke of Westminster.* London: Weidenfeld and Nicolson, 1986.

Fiemeyer, Isabelle. *Coco Chanel: Un parfum de mystère.* Paris: Petite Bibliothèque Payot, 1999.

Fleischhauer, Ingeborg, and Benjamin Pinkus. *The Soviet Germans Past and Present.* New York: St. Martin's Press, 1986.

Flügge, Manfred. *Amer azur. Artistes et écrivains à Sanary.* Paris: Éditions du Félin, 2007.

Foulon, Charles-Louis. *André Malraux et le rayonnement culturel de la France.* Brussels: Éditions Complexe, 2004.

Fry, Varian. *La liste noire.* Translated by Edith Ochs. Paris: Éditions Plon, 1999. Originally published as *Surrender on Demand,* New York: Random House, 1945.

Galante, Pierre. *Les Années Chanel.* Paris: Mercure de France, 1972.

————. *Mademoiselle Chanel.* Chicago: Henry Regnery Company, 1973.

Gallet, Danielle. *Mme de Pompadour ou le pouvoir féminin.* Paris: Librairie Arthème Fayard, 1985.

Gidel, Henry. *Coco Chanel.* Paris: Éditions J'ai lu/Flammarion, 2000.

Glass, Charles. *Americans in Paris: Life and Death under Nazi Occupation, 1940–44.* London: Harper's Press, 2009.

Gold, Arthur, and Robert Fizdale. *Misia.* London: Macmillan, 1980.

————. *Misia: La Vie de Misia Sert.* Translated by Janine Herisson. Paris: Éditions Gallimard, 1981.

Goñi, Uki. *The Real Odessa.* London: Granta Books, 2002.

Grandjonc, Jacques, and Theresia Grundtner. *Zones d'ombres, 1933–1944: Exil et internement d'Allemands dans le Sud-Est de la France.* Aix-en-Provence: Alinea, 1990.

Green, Nancy L. *Ready-to-wear and Ready-to-work: A Century of Industry and Immigrants in Paris and New York City.* Durham, N.C.: Duke University Press, 1997.

Greene, Graham, and Hugh Greene. *The Spy's Bedside Book.* New York: Bantam Books, 2008.

Griffith, Aline, Countess of Romanones. *The Spy Wore Red.* New York: Random House, 1987.

Haedrich, Marcel. *Coco Chanel.* Paris: Pierre Belfond, 1987.

————. *Coco Chanel: Her Life, Her Secrets.* Translated by Charles Lam Markmann. Boston: Little, Brown and Company, 1972.

Hassell, Agostino von, and Sigrid MacRae. *Alliance of Enemies.* New York: Thomas Dunne Books, St. Martin's Press, 2006.

Higham, Charles. *The Duchess of Windsor: The Secret Life.* Somerset, N.J.: John Wiley & Sons, Inc., 2005.

————. *Trading with the Enemy.* New York: Delacorte Press, 1983.

Hodson, James Lansdale. *Through the Dark Night.* London: Victor Gollancz Ltd., 1941.

Hoffman, Tod. *The Spy Within.* New York: Random House, 2008.

Hoisington, William A., Jr. *The Assassination of Jacques Lemaigre Dubreuil.* London and New York: RoutledgeCurzon, Taylor & Francis Group, 2005.
Ingrao, Christian. *Croire et détruire—les intellectuels dans la machine de guerre SS.* Paris: Fayard, 2010.
Jenkins, Roy. *Churchill.* New York: Plume, 2002.
Josephs, Jeremy. *Swastika Over Paris.* New York: Arcade Publishing, 1989.
Kahn, David. *Hitler's Spies: German Military Intelligence in World War II.* Cambridge, Mass.: Da Capo Press Edition, 2000.
Kaplan, Justine, ed. *Bartlett's Familiar Quotations,* 70th Ed. New York: Little, Brown and Company, 2003.
Karbo, Karen. *The Gospel According to Coco Chanel: Life Lessons from the World's Most Elegant Woman.* Illustrated by Chesley McLaren. Guilford, Conn.: Globe Pequot Press, 2009.
Karski, Jan. *Mon témoignage devant le monde. Histoire d'un État clandestin.* Paris: Robert Laffont, S.A., 2010.
Kersaudy, François. *De Gaulle et Roosevelt, le duel au sommet.* Paris: Perrin, 2004.
Kirkland, Douglas. *Coco Chanel: Three Weeks 1962.* Foreword by Judith Thurman. New York: Glitterati Incorporated, 2009.
Kitson, Simon. *The Hunt for Nazi Spies: Fighting Espionage in Vichy France.* Chicago: University of Chicago Press, 2007.
Kladstrup, Donald, and Petie Kladstrup. *Wine and War: The French, the Nazis, and the Battle for France's Greatest Treasure.* New York: Broadway Books, 2002.
Krauze, Jan, and Didier Rioux. *Le Monde: Les Grands Reportages, 1944–2009.* Paris: Éditions Les Arènes, 2009.
Kurowski, Franz. *The Brandenburger Commandos: Germany's Elite Warrior Spies in WWII.* Mechanicsburg, Pa.: Stackpole Books, 2005.
Lawford, Valentine. *Horst.* New York: Alfred A. Knopf, 1984.
Lazareff, Pierre. *Deadline: The Behind the Scenes Story of the Last Decade in France.* Translated by David Partridge. New York: Random House, 1942.
Leese, Elizabeth. *Costume Design in the Movies.* New York: Dover Publications, 1991.
Livre Troisième: Des crimes, des délits et leur punition, Code Pénal et Code de Justice. Paris: Armée de Terre. Paris: Librairie Dalloz, 1994.
Lloyd, Alan. *Franco.* New York: Doubleday & Company, 1969.
Luce, Clare Boothe. *Europe in the Spring.* New York: Alfred A. Knopf, 1940.
Madsen, Axel. *Chanel: A Woman of Her Own.* New York: Owl Books/Henry Holt and Company, 1990.
Manchester, William. *The Last Lion: Winston Spencer Churchill: Alone 1932–1940.* Boston, New York, London: Little, Brown and Company, 1988.
Marcus, Stanley. *Minding the Store.* Denton, Tex.: University of North Texas Press, 2001.
Marrus, Michael R., and Robert O. Paxton. *Vichy France and the Jews.* Stanford, Calif.: Stanford University Press, 1995.
Marty, Allan T. "A Walking Guide to Occupied Paris: The Germans and Their Collaborators." Unpublished manuscript.
Meyer-Stabley, Bertrand. *Les Dames de l'Élysée. Celles d'hier et de demain.* Paris: Librairie Académique Perrin, 1999.
Mitchell, Allan. *Nazi Paris: The History of an Occupation, 1940–1944.* New York: Berghahn Books, 2008.

Montagnon, Pierre. *La France dans la guerre de 39–45.* Paris: Pygmalion, 2009.
Morand, Paul. *L'Allure de Chanel.* Illustrations by Karl Lagerfeld. Paris: Hermann Éditeurs des sciences et des arts, 1996.
———. *The Allure of Chanel.* Translated from the French by E. Cameron. London: Pushkin Press, 2008.
———. *Journal inutile, 1968–1972.* Paris: Éditions Gallimard, 2001.
Murphy, Robert. *Diplomat Among Warriors.* New York: Doubleday & Company, 1964.
Nieradka, Magali. *Waiting Room by the Mediterranean: Marta and Lion Feuchtwanger in French Exile.* N.P., n.d.
Norwich, John Julius. *The Duff Cooper Diaries 1915–1951.* London: Wiedenfeld & Nicolson/Orion Publishing Group, 2005.
Ousby, Ian. *Occupation: The Ordeal of France 1940–1944.* London: Pimlico, 1999.
Padfield, Peter. *Himmler: Reichsführer-SS.* London: Macmillan London, 1990.
Paxton, Robert O. Translated from English by Pierre de Longuemar. *L'Armée de Vichy.* Paris: Tallandier Éditions, 2004.
———. *Vichy France: Old Guard and New Order, 1940–1944.* New York: Alfred A. Knopf, 1972.
Paxton, Robert O., and Michael R. Marrus. *Vichy France and the Jews.* New York: Basic Books, 1981.
Peyrefitte, Roger. *Les Juifs.* Paris: Flammarion, 1965.
Picardie, Justine. *Coco Chanel.* London: Harper Collins, 2010.
Porch, Douglas. *The French Secret Services: From the Dreyfus Affair to the Gulf War.* New York: Farrar, Straus & Giroux, 1995.
Pourcher, Yves. *Pierre Laval vu par sa fille.* Paris: Le Cherche midi, 2002.
Poznanski, Renée. *Jews in France during World War II.* Waltham, Mass.: Brandeis University Press, 2002.
Pryce-Jones, David. *Paris in the Third Reich.* London: William Collins Sons & Co., 1981.
Rector, Frank. *The Nazi Extermination of Homosexuals.* New York: Stein & Day Publishers, 1981.
Reese, Mary Ellen. *General Reinhard Gehlen: The CIA Connection.* Fairfax, Va.: George Mason University Press, 1990.
Reile, Oscar. *L'Abwehr, le contre-espionnage allemand en France de 1935 à 1945.* Paris: Éditions France-Empire, 1970.
Richelson, Jeffrey T. *A Century of Spies: Intelligence in the Twentieth Century.* Oxford: Oxford University Press, 1997.
Ridley, George, with Frank Welsh. *Bend'Or, Duke of Westminster.* London: Robin Clark, Namara Group, 1985.
Robert-Diard, Pascale, and Didier Rioux. *Le Monde: Les Grands Procès 1944–2010.* Paris: Éditions Les Arènes, 2010.
Roulet, Claude. *Ritz: A Story That Outshines the Legend.* Paris: Quai Voltaire, 1998.
Roussel, Éric. *Le Naufrage.* Paris: Gallimard, 2009.
———. *Paris libéré!* Paris: Gallimard, 2002.
Sachs, Maurice. *La décade de l'illusion* Paris: Gallimard, 1950.
Sadosky, Louis, and Laurent Joly. *Berlin 1942: Chronique d'une détention par le Gestapo.* Paris: CNRS Editions, 2009.
Scheijen, Sjeng. *Diaghilev: A Life.* New York: Oxford University Press, 2009.

Schellenberg, Walter. *The Labyrinth.* Translated by Louis Hagen. New York: Harper & Brothers, 1956.

Schwarberg, Günther. *The Murders at Bullenhuser Damm.* Translated by Erna Baber Rosenfeld with Alvin H. Rosenfeld. Bloomington: Indiana University Press, 1984.

Shirer, William L. *Berlin Diary.* Baltimore, Md.: Johns Hopkins University Press, 1941.

———. *The Rise and Fall of the Third Reich: A History of Nazi Germany.* New York: Simon and Schuster Paperbacks, 1990.

Smith, Richard Harris. *OSS: The Secret History of America's First Central Intelligence Agency.* Guilford, Conn.: The Lyons Press, an imprint of The Globe Pequot Press, 2005.

Spotts, Frederic. *The Shameful Peace: How French Artists and Intellectuals Survived the Nazi Occupation.* New Haven, Conn.: Yale University Press, 2008.

Steegmuller, Francis. *Cocteau: A Biography.* Boston: David R. Godine, 1992.

Templewood, Viscount. *Ambassador on Special Mission: Sir Samuel Hoare.* London: Collins, 1946.

Thompson, David. *A Biographical Dictionary of War Crimes Proceedings, Collaboration Trials and Similar Proceeding Involving France in World War II.* Written and compiled for the Grace Dangberg Foundation, Inc. http://reocities .com/Pentagon/bunker/7729/FRANCE/French_Trials.html, 1999–2002.

Trachtenberg, Joshua. *The Devil and the Jews: The Medieval Conception of the Jew and Its Relation to Modern Anti-Semitism.* Philadelphia: Jewish Publication Society, 2002.

Vaughan, Hal. *Doctor to the Resistance: The Heroic True Story of an American Surgeon and His Family in Occupied Paris.* Dulles, Va.: Potomac Books, 2004.

———. *FDR's Twelve Apostles: The Spies Who Paved the Way for the Invasion of North Africa.* Guilford, Conn.: The Lyons Press, an imprint of The Globe Pequot Press, 2006.

Veillon, Dominique. *La Mode sous l'Occupation, nouvelle édition revue et augmentée.* Paris: Éditions Payot & Rivages, 2001.

———. *Vivre et survivre en France 1939–1947.* Paris: Éditions Payot & Rivages, 1995.

Verheyde, Philippe. *Les mauvais comptes de Vichy: L'aryanisation des entreprises juives.* Paris: Perrin, 1997.

Vilmorin, Louise de. *Mémoires de Coco.* Paris: Éditions Gallimard, 1999.

Vreeland, Diana. *DV.* New York: Alfred A. Knopf, 1984.

Waite, Robert G. L. *Vanguard of Nazism: The Free Corps Movement in Postwar Germany, 1918–1923.* Cambridge, Mass.: Harvard University Press, 1952.

Wallach, Janet. *Chanel: Her Style and Her Life.* New York: Nan A. Talese/Doubleday, 1998.

Wistrich, Robert S. *Who's Who in Nazi Germany.* London: Routledge, 1995.

Zdatny, Steven. *Fashion, Work, and Politics in Modern France.* New York: Palgrave Macmillan, 2006.

WEBSITES

www.ancestry.com
www.camp-de-drancy.asso.fr

http://www.essortment.com/all/perfumefrench_rlot.htm
www.fmd.asso.fr
www.jpost.com
www.larousse.fr
www.lemonde.fr
www.lexpress.fr
www.meteo-paris.com/chronique/?d=1943
http://pagesperso-orange.fr/d-d.natanson/etoile.htm, Mémoire juive et éducation
www.press.uchicago.edu
http://pubs.acs.org/doi/abs/10.1021/cr950068a
www.sanarysurmer.com/culture/index.html
www.suite101.com/content/icons-chanel-no-5-perfume-a44263
www.thepeerage.com
www.usmbooks.com

ACKNOWLEDGMENTS

To friends, colleagues, and supporters who helped me discover little-known details of Gabrielle Chanel's life I owe a debt of gratitude. If I have failed to thank someone—please be thanked here and now. Some who assisted in this work wish to go unnamed: to them I offer a special *merci, messieurs!*

To all I beg indulgence—any errors in this work are my own.

My foremost thanks must go to Edward Knappman and his wife, Elisabeth, to Ernst Goldschmidt and to Charles Robertson, all friends and colleagues for many years. Their advice and assistance have been a godsend. To my research colleagues a heartfelt thanks, and to Sally Gordon Mark in Paris, Michael Foedrowitz in Berlin, and Philip Parkinson in London a monumental *merci* for their diligent approach to historical research at the complicated labyrinths of national and family archives. Susannah Kemple in New York helped with excellent translations of Dincklage and German material.

My assistant in New York, Pamela Zimmerman, has helped me through three books now—to Pam and her husband, Gerry, a million thanks. And to Dr. Alain T. Marty, thanks for sharing his unpublished and monumental "A Walking Guide to Occupied Paris: The Germans and Their Collaborators."

Mlle Chanel's grand-niece, Mme Gabrielle Palasse Labrunie, offered a unique vision of Chanel. Her warm and gracious hospitality helped me appreciate and admire Coco Chanel's work. Mme Labrunie knew I would follow the Chanel story wherever the documents took me.

Thanks are due to my lawyer, John Logigian; my agent, Tina Bennett, at Janklow & Nesbitt; and legal counsel. Bennett Ashley, for help in dealing with a host of thorny problems. In France, special thanks go to attorneys André Schmidt, Jean-Marc Baudel, and Wallace Baker who helped unknot tricky French legal questions, as did Yves Ozanam at the Paris Palais de Justice. And thanks are due to friend and CUI colleague, historian Pierre de Longuemar.

Many thanks to copyeditor Laura Starrett for a superb job. I haven't words enough to thank Carmen Johnson at Alfred A. Knopf for her attention to detail and her assistance throughout the last months of my work.

Finally, I am forever indebted to Victoria Wilson, senior editor and vice president of Alfred A. Knopf, for her support on the long road to editing and completing this book.

I could not have written this book without the help of my wife, Dr. Phuong Nguyen, and B.B.B.

INDEX

A Note on the Type

The text of this book was set in Garamond No. 3. It is not a true copy of any of the designs of Claude Garamond (ca. 1480–1561), but an adaptation of his types, which set the European standard for two centuries. It probably owes as much to the designs of Jean Jannon, a Protestant printer working in Sedan in the early seventeenth century, who had worked with Garamond's romans earlier, in Paris, but who was denied their use because of Catholic censorship. Jannon's matrices came into the possession of the Imprimerie nationale, where they were thought to be by Garamond himself, and were so described when the Imprimerie revived the type in 1900. This particular version is based on an adaptation by Morris Fuller Benton.

COMPOSED BY *North Market Street Graphics, Lancaster, Pennsylvania*

PRINTED AND BOUND BY *Berryville Graphics, Berryville, Virginia*

DESIGNED BY *Iris Weinstein*